Does Economic Governance Matter?

NEW DIRECTIONS IN MODERN ECONOMICS
Series Editor: Malcolm C. Sawyer
Professor of Economics, University of Leeds, UK

New Directions in Modern Economics presents a challenge to orthodox economic thinking. It focuses on new ideas emanating from radical traditions including post-Keynesian, Kaleckian, neo-Ricardian and Marxian. The books in the series do not adhere rigidly to any single school of thought but attempt to present a positive alternative to the conventional wisdom.

For a full list of Edward Elgar published titles, including the titles in this series, visit our website at www.e-elgar.com.

Does Economic Governance Matter?

Governance Institutions and Outcomes

Edited by

Mehmet Ugur and David Sunderland

University of Greenwich, UK

NEW DIRECTIONS IN MODERN ECONOMICS

Edward Elgar

Cheltenham, UK • Northampton, MA, USA

Published by
Edward Elgar Publishing Limited
The Lypiatts
15 Lansdown Road
Cheltenham
Glos GL50 2JA
UK

Edward Elgar Publishing, Inc.
William Pratt House
9 Dewey Court
Northampton
Massachusetts 01060
USA

A catalogue record for this book
is available from the British Library

Library of Congress Control Number: 2011925759

MIX
Paper from
responsible sources
FSC® C018575

ISBN 978 0 85793 176 4

Typeset by Servis Filmsetting Ltd, Stockport, Cheshire
Printed and bound by MPG Books Group, UK

Contents

v

PART III   THE GOVERNANCE AND REGULATION INTERFACE

Contributors

José Antonio Alonso is Professor of Applied Economics at Universidad Complutense de Madrid and director of the Instituto Complutense de Estudios Internacionales (ICEI). He specializes in development economics, growth and international economic relations and has written numerous articles in academic journals such as *Applied Economics*, *Journal of Post Keynesian Economics*, *European Journal of Development Research*, *International Journal of Development Planning Literature* and *CEPAL Review*. He has worked as a consultant for several national government agencies and international organizations.

Ahmet Faruk Aysan, Associate Professor of Economics at Bogazici University (Istanbul), holds a PhD in Economics from the Department of Economics, University of Maryland College Park, US (2005). He has served as a consultant at the Social and Economic Development Division of Middle East and North Africa region as well as in Eastern and Central Asia Departments at the World Bank. He also administers projects on banking and credit cards for the Central Bank of the Republic of Turkey and The Scientific and Technological Research Council of Turkey. He had visiting positions at Boston and Suffolk Universities. He is a specialist in governance, private investment, banking and financial markets and has authored or co-authored a number of articles on these issues. He is on the editorial board of several academic journals and also serves as the national delegate of Turkey at the Seventh Framework Programme (FP7) of the European Union.

Ömer Faruk Baykal graduated in Economics from Bogazici University. He later completed an MA program in Economics at Bilkent University and holds an MA from the University of Maryland, College Park, where he studied microeconomics and industrial organization. Ömer started his career at the World Bank in Washington, DC and worked in various departments including Europe and Central Asia (ECA) and Middle East and North Africa (MENA). In 2007, Ömer joined the ECO Trade and Development Bank (ETDB) as Chief Economist where his responsibility is to design development strategies at the national and sectoral level to promote economic growth and trade in ECO region economies.

John Cullen is Professor of Management Accounting at the Management School, University of Sheffield. He worked in senior finance and commercial roles in industry before joining academia. His research interests cover inter-organizational accounting, supply chain management, management control and organizational governance. He has undertaken qualitative research in numerous private and public sector organizations and has a particular interest in institutional theories. His research portfolio also includes action research in a number of different industrial sectors and he has undertaken consultancy projects in a range of organizations. He has published widely in academic and practitioner journals and books.

Peter-Jan Engelen is Associate Professor of Finance at Utrecht University, the Netherlands. He holds a PhD and an MSc in Applied Economics. He also read law, obtaining an LLB and LLM. Some of his recent research topics include real options, law and finance, initial public offerings (IPOs), insider trading, reputational penalties and the ethics of financial markets. In 2002 he was awarded the prestigious European *Joseph de la Vega Prize*, and in 2006 he was awarded Best Researcher in Economics at Utrecht University. He has published in several journals including the *Journal of Banking and Finance, Research Policy*, the *Journal of Business Finance and Accounting*, the *Review of Law and Economics* and the *Journal of Business Ethics*.

Korkut Alp Ertürk graduated in economics from New York University and completed his PhD at the New School for Social Research. He has worked as a consultant for various UN agencies over the years and is currently Professor of Economics at the University of Utah, where he was department chair 2002–2008.

Carlos Garcimartín is Professor of Economics at Universidad Rey Juan Carlos, Madrid, Spain, and researcher of the Instituto Complutense de Estudios Internacionales (ICEI). He has been affiliated with the Universities of Salamanca, Complutense de Madrid and Rey Juan Carlos. He has worked as a consultant for several national government agencies and international organizations. His main research topics are focused on public economics, international economics and development economics. He has been involved in national and international research projects, and has published articles in prestigious international journals.

Vladimir Hlasny is Assistant Professor of Economics at Ewha Womans University in Seoul, and is currently a visiting fellow at the International Centre for Economic Research. His research centres on industrial organization and environmental economics. He has studied causes and consequences of recent regulatory reforms in utility industries, including natural gas, electricity and telecommunications. Vladimir has also evaluated environmental policies dealing with air pollution and biological invasions. He holds a doctorate in economics from Michigan State University.

Grazia Ietto-Gillies is Emeritus Professor of Applied Economics at London South Bank University and Visiting Professor at Birkbeck University of London. She has been Director of the Centre for International Business Studies at London South Bank University from 1992 to 2010. Her main research areas are transnational companies, their theories, activities and effects; indices of internationalization; globalization; impact of internationalization on innovation. She has also worked on methodology of economics; demarcation of services and manufacturing; healthcare in UK; and de-industrialization. She has written several books, co-edited three volumes, and published over 40 articles in academic journals and many chapters in edited books.

Emmanuel Lazega is Professor of Sociology at the University of Paris-Dauphine, a member of the Institut de Recherche Interdisciplinaire en Sciences Sociales (IRISSO-CNRS). His current research focuses on social, intra- and inter-organizational networks in the economy, with a substantive focus on the social control of business and a methodological focus on the dynamics of these multi-level networks. Publications include *Conventions and Structures in Economic Organization: Markets, Networks, and Hierarchies* (Edward Elgar, 2002, edited with Olivier Favereau); *The Collegial Phenomenon: The Social Mechanisms of Cooperation Among Peers in a Corporate Law Partnership* (Oxford University Press, 2001); and *Micropolitics of Knowledge: Communication and Indirect Control in Workgroups* (Aldine-de Gruyter, 1992).

Lise Mounier is a research fellow at Centre National de la Recherche Scientifique in Paris. Her work focuses on professional groups and social networks. With Emmanuel Lazega she has undertaken several research projects in the field of structural economic sociology, analysing the business world and judicial institutions in France.

Constantine E. Passaris is Professor of Economics and Chairman of the Department of Economics at the University of New Brunswick, Canada. His scholarly publications have appeared as monographs, encyclopaedia entries, book chapters and refereed journal articles. Constantine has been a member of the Economic Council of Canada, chairman of the New Brunswick Human Rights Commission, Canadian advisor to the Canadian Commission for UNESCO, a member of the Premier's Roundtable on New Brunswick Self Sufficiency and chairman of the New Brunswick Advisory Board on Population Growth.

Luis Rivas is professor of Economics at IE University, Segovia, Spain, and Universidad Pontificia de Salamanca, Spain. He has supervised and participated in several national and international research projects. He has been a researcher at several universities in the US, France and Portugal, and at the Ministry of Economics and Institute of Fiscal Studies in Spain. He specializes in growth, public economics and international economics and has written articles in prestigious international journals. As a professor he has lectured, besides Spain, in countries such as Ireland, Bolivia, the US, Poland, Germany, Dominican Republic, Mexico and the UK.

David Sunderland is Reader in Business History at the University of Greenwich, London. He is the author of *Managing the British Empire* (Boydell & Brewer, 2004); *Managing British Colonial and Post-Colonial Development* (Boydell & Brewer, 2007); *Social Capital, Trust and the Industrial Revolution, 1780–1880* (Routledge, 2007); and *An Economic History of London, 1800–1914* (co-authored with Dr Michael Ball) (Routledge, 2006).

Mathew Tsamenyi is Professor of Accounting at the University of Birmingham, UK and Visiting Professor of Accounting at the China Europe International Business School (CEIBS) where he teaches on their African programme. His main research interests are in the areas of management accounting and control systems, accounting systems in emerging economies and public sector reforms, privatization and accounting and accountability systems. Professor Tsamenyi has consulted widely for various organizations including the United Nations Conference on Trade and Development (UNCTAD) and the Netherlands Development Organization. He has delivered courses in several countries including the UK, Hong Kong, Singapore, Malaysia and Ghana. Professor Tsamenyi has published over 20 articles in leading international journals and he is the co-editor of the *Journal of Accounting in Emerging Economies* and the *Research in Accounting in Emerging Economies* series.

Paola Tubaro is Lecturer in Economic Sociology at the University of Greenwich, London, UK. She has a PhD in Economics, jointly awarded by the University of Paris Ouest, France, and the University of Frankfurt, Germany. Her current research interests include intra- and inter-organizational relationships in markets, with focus on regulation and governance systems, both formal and informal; and consumer choice, particularly behavioural changes induced by ubiquitous computer-based communication and their ethical and societal effects. Methodologically, her work is grounded in empirical social network analysis techniques and agent-based computer simulation, emphasizing the emergence of system-level regularities from individual behaviours and interactions.

Mehmet Ugur is Jean Monnet Reader in Political Economy in the Department of International Business and Economics at the University of Greenwich Business School. He researches the impact of credible commitment mechanisms and governance structures on economic, organizational and political outcomes. He has applied this framework to a large number of issues ranging from corporate governance through European integration to economics of regulation in network industries. He is currently the convenor of the MA/MSc in Business and Financial Economics and departmental research coordinator. He is a member of the Economic Governance Research Group (EGRG) and of the Centre for Governance, Risk and Accountability in the Business School, University of Greenwich. He has published five monographs and edited books, and over 40 journal articles and book chapters.

Marie-Ange Véganzonès-Varoudakis is a research fellow at the Centre National de la Recherche Scientifique (CNRS), Centre d'Etudes et de Recherches sur le Développement International (CERDI), Université d'Auvergne, France. She holds a PhD from the Institut d'Etudes Politiques (IEP) of Paris. She has held assignments with the World Bank, the OECD, the French Ministry of Economy and the UN. Her research is in economic policy and economic growth, exchange rate regimes and export performance, trade openness and foreign direct investment (FDI), governance institutions and private investment, investment climate and firms' productivity. She has published the results of her research in a large number of scholarly journals.

Cláudio de Araújo Wanderley is PhD in Accounting from the Management School, University of Sheffield. He is also a lecturer of Accounting at Federal University of Pernambuco, Brazil. His main research interests are in the areas of management accounting and performance measurement, accounting systems in emerging economies, public sector reforms, privatization and accounting and regulatory accounting in the Electricity sector.

1. Does economic governance matter? New contributions to the debate

Mehmet Ugur and David Sunderland

Institutions form the incentive structure of a society, and the political and economic institutions, in consequence, are the underlying determinants of economic performance. (North, 1994: 359)

INTRODUCTION

In the 1990s, the emergence of an extensive literature on the relationship between institutional quality and economic performance was associated with two stylised facts. The first was the dramatic worsening of all economic performance indicators of the ex-Soviet space in the wake of the institutional vacuum created by the collapse of what was dubbed 'real socialism'. As Coase (1992: 714) indicated in his Nobel Prize lecture, the transition experience of the ex-Soviet regimes demonstrated that the inclusion of '. . . institutional factors in the corpus of mainstream economics' could be avoided no longer. The second stylised fact was the persistence, and even widening, of the gap between low-income and developed countries. This 'convergence failure' eventually prompted the World Bank (2002: 2) to state that the main challenge for development policy at the turn of the twenty-first century was the supply of effective market-supporting institutions, and the creation of demand for such institutions.

Although the incorporation of institutions into economic analysis has been a welcome step in the right direction, one should not overlook the fact that the change has been a belated reaction on the part of mainstream economics. Early references to the importance of institutions date back to Adam Smith. In his *Wealth of Nations*, Smith (1976[1776]: 910) postulates that 'Commerce and manufactures can seldom flourish in any state . . . in which there is not a certain degree of confidence in the justice of government'. In another section of the book, he more explicitly relates differences in investment rates (hence, differences in growth rates) to the extent to which the rule of law and property rights exist:

> In all countries where there is tolerable security, every man of common under-
> standing will endeavour to employ whatever stock he can command in procur-
> ing either present enjoyment or future profit . . . In those unfortunate countries
> . . . where men are continually afraid of the violence of their superiors, they
> frequently bury and conceal a great part of their stock. (Smith, 1976[1776]:
> 284–285)

Yet neo-classical economics has ignored these early insights for a long time as it strived to explain economic activity by reference to a set of choices made under structural/technical constraints and utility functions that depict the levels of utility associated with different choices made. Once the wider institutional context is assumed away in this manner, it is relatively straightforward to demonstrate that resource allocation would be Pareto-optimal if there was perfect competition. In addition, any Pareto-optimal resource allocation that is technically feasible can be achieved by establishing free markets. The problem with this institution-free view of the world has always been that it cannot explain why different non-market institutions coexist with markets and within markets, how market and non-market institutions interact and whether different rates of growth performance may be related to differences in the institutional characteristics of national economies.

Another, but potentially more significant, problem with the neo-classical view is that its 'technical' analysis of economic activity has never been compatible with its 'background' assumptions concerning the exist-ence of property rights and the extent to which contracts are concluded and implemented with a degree of confidence (Rodrik, 2000). It does not require immense imagination to see that *technically-feasible* economic outcomes may remain *socially-unfeasible* if the existing definition of property rights is not credible due to the existence of a highly intrusive or excessively weak state; if inadequate trust levels discourage the forma-tion of contracts (Fukuyama, 1996); or if contracts are costly to enforce due to lack of trust in the legitimacy of the economic/political regime or because of poor judicial quality. As the transition experience of the ex-Soviet countries has demonstrated, the creation of markets and private property rights was not sufficient for the emergence of efficient entrepre-neurs. Instead, there has been the emergence of entrepreneurs excelling in anti-competitive behaviour and tax avoidance, and corporate governance failures that range from insider dealing to outright fraud. As Coase (1992: 714) has indicated, the countries of the ex-Soviet space 'may be advised to move to a market economy . . . but without the appropriate institutions no market economy is possible'. The appropriate institutions in this context refer to more than 'the rule of law' and 'property rights institutions' that Djankov et al.. (2003) consider as the remedy to the problems in transition countries. Also necessary are regulatory institutions, institutions of social insurance, quality of networking institutions, institutions of conflict resolution and institutions supportive of the production of 'public goods' in the general sense, including an efficient public policy.

The studies in this book were presented at a conference on economic governance and economic outcomes, held at the University of Greenwich in June 2010. The aim of the conference was to build on the extensive literature on the relationship between governance quality and macro-economic outcomes such as growth, investment and income inequality; but also to encourage debate on how the impact of governance quality unfolds at the micro-economic level to affect individual or corporate behaviour. The outcome is the nine articles that follow this introduction – four of which focus on micro-level behaviour, three on macro-level outcomes and two on the meso-level of privatised utility regulation. In what follows, we first provide a brief overview of the evolution of the debate on the relationship between economic governance institutions and economic outcomes. The aim here is to introduce the reader to the economic governance debate that has inspired the work in this volume directly or indirectly. Then, we summarise the main issues questions addressed by the studies and the conclusions derived.

QUALITY OF GOVERNANCE INSTITUTIONS: DEFINITION, FUNCTIONS AND MEASUREMENT

According to North (1994), institutions can be defined as 'rules of the game' between economic actors. Rules of the game consist of either 'formal constraints' (for example, rules, laws, constitutions) or 'informal constraints' (for example norms of behaviour, conventions, voluntary codes of conduct) and their enforcement characteristics. Institutions can also refer to routines and ways of behaving that are based on formal rules, past decisions, tacit knowledge and norms and are only modified if the environment changes (Nelson and Winter, 1982). In this definition, the emphasis is on how institutions define the 'cost/incentive structure' of societies and economies. Lin and Nugent (1995: 2306–2307), among others, concur with this view by defining institutions as 'a set of . . . behavioural rules that shape and govern interactions between human beings, partly by helping them to form expectations . . .'.

The second definition of institutions is associated with Williamson (1975; 1985), but it in fact dates back to Coase (1937). In this definition, institutions are considered as 'governance structures' rather than as 'rules of the game'. The emphasis here is on ownership structures, hierarchies, corporate culture or information asymmetries that lead to principal–agent problems. The question addressed by this approach is: how do institutions enable economic actors to avoid prisoners' dilemma outcomes or prevent the collective action failures in their repeated interactions (Milgrom and Roberts, 1992). One way in which institutions can help to resolve such problems is the guarantee they provide for well-defined property rights (Coase, 1937). Another would be statutory or voluntary governance standards that could alleviate agency problems which emerge when agents (public or private actors) act against the interests of the principals (citizens, consumers, stakeholders, and so on) who appoint them to carry out a function on their behalf. The difference between institutions as 'governance structures' and as 'rules of the game' may not be easy to pin down, but can be clarified as follows: 'institutions as governance structures' are a system of rules that enable economic actors to avoid sub-optimal collective action outcomes that might emerge when 'institutions as rules of the game' are either inadequate or absent.

The third approach to institutions is associated with Axelrod (1984). In his analysis of cooperation, Axelrod explores how cooperation can emerge in a world of self-interested actors (superpowers, businesses or individuals) when there is no central authority to police their actions. He points out the importance of internalised network norms that encourage cooperative behaviour within large groups that, according to Olson (1965 and 1982), face collective action problems preventing them from cooperation. In this setting, governance institutions can be conceptualised as 'private ordering' outcomes that can resolve information and sanctioning problems in a decentralized manner (Dixit, 2008; Ostrom, 1990). In this setting, institutions are rather informal and they emerge as a result of repeated actions to provide information about trading partners and/or to punish the partners when the latter cheat.

Three conclusions can be derived from the definitional debate on institutions. First, institutions differ from organisations that may also be referred to as 'institutions' in the language of public debate – and this is for two reasons. First, organisations such as firms, central banks or regulatory agencies are essentially goal-oriented economic actors. Organisations may well be guided and/or constrained by institutional norms, or they may be the enforcers of those norms. However, organisations differ from institutions because the latter are not specific to a particular organisation and should not be confused with the rules/by-laws that govern the operation of the organisations. Rather, institutions (either as 'rules of the game' or as 'governance structures') operate at a deeper level as endogenous solutions to the collective action problems that organisations may be established to address. Secondly, the distinction between institutions and organisations enables us to focus on 'governance quality' rather than organisational structure per se. In this context, governance quality refers to the extent to which public or private sector organisations are subject to the right mix of incentives and constraints that induce them to deliver optimal outcomes. Therefore, institutions as governance quality are more pervasive in their effects not only on the economy as a whole, but also on the organisations within the economic sphere.

The second conclusion that can be derived here is that governance institutions are products of collective action and public choice. In that sense, they can be conceived of as constituent parts of the social contract between members of a community that consist of individual, corporate and political economic actors – with different levels of power endowment at the beginning and during the historical period within which the contract takes shape (Lessnoff, 1990). As such, institutions emerge as endogenous choices and are not necessarily optimal in terms of either efficiency or equity. The endogenous nature of institutions and the determinants of their optimality/sub-optimality have been discussed widely not only by Marx (1872), but also by a wide-range of non-Marxist social scientists including von Mises (1949), Hayek (1960), Olson (1965; 1982), Buchanan and Tullock (1962), Stigler (1971) and North (1990). What emerges from this debate is that the incumbents with economic/political/social power can influence the choice of institutions that serve their interests. More recently, Acemoglu (2003) has also demonstrated new theoretical grounds and provided empirical evidence indicating that inefficient institutions may be both prevalent and persistent – mainly because they are chosen to 'serve the interests of politicians or social groups that hold political power at the expense of the rest'.

Yet, the endogenous nature of institutions is not always conducive to the choice of sub-optimal institutions. Elinor Olstrom's extensive work has demonstrated that local communities have managed common pool resources (CPRs) successfully for long periods and distilled a range of rules and enforcement mechanisms that determine both success and failure (Ostrom, 1990). She has also demonstrated that bottom-up or local institutions tend to perform better than formal (government-imposed) rules or market-based discipline through privatisation. Ostrom identified a number of principles for successful management of CPRs, the most important of which are: (1) rules should clearly define who is entitled to what; (2) there should be adequate conflict resolution mechanisms in place; and (3) there should be a good alignment between an individual's duty to maintain the resource and the benefits that they will derive from that resource. Put differently, reciprocity, fairness and clear enforcement mechanisms are essential ingredients for efficient institutions.

The third conclusion is that governance institutions can be essentially of two types. *Type One institutions* that include institutions as rules of the game (North, 1990; Axelrod, 1984) and *Type Two institutions* that include institutions as governance structures (Coase, 1937; Williamson, 1975, 1985). Type One institutions tend to have a *market-creating effect* by encouraging/supporting the emergence of new markets where economic actors can engage in mutually beneficial economic exchange. The higher the quality of Type One institutions, the lower the transaction costs, the higher the transaction volumes and the higher the probability that economic actors will extend their activities into new areas or sectors. The overall result is an expansion in the set of mutually-beneficial economic activities and an increase in economic performance. This result is underpinned by institutional quality that encourages trust/cooperation, higher levels of contracting and provides incentives for investment in human as well as physical capital. The quality of Type One institutions can be measured by the quality of the following indicators: rule of law, contract enforceability, risk of expropriation, power and accountability, judicial competence and impartiality and trust.

Type Two institutions, on the other hand, tend to have a *market-deepening* effect, which refers to increased efficiency of the existing markets in which economic actors interact and conclude mutually-beneficial contracts. This effect is felt as a result of improved quality of public and private governance structures, which enables economic actors to secure higher overall returns on a given volume of contracting. In other words, higher quality of Type Two institutions leads to higher levels of governance quality that, in turn, leads to: (1) reduced risks of coordination failures and agency problems; (2) lower incidence of externalities and market failures; and (3) improved policy credibility and reduced macroeconomic volatility. As the quality of Type Two institutions increases, economies will be less likely to suffer welfare losses that arise from resource misallocation and distortions. The quality of Type Two institutions, on the other hand, can be measured by the quality of the following indicators: bureaucratic/government efficiency, policy predictability, company law and corporate governance regimes and transparency/accountability.

Having clarified some definitional issues and identified the types of institutions, we can now try to distil some conclusions about the functions of governance institutions and address the issues concerning the use of existing institutional quality measures/indicators. With respect to the functional classification, we draw on Rodrik (2000), who identifies the functional range of institutions and elaborates on how they impact on economic performance.

Property Rights Institutions

Property rights institutions are norms and rules that confer rights and guarantees concerning returns to the assets invested or values produced. The institutions in this category refer to the rule of law, law enforcement quality, contract enforceability, risk of appropriation, political discretion, accountability and procedures for change of executive. Property rights institutions affect economic performance by affecting the economic actors' decisions to save and invest in physical as well as human capital, and all decisions related to the conclusion of mutually-beneficial contracts. They also affect economic performance by establishing a certain level of trust, which reduces the risks associated with given levels of returns on investment and contracting.

Regulatory Institutions

The institutions in this category correspond to norms, rules and regulations that can prevent or mitigate market failures and agency problems. They indicate the extent to which the civil service is independent from politicians, the extent to which policy-makers and regulators are open to capture by interest groups and the extent to which economic policy-makers as well as corporate actors are accountable to the public in general and stakeholders in particular. They can be measured by the extent of corruption, tax evasion, regulatory burden, quality of bureaucracy, and so on. These norms and regulations affect economic performance by enhancing the efficiency of public policy and by mitigating the risk of anti-competitive behaviour, free-riding and rent-seeking by corporate actors.

Institutions for Macroeconomic Stabilisation

Institutions for macroeconomic stabilisation are institutions that could reduce macro-economic instability either by minimising the incidence of policy-induced macro-economic volatility or by increasing the resilience of the economy to adverse external shocks. The strength of the stabilisation institutions can be measured by the independence of the central bank, by the transparency and credibility of the budgetary process and by the extent to which competences are distributed and accountability is ensured by transparent rules and procedures. Stabilisation institutions can affect economic performance by reducing uncertainty and making economic growth sustainable.

Institutions for Conflict Resolution

Institutions for conflict resolution are the norms, rules and principles that are in place to resolve social/economic and political/ethnic conflicts. The economic/social conflict resolution institutions address coordination failures, distribution problems and issues of inclusion/exclusion into the formal economy. The ethnic/political conflict resolution institutions address issues such as violence, exclusion, solidarity, personal security, and so on. While economic/social conflict resolution institutions affect economic performance by reducing the risk of prisoners' dilemma situations and associated sub-optimal outcomes, ethnic/political conflict resolution institutions have an impact on economic performance by enhancing inclusion and solidarity.

The final issue to be addressed in this section relates to measures of institutional quality used in the empirical literature. The large majority of empirical studies use three main sources of governance quality data: (1) the International Country Risk Guide of the Political Risk Services (ICRG); (2) the Word-wide Governance Indicators (WGI) of the World Bank; and (3) the Corruption Perception Index of Transparency International (TI). The remaining studies use other sources, which include the Business Environment Risk Intelligence (BERI) indices, the Economist Intelligence Unit Country Risk Service and Democracy Index and Polity IV data.

The institutional quality measures provided in these sources consists of scores between a minimum and a maximum value for each country/year. The country score consists of the average of all scores assigned by individual interviewees or country experts. Hence, existing measures of institutional quality tend to consist of subjective scores. As such, use of institutional quality measures poses a number of problems for empirical research.

One problem is what is described as 'halo effect' or reverse causality, whereby institutional quality measures may be influenced by the extent to which respondents to surveys are satisfied with the economic performance (say, growth) in a particular year rather than the true level of governance quality per se. This endogeneity or reverse causality problem has been discussed widely in the literature, of which Kurtz and Schrank (2007) is a recent example. However, endogeneity due to perception-based nature of the data or the dependence of governance quality on economic development can be and has been addressed in the empirical literature.

For example, Acemoglu et al. (2001) have introduced instrumental variables that are correlated with institutional quality but are not likely to be influenced by economic performance in a particular year – for example, settler mortality rates in the early colonial period. They have demonstrated that institutional quality is the determinant of economic performance rather than the other way round. Knack and Keefer (1997b), on the other hand, used a measure of ethnic cleavage and the number of law students as instrumental variables. They also reported that survey-based institutional indicators such as rule of law, pervasiveness of corruption, the risk of contract repudiation, and so on, are significant predictors of a country's ability to catch up. Finally, using Granger causality tests for panel data, Rodrik et al. (2004) have also demonstrated that the endogeneity problem can be addressed and that institutions tend to be more powerful determinants of economic performance compared to policy variables such as openness to trade.

Nevertheless, there is an additional problem posed by the use of perception-based measures of institutional quality: the risk of 'business bias' that may originate from survey design, which may involve over-representation of business representatives and/or selective choice of survey questions. However, this risk may be less serious than suspected. For example, Kaufmann et al. (2007) report that scores obtained from business surveys are highly correlated with governance quality scores obtained from household surveys conducted by non-governmental organisations (NGOs). For example, in the case of the 'government effectiveness' indicator for 2005, the correlation between two major business surveys was 0.74. This correlation, however, is quite similar to the correlation between the results of these two business surveys and a survey of households in Africa – which was 0.70.

The problems highlighted above suggest that governance indicators may not present perfect measures of perceived governance quality, but the empirical studies have developed instrumentation methods to address the endogeneity problem. In addition, the existing indicators are based on clearly specified methodologies and are open to verification. In that sense, they satisfy the so-called 'substantive significance' test proposed by Taylor and Frideres (1972). Taylor and Frideres state that 'configured data' satisfy the admissibility test if it allows for subsequent error checks and it is relevant to test for two or more alternative theoretical predictions. Institutional quality data satisfies this admissibility condition because it has been used widely in the literature estimating the impact of institutional quality on different performance measures and has led to different estimation results depending on the country or time dimensions of the data used.

Keefer (2004) sums up the relevance of institutional quality research and the emerging patterns for future research fairly well. He indicates that significant progress has been made in understanding the sources of 'good governance' and the latter's effects on economic development. However, governance quality has been used to capture a heterogeneous range of concepts and consequences for economic outcomes. Therefore, future research should focus more on separate indicators of governance quality such as security of property rights, quality of bureaucratic performance, corruption and voice and accountability. Future research should also focus more explicitly on the linkage between governance quality and the incentives for governments to correct poor institutional quality. The studies included in this volume take valuable steps in that direction by examining the effects of different dimensions of governance quality, the determinants of governance quality and the relationship between formal and informal institutions as well as the relationship between governance institutions, networks and regulatory regimes.

DOES ECONOMIC GOVERNANCE MATTER? THE EXISTING EVIDENCE

We have identified 21 empirical studies examining the relationship between institutional quality and economic performance. These studies, which were all published between 1995 and 2004, tend to report a positive and statistically significant association. Some of them demonstrate that the direction of causation is from institutions to economic performance and not the other way round. Some others report that variations in institutional quality are more significant than other variables that also affect economic performance (for example, geography or openness to trade).

These studies draw on cross-country and/or panel data and the majority address the endogeneity problem mentioned above – that is, the possibility of reverse causality or interdependence between the measures of institutional quality and economic performance. For example, Knack and Keefer (1995) report that institutions protecting property rights are significant predictors of economic growth.

In a subsequent study, Knack and Keefer (1997a) estimate the impact of differences in trust and civic cooperation norms on investment/GDP ratios and per-capita GDP growth rates during the period 1980–1992. They find that both trust and civic cooperation are positively associated with investment/GDP ratios and per capita GDP growth rates. The authors control for endogeneity by using ethnic cleavage and the number of law students as instrumental variables – that is, as institutional proxies that are less likely to be influenced by the level of development itself. In a parallel study, Knack and Keefer (1997b) examine the impact of institutions on a developing country's ability to catch up with developed countries. This is an innovative exercise as it constitutes the first attempt to re-specify the neo-classical convergence model. They find that institutional indicators such as rule of law, pervasiveness of corruption, the risk of contract repudiation, and so on, have significant effects on a country's ability to catch up. The authors conduct robustness tests and report that institutional factors remain significant determinants of convergence.

Another set of studies published between 1996 and 1999 report similar results. For example, Ades and di Tella (1996) review the empirical literature on the relationship between corruption and investment. They report that the majority of the work reviewed leads to two unequivocal conclusions: (1) corruption and judicial system quality are associated positively; and (2) higher levels of corruption are associated with lower investment levels. Brunetti et al. (1997a and 1997b) focus on institutional factors that affect the credibility and predictability of the rules affecting business establishments. Brunetti et al. (1997a) use company-level data for 3,600 companies from different countries and report that rule credibility is a significant determinant of investment decisions by the firms and growth rates recorded by the countries. In Brunetti et al. (1997b), the authors regress foreign direct investment and economic growth on indicators of institutional predictability. They report that institutional predictability explains a large part of the differences in foreign investment flows attracted and economic growth rates recorded. Political stability and security of the property rights are found to be especially important.

Clague et al. (1997) use a combination of institutional quality and contract intensity measures (defined as contract-intensive money) and report that institutional measures have positive and statistically significant impacts on investment and output growth. The results hold irrespective of whether the sample consists of all countries for which data is available or only less developed countries. Three more studies published in 1999 also report similar results. For example, Hall and Jones (1999) examine the impact 'social infrastructure' (measured as composite index of law and order, bureaucratic quality, risk of appropriation, corruption, and so on) report that social infrastructure account for much of the difference in productivity measured as output per worker. Similarly, Kaufmann et al. (1999) examine the impact of institutional quality indicators on development outcomes such as per-capita GDP, infant mortality and adult literacy. The authors report a strong relationship between governance quality and development outcomes. Their results remain robust to inclusion or exclusion of OECD countries. Finally, Rodrik (1999) reports that internal social conflicts and weak conflict resolution institutions explain why high growth rates experienced in some periods did not persist and why a large number of countries experienced growth collapses after the mid-1970s. This finding suggests that institutional quality is a predictor not only of economic growth but also of its sustainability.

The empirical findings summarised above lend support to the argument that institutional quality is a significant predictor of cross-country variations in economic performance. However, they should not detract attention from two empirical/methodological problems encountered in quantitative estimations of the institutions–economic performance relationship.

First, both institutional quality and economic performance may be determined endogenously. In other words, institutional quality (that is, the explanatory variable) may be affected by the level of development itself (that is, by the dependent variable); or both variables may be affected by other variables that are excluded from the regression equations. The endogeneity problem is also posed by the subjective nature of the institutional indicators. The latter are collected through surveys of experts or other actors, whose perceptions of institutions at a particular time are likely to be influenced by how well the economy is performing at the time of the survey. Unless further robustness tests and instrumentation techniques are used, the endogeneity problem may lead to upward bias in reported estimates.

Acemoglu et al. (2001) came up with an interesting solution to the endogeneity problem by using data on settler mortality rates as an instrument for institutional quality. Settler mortality rates enable the authors to identify regions/lands where colonial settlers were less likely to settle for long because of high health hazards. Settlers in high-health-risk areas would be inclined to secure extraction in the short run and would be less concerned about building institutions guaranteeing property rights in the long run. Settlers in low-health-risk areas, however, can be expected to have an interest in building institutions guaranteeing property rights. Because variations in settler mortality rates and the following variations in institution-building efforts preceded divergence in economic performance, a negative relationship between settler death rates and economic performance would suggest that: (1) institutional quality is a good predictor of economic performance; and (2) the causality would be from institutions to economic performance rather than the other way round. Acemoglu et al. (2001) report that settler death rates (hence, institutional quality) are good predictors of the current discrepancy in economic performance. This innovative approach to instrumentation has encouraged the adoption of other methods of controlling for endogeneity – including simultaneous estimations through two-stage or three-stage least squares, use of the general method of moments (GMM) that uses the optimally-lagged values of the institutional measures that is not correlated with the error term and use of ethnic tensions/cleavages as instruments for institutional quality.

The second problem we need to consider relates to the effect of other variables – for example, openness to trade and geography – on economic performance. For example, Frankel and Romer (1999) use the nominal trade/GDP ratio as a measure of openness and report that the degree of openness is a significant predictor of the cross-country variations in economic performance. Later, Alcala and Ciccone (2004) use the ratio of nominal trade to purchasing-power-parity-adjusted GDP (the so-called 'real openness' indicator) and report a similar result. In fact, Alcala and Ciccone demonstrate that their results obtained by using the real openness indicator are more robust than those reported by Frankel and Romer (1999).

Similar results are also reported with respect to the effect of geography. For example, Gallup et al. (1998) examine the relationship between geography and economic growth, controlling for economic policies and institutions. They find that geographical location and climate have large effects on income levels and growth rates. Geographical factors affect economic performance via transportation costs, disease burden and low productivity in agriculture. Sachs (2001) also reports that geographical location is a significant predictor of low technology in two sectors: agriculture and healthcare. As a result, countries located in tropical areas tend to record lower growth rates. Finally, Sachs (2001) controls for institutional quality and demonstrates that malaria transmission has a direct and significant effect on per capita income levels.

Given these findings on the impact of openness to trade and geography (that is, non-institutional factors), it is necessary to disentangle the partial effects of both institutional and non-institutional variables, and establish whether collinearity exists between them. To address these issues, Dollar and Kraay (2003) examine the partial effects of openness to trade and institutional quality on per capita GDP. They report that cross-country regressions of per capita GDP trend on proxied measures of openness and institutional quality do not provide reliable information about the partial effect of either institutions or trade in the long run. This is mainly because of the high level of correlation between openness and institutional quality. To avoid this problem, Dollar and Kraay regress decade-long changes in growth rates on decade-long changes in the degree of openness to trade and institutional quality. They find that trade has a significant effect on GDP growth, but institutions do not.

Rodrik et al. (2004) respond to Dollar and Kraay (2003) by conducting a two-stage regression to estimate the direct and indirect effects of institutions, trade and geography on economic performance. They report that the 'quality of institutions' is more significant than either geography or trade. In fact, they demonstrate that when institutions are controlled for, conventional measures of geography have at best weak direct effects on incomes whereas trade is insignificant and enters into the equation with the wrong (that is, negative) sign. The estimated direct effect of institutions on incomes is positive and large. A unit improvement in institutional quality increases log income by 2.15. The estimated direct effect of trade on income is negative but statistically insignificant. Finally, the estimated effect of trade on institutions is positive but small. As a result, Rodrik et al. (2004) argue that 'institutions rule' as far as partial direct effects are concerned.

This finding suggests that it is difficult to accept Dollar and Kraay's argument that 'multicollinearity blurs the individual effects of institutions and trade'. Although geography and trade may affect institutional quality, it is possible to control for such effects and identify the institutions' partial effects independently. In addition, Rodrik et al. (2004) demonstrate that Dollar and Kraay's scepticism about the tractability of the partial effects are due to arbitrariness in their sampling (for example, omission of some European countries that are not essentially outliers) and their choice of independent variables (for example, the substitution of nominal openness with 'real' openness). That is why it is not surprising to observe that the significance of the partial effects of institutions is confirmed by other studies too. For example, Nsouli et al. (2004) examine the partial effects of institutions and IMF programme implementation on the basis of data for 197 IMF programmes approved between 1992 and 2002. They report the following findings: (1) improvement in institutional quality during the programme implementation period is associated with better growth performance; (2) although institutional quality and programme implementation are both important determinants of growth, institutional factors have a quantitatively larger effect; and (3) although programme implementation is the major influence on current account balance in the first year of the implementation period, institutional factors have a larger effect in the long run.

The studies summarised above have made a significant contribution to making the role of governance institutions a central issue in the study of economics in general and development economics in particular. Written against this background, more recent studies have made further contributions by modelling the interaction between economic governance institutions, political institutions and economic performance and by differentiating between formal (government-imposed) and informal (private ordering) institutions.

With respect to the former, Acemoglu et al. (2004) have analysed the choice of economic governance institutions, the relationship between the latter and political institutions and the implications of political institutions for power asymmetry between social groups. In their model, social choices concerning economic institutions tend to favour groups with greater political power, which consists of de jure and de facto power. Both political institutions and the distribution of power change over time as economic governance institutions affect the distribution of resources; and groups with de facto power now try to change the political institutions with a view to increase their de jure power in the future. In this setting, economic governance institutions favouring growth emerge when: (1) political institutions allocate power to groups with interests in broad-based property rights enforcement; (2) when political institutions create effective constraints on power-holders; and (3) when there are relatively few rents to be captured by power-holders. With respect to the difference between formal/informal institutions, Dixit (2003) examines the resolution of asymmetric prisoners' dilemmas between economic actors. In this model, games are played repeatedly, but information about cheating is inadequate and there is no official legal system of contract enforcement to encourage or sustain cooperation. Dixit (2003) demonstrates that private ordering institutions can emerge as profit-maximising supply of private intermediation that provides the necessary information and enforcement mechanisms. Although these types of private ordering institutions represent an improvement compared to total absence of formal governance institutions, they may fail to achieve social optimality.

DOES ECONOMIC GOVERNANCE MATTER? CONTRIBUTIONS OF THE STUDIES IN THIS VOLUME

The chapters in this volume are organised in three parts. The chapters in the first part examine the relationship between governance institutions and micro-economic behaviour. Chapters in the second examine the relationship between governance institutions and macro-economic outcomes such as investment, taxes and employment. The third part examines the interface between governance institutions and regulation of privatised utilities. In what follows, we will provide a brief overview of the questions addressed and the findings reported in individual studies.

Part I brings together four chapters that examine the relationship between governance institutions and micro-economic behaviour. The two chapters by Ertürk and Ietto-Gillies draw on qualitative evidence, whereas the other two by Lazega et al. and Engelen combine both qualitative and quantitative evidence. With respect to context, Ertürk provides a theoretical/analytical account that may be applicable to different markets and/or contracts within each market. The other three focus on specific contexts that include conflict resolution in the Commercial Court of Paris

(Lazega et al.), legal versus reputational penalties in deterring corporate misconduct in a set of European and American companies (Engelen) and the interaction between national governance systems and transnational companies (Ietto-Gillies).

What unifies these chapters is a common research question: how do economic governance institutions influence the behaviour of economic agents and what can be said about the optimality or effectiveness of chosen governance institutions?

To address this general question, Ertürk (in Chapter 2) analyses how institutions could give order to a Hobbesian 'state of nature' when the Leviathan has fallen asleep – that is, when the autonomy and authority of the state has been eroded by globalisation or by the dominance of policies in tune with the interests of the powerful economic actors. He seeks to find out whether self-interested agents could rely on their own devices to enforce contracts. This is akin to the question addressed by Dixit (2003), who examines the scope for and consequences of private for-profit institutions that emerge either in the absence of, in parallel to, formal institutions. Yet Ertürk develops his analysis in a different (and we would argue, in an innovative) direction to establish what effect(s) power asymmetry between agents would have on the latter's commitments in the long run – and thereby on the scope for higher levels of contracting (that is, the scope for market creation) and on the cost of contract enforcement (that is, the scope for market deepening).

Drawing on the concept of disembedded markets and the work of Axelrod (1984) and Gintis (2007), Ertürk demonstrates that power asymmetry increases the cost of contract enforcement when formal (that is, government-backed) institutions and enforcement mechanisms exist, and would reduce the efficiency of contracting when economic agents rely solely on repeated market exchanges as commitment devices. He then goes on to examine the commitment problems faced by the 'powerful' and 'weak' agents when formal institutions designed to address power asymmetry are weak or absent. He concludes that, in such situations, the ability of the 'weak' agent (for example, consumers or workers) to engage in collective action or coalition building may emerge as a solution to the commitment problem faced by the weak agents (workers, consumers, and so on) as well as powerful agents (employers or firms in imperfect markets). For Ertürk, institutional norms that underpinned strong safety nets and powerful unions in the post-1945 period had contributed to easing of both challenges as they reduced the incidence of free-riding and opportunistic competition between the weak agents and helped the powerful agents solve their commitment problem. In a way, Ertürk's contribution also ties in with Acemoglu's theoretical finding suggesting that economic governance institutions favouring growth are more likely to emerge when political institutions create effective constraints on power-holders and allocate power to groups with interests in broad-based property rights enforcement rather than protection of rents or ability to extract rents.

In Chapter 3, Lazega, Mounier and Tubaro adopt a 'joint governance' approach that combines formal governance with self-governance that is similar to what Dixit (2003) describes as institutions of private ordering under the umbrella of the state. Their innovation consists of introducing a social networks perspective that enables them to analyse the impacts of inter-actor resource dependencies on the performance of private ordering institutions in the area of business conflict resolution. Their case study and data are based on the procedures and decisions of the first Commercial Court in Paris – a consular court to which the French state delegates conflict-resolution powers with respect to business disputes and to disputes between shareholders and management boards.

One of Lazega et al.'s contributions is that the nature of the advice network that judges are involved in affects the normative orientation of the court and eventually its decisions. The network in this context represents the channels through which knowledge, norms, ideas and guidance circulate. This network effect is in addition to the effect of the organisational structure of the court – that is, its chambers and internal hierarchy. As such, the network effect reported by Lazega et al. contributes to our understanding of the difference between organisations and institutions – a difference referred to above – and highlights the importance of institutional norms as an additional determinant of organisational performance.

Another contribution relates to how different business sectors with different inclinations towards an interventionist approach to resolution of business conflicts may influence the interpretation of the legal norms and the decisions of the court. Here Lazega et al. demonstrate that different business sectors can exercise influence not only by lobbying or having their own representatives appointed as judges, but also by being part of the advice networks that provide information to the latter. Put differently, Lazega et al. point out the risk of additional sources of institutional capture that may affect not only the quality of the norms adopted but also the performance of joint governance institutions established under the umbrella of the state.

Finally, Lazega et al. extend the space over which private ordering institutions backed by the state (that is, joint governance institutions) may be better than institutional vacuum, but they may still produce socially sub-optimal outcomes. Dixit (2003) indicates that sub-optimal outcomes can result under certain conditions and with respect to the market-based private ordering institutions that provide information and enforcement.

Lazega et al. extend this finding by demonstrating that joint governance can also lead to suboptimal conflict resolution. Joint governance institutions may be efficient in terms of speed, but its combination of relation-based and rule-based modes of governance can lead to sub-optimal outcomes – by allowing certain parties to 'cheat' more easily, to protect their rent and power, or to double cross any other party in a conflict.

Engelen examines another version of the joint governance model in Chapter 4, where he focuses on the interaction between law (public and private law) enforcement and enforcement through market discipline. In this chapter, the financial market is taken to be an institution that disseminates information about corporate insider dealings and exerts penalties through lower share values. Engelen reports existing evidence on public enforcement power in six European countries and the United States, and then tests whether there is any interaction between a country's public enforcement power and the magnitude of reputational penalties companies experience in the wake of illegal insider trading. He uses an event study methodology, with data for average abnormal returns aligned with the time when the event of corporate misconduct becomes public knowledge.

Engelen's work provides interesting insights into the relationship between public and private law enforcement characteristics and between the latter and the reputational penalties imposed by the market when company insiders engage in corporate misconduct. Engelen first distinguishes between public law enforcement through actions of regulatory bodies and private law enforcement through 'class actions' of the shareholders. Examining the evidence on the number of legal actions taken and penalties imposed, he reports that private law actions combined with public law actions tend to yield higher penalties and quicker settlements compared to private law actions only. This evidence indicates that there are complementarities between public and private law institutions governing corporate insider dealing.

Engelen takes the next step and tests for existence or absence of complementarities between public and private law enforcement characteristics of the countries in the sample and the enforcement through the stock market as a private ordering institution. Using a dataset for 202 insider dealings announcements in seven countries, he first estimates the average abnormal returns due to the announcement of the insider dealing event and then calculates the correlations between the latter and the countries' public and private law enforcement scores. He reports that both the Pearson's rank correlation and the polyserial correlation coefficients are small and statistically significant. Hence, he concludes that there is no substitution between reputational penalties and legal penalties. As such, the overall conclusion is that reputational penalties imposed by stock market participants can be taken as an additional enforcement channel that operates alongside the private and public law enforcement channels. The loss due to reputational penalties is usually larger than the legal penalties imposed pursuant to public and/or private law actions, but this does not suggest that market-based private ordering institutions should replace formal legal institutions. It merely indicates that a more detailed analysis of the interaction between two types of institutions is necessary. One potential avenue could be to model and estimate abnormal returns not only as a function of the 'news' about insider dealing incidents, but also of the 'news' about whether a public or private law action has been taken during the estimation period.

The fifth chapter in this section is by Ietto-Gillies, who takes the governance debate beyond Williamson's analysis of the transnational companies. While Williamson analyses the firm in general and the transnational companies in particular as governance structures for minimising transaction costs, Ietto-Gillies looks at how the transnational companies may exploit the differences between national governance regimes.

Ietto-Gillies argues that differences between regulatory regimes of different countries create scope for advantages and for strategic behaviour by TNCs vis-à-vis other actors such as labour, suppliers, governments as well as rival firms in relation to factors such as knowledge acquisition and risk spreading. She then goes on to examine how transnational companies exploit differences in governance regimes and further widen the asymmetry of power between TNCs and other actors who do not have transnational power. Ietto-Gilles continues her analysis to demonstrate that the exacerbated power asymmetry leads to re-distribution in favour of transnational companies and to the disadvantage of other actors. Specifically, the interaction between national governance structures and transnational companies leads to redistribution from wages to profits and from the social to the private spheres. Ietto-Gillies' contribution to the governance debate can be stated as follows: what affects the distribution of wealth and resources between different actors is not only the quality of national governance structures, but also the extent to which transnational companies can play off these national governance structures against each other. Hence, high levels of governance quality in a particular country cannot be relied upon to deliver optimal outcomes in terms of equity or efficiency. This is a significant contribution and can inspire future empirical research focusing on the relationship between economic outcomes such as income inequality, poverty, health, regional disparity, etc, and measures the interaction between governance quality and prevalence of transnational corporations within a jurisdiction.

Part II contains three chapters on the relationship between governance institutions and macro-economic outcomes. As indicated in the brief review of the empirical evidence above, the impact of governance institutions on macro-economic outcomes such as growth and investment is a well-researched issue in the literature. This observation, however, does not imply less scope for innovation – and the chapters in Part II embrace the challenge of innovation willingly and effectively. The first two chapters, Aysan et al. in Chapter 6 and Alonso et al. in Chapter 7, examine the relationship between governance institutions on the one hand and investment, taxes and foreign aid on the other, and report a rich a set of findings that make valuable contributions to the debate. The third study by Passaris is normative in nature and makes its contribution by exploring the extent to which one can draw on the economic governance framework to devise a scheme for full employment in the wake of the global financial crisis and within a globalising world economy.

Aysan et al. extend the empirical content of the literature by focusing on a relatively under-studied region – namely the Black Sea Economic Cooperation Zone (BSEC). The authors first investigate the relationship between governance institutions and investment for a sample of 43 developing countries, using a dynamic system GMM estimation methodology to control for endogeneity between investment and institutional quality indicators. They innovate by adopting a comprehensive approach to the range and classification of the governance institutions included in the analysis. As such, their work responds to the task for future research identified by Keefer (2004): systematic disaggregation of institutional quality indicators instead of using composite indices.

Aysan et al. classify the governance institutions analysed widely in the literature into three categories: administrative quality institutions (AQ), political stability institutions (PS) and democratic accountability institutions (PA) through principal component analysis. They also construct two general governance indices (GOV1 and GOV2), using most of the information contained in all governance indicators. This categorisation enables them to incorporate all available information about institutional quality and minimise the collinearity problem at the same time. They report empirical results that confirm the importance of institutional variables for investment. The positive association between investment and measures of institutional quality holds and remain significant with respect to administrative quality (AQ), political stability (PS) and democratic accountability (PA) – as well as for the general indices of governance (GOV1) and (GOV2).

The second contribution of Aysan et al. is the simulation results they report for BSEC countries. The authors conduct a simulation exercise to estimate how much capital accumulation would be enhanced if governance institutions reached the levels of EU-12 average. Calculations were conducted by using the proportion of each governance index affecting the GOV2 index, the coefficient coming from the regression and the gap between BSEC and EU-12 averages. Their results for the final year show that the investment/GDP ratio could increase by 0.58 per cent over the baseline if the quality of bureaucracy and control over corruption caught up with EU-12 average. A similar improvement in the law and order and democratic accountability indicators would lead to lower but still significant increases in investment/GDP ratio – by 0.17 per cent and 0.18 per cent, respectively.

The third contribution by Aysan et al. relates to the linkage they establish between the economic governance literature and regionalisation literature that examines the causes and consequences of regional bloc formation. The authors provide detailed evidence on the trend in BSEC governance indicators since the establishment of the cooperation zone and on the extent of convergence towards governance quality levels in EU-12.

In Chapter 7, Alonso et al. examine the relationship between aid, institutions and tax revenues. The main innovation here concerns the examination of the two-way relationship between aid, institutions and taxes. The authors first examine the impact of international aid on institutional quality. Then, they examine the impact of aid on the incentives to mobilise tax revenue and show that this effect is mediated through institutional quality.

One contribution by Alonso et al. is to provide evidence that contradicts the consensus among the small number of studies that reported a negative impact of aid on institutional quality. The authors demonstrate that the negative effect reported in those studies does not hold when the determinants of institutional quality are analysed explicitly in the estimation model and the decreasing returns on aid are taken into account. With this approach, we can state with justified confidence that Alonso et al. provide a comprehensive framework for analysing and estimating the relationship between aid and institutional quality.

The second contribution that Alonso et al. must be credited for concerns their analysis of whether aid reduces the incentives to raise tax revenue – that is, whether aid has a substitution effect. The findings reported in the empirical literature are ambiguous on this issue. However, Alonso et al. demonstrate that these findings may not be reliable because they are based on easy-to-obtain but essentially inappropriate data for tax revenues – which consists only of central government revenues. In samples including highly-decentralised countries and/or nations with high social contributions, central government revenues may be misleading and causes significant measurement errors. Therefore, the authors construct a new database for general government tax revenues, inclusive of social contributions, and demonstrate that the impact of aid on tax revenues is positive if the institutional quality indicator is above –1.1 on a scale from –2.5 to +2.5. This finding indicates that aid has a positive effect on tax revenues and this effect may be amplified or dampened by the level of governance quality.

A third and more general contribution of Alonso et al. is their painstakingly careful and detailed analysis of the determinants of institutional quality. The authors go well beyond the narrow, and one would argue ideological, approach to institutions adopted by the World Bank or western 'advisors' of the transition regimes in central and eastern Europe – that is, by the shadow elite of the early 1990s studied in fine details and with sobering findings by Wede (2009). In this 'ideological' take on institutions, the latter are co-extensive with property rights and (law and) order institutions. We take the words 'law and' into brackets here to emphasise the importance accorded to 'order' in this approach and to indicate that 'law' is considered to have performed its function as long as 'order' is secured. This approach is epitomised in the World Bank working paper by Djankov et al. (2003) referred to above, and its main insight into institutions can be summed up as follows: there are four common strategies for social control of business: private orderings, private litigation, regulation and state ownership, and these categories are associated with falling social cost of disorder and rising social cost of dictatorship. Then, the optimal institutional choice for a particular country consists of the combination of 'disorder' and 'dictatorship' that maximises its 'objective function' – mainly growth. Translated into the transition jargon, all Djankov and his colleagues could think of when analysing institutions boil down to combinations of 'socialist dictatorship' and 'market freedom' that countries can choose from.

Alonso et al. question this instrumentalist approach to institutions and argue that institutions have to two basic economic functions: (1) reducing transaction costs, thus granting certainty and predictability to social interaction; and (2) facilitating coordination between economic agents. Then, the quality of governance institutions depends on four basic properties: (i) static efficiency, that is, the institution's capacity to promote efficient equilibria; (ii) legitimacy, that is, the institution's capacity to frame credible inter-temporal contracts; (iii) predictability, that is, an institution's capacity to reduce the uncertainty associated with human interaction; and (iv) adaptability or dynamic efficiency, that is, the extent to which an institution facilitates rather than hinders social changes, or at least generates incentives that facilitate agents' adjustment to social change. This approach represents a breath of fresh air and demonstrates how the debate on governance institutions can move beyond the instrumentalist approach that either establishes a short-cut relationship between institutions and economic performance, or justifies any given institutional choice as long as the latter is associated with growth.

The final chapter in Part II is by Passaris, who explores the scope for the creation of an 'employer of last resort' in the age of globalisation. As indicated above, Passaris is defiantly normative in his approach because, as an economist with strong interest in public policy, he is concerned about the unsustainability of current growth strategies pursued in developed countries. He argues that the institutional architecture of economic governance requires change with a view to providing an anchor for economic policy options concerning full employment. He then goes on to propose a new set of guiding principles for economic governance and articulates a road map for achieving full employment, which is congruent with the structural parameters of the new global economy.

Passaris draws on his earlier work on technological innovation and the difference between the innovation processes of the nineteenth and late-twentieth/early-twenty-first centuries. In the former, it was relatively easy and less costly to re-employ the workers made redundant by the new technology. This was due to relatively longer spells over which technological changed evolved and matured; and because of the scope this had created for re-skilling and re-employing the redundant work force. It was also due to the fact that a significant chunk of the cost of investing in human capital (that is, skill acquisition and re-skilling) was borne by employers and therefore wage claims were moderated. In the new era, however, both the cost of investing in human capital is higher and employers are less willing to contribute towards this through training or internship – mainly due to competitive pressures unleashed by globalisation. Passaris argues that these new conditions require alignment of the norms that underpin public policy design.

His concrete proposal involves the establishment of an employment commission, which will act as employer of last resort – a function similar to the stability function of the central banks as lenders of last resort. Of course, just as it is the case with role of the central bank, an employer of last resort raises the issue of moral hazard. It also raises additional issues such as financing of its operations and the quality of the jobs and training that it can offer to the unemployed for the duration of their unemployment spell. Passaris is aware of these issues, but he is also aware that the status quo is not a viable alternative. Therefore, his contribution should be seen as an attempt to challenge the existing orthodoxy and policy lethargy rather providing a 'finished' blueprint. Its added-value consists of the way in which it demonstrates how the economic governance framework can be drawn upon to propose and perhaps refine new policy regimes in an area (labour market) where pro-active public policy has been all but abandoned under the competitive pressures associated with globalisation.

Part III includes two chapters that examine the relationship between governance institutions and the choice/performance of regulatory regimes in the wake of utilities privatisation. In Chapter 9, Hlasny examines the factors behind regulatory reform in utility industries, using panel data on all natural-gas utilities in the United States. His aim is to identify the political institutional factors and other factors that affect the choice of regulatory regimes – mainly price cap regulation, consumer choice regulation and sliding scale regulation. Drawing on a rich dataset and using a proportional-hazard model for estimation, Hlasny reports that frequency and timing of commissioner re-elections, system of selection of commissioners and party composition of the commissions and state legislatures are significant in explaining the patterns of regulatory choice and reform of the gas utilities in the US. Among other factors, demonstration effects from regulatory regimes in neighbouring states and in other utility industries in each state also appear to play a role. Hlasny also reports a negative association between the prevalence of restructuring and the incidence of price cap regulation across states. He explains this association by limiting of the price cap regulation to block restructuring only.

The final chapter in Part III is by Wanderley et al., who examine the evolution of the regulatory regime for the Brazilian electricity sector. The authors view the tariff review process as a governance regime with rules and contract types for shaping incentives and constraints faced by the agents, including the government, the regulator, companies and consumers. They argue that a well-designed and well-implemented tariff review framework leads to good results in terms of the two main output measures for utility regulation: the level and rate of growth of technical efficiency and productivity, and the level of capacity. They develop and test this argument by comparing two phases of the regulatory process – the first phase from 1995–2003 when the regulatory regime was based on ad hoc and 'imported' blueprints; and the second phase from 2004 when the regulatory regime and the tariff review process became characterised by more centralisation of decision-making and a greater weight for government policy than the first phase. Wanderley et al. relate the shortcomings of the regulatory regime in the first phase to weaknesses in the governance principles that underpin the design of the regulatory agencies, and argue that low governance quality is a significant factor that led to inefficiencies and a supply crisis in 2001.

The unique and novel contribution of Hlasny and Wanderley et al. to the governance debate is their attempt to extend the application of the economic governance framework to the study of regulation. Although the link between the two areas of study seems obvious, there has been little attempt to examine the interface between economic governance and regulation. We hope that the insights provided in these chapters will contribute to the development of a novel look at the issues of regulatory capture or regulatory failures. The findings in Chapters 9 and 10 suggest that regulatory capture or regulatory failures should be considered not only as 'typical' examples of government failures, but also as symptoms of shortcomings in the underlying governance quality that, in turn, determines the risk of government failure.

CONCLUDING REMARKS

This chapter has turned out to be longer than the introductory chapters that the reader usually encounters in edited volumes. We hope that the reader will not only tolerate but also enjoy reading it because we sincerely wished to do justice to the existing literature and to spell out how the chapters in this volume are related and what contributions they make to that literature. In the remaining few paragraphs, we would like to flag up a number of general observations we have made during the conference stage and the editing stage – rather than summarising the narrative above.

One general observation about the contributions to this volume is that they are all based on original research that preceded the conference, which functioned mainly as catalyst and platform that brought together researchers grappling with similar conceptual and theoretical issues. As editors, we are thankful to all contributors who demonstrated unreserved willingness to make their work available for this volume rather than considering alternative outlets for publication.

The second observation is about our belief that the chapters in this volume do take the economic governance debate forward by extending the range of issues analysed, data used and hypotheses tested in the area. We do not claim, and nor do the contributors, that the wider perspective reflected in this volume is defined fully or constitutes a final delineation of the scope for innovation in the area of economic governance research. Nevertheless, we are confident that this volume does provide a good indication about ongoing efforts aimed at better understanding the role of governance institutions, development of new methods of analysis and use of new and/or more refined data. As such, we hope that it will not only contribute to existing knowledge but will also inspire new research questions.

The third observation is that the studies in this volume, despite their evident variety in terms of focus, context or level of analysis, reflect a common core that makes this volume coherent and cumulative in terms of the knowledge/information it provides. The common core is that the quality of governance institutions matters theoretically, empirically and at the level of policy analysis. This common theme runs across all contributions and makes the variety with respect to context, analysis or theoretical perspectives a source of richness rather than incoherence.

Finally, an observation that may help potential readers maximise the benefits of reading this volume: we must indicate that the chapters in this volume differ with respect to the 'technicality' of their analysis – ranging from verbal reasoning to estimation of highly-abstract models. Therefore, readers may have to adjust their expectations as they move from one chapter to another. This may be seen as a reason for concern, but we do not subscribe to this view for three reasons. First, the level of 'technicality' is kept to a minimum without compromising the rigour of the analysis. Secondly, the technical aspects of the analysis are embedded within a clear and easy-to-follow narrative. Thirdly, the relatively more 'technical' studies do provide diagrammatical expositions of their models as far as possible. With these 'assurances' made, all that is left to say is the following: the ultimate proof of the pudding is in the eating.

REFERENCES

Acemoglu, Daron (2003), 'Why not a political Coase theorem: social conflict, commitment, and politics', *Journal of Comparative Economics,* **31**, 620–652.
Acemoglu, Daron and James Robinson (2000), 'Political losers as a barrier to economic development,' *American Economic Review*, **90** (2), 126–130.
Acemoglu, Daron and James Robinson (2002), 'Economic backwardness in political perspective', *NBER Working Paper*, **8831**.
Acemoglu, D., S. Johnson and J.A. Robinson (2001), 'The colonial origins of comparative development: an empirical investigation', *American Economic Review*, **91** (5), 1369–1401.
Acemoglu, D., S. Johnson and J. Robinson (2004), 'Institutions as the fundamental cause of long-run growth', *NBER Working Paper*, **10481**.
Ades, A. and R. di Tella (1996), 'The causes and consequences of corruption: a review of recent empirical contributions', *IDS Bulletin*, **27** (2), 6–11.
Aghion, Philippe, Alberto Alesina and Francisco Trebbi (2002), 'Endogenous political institutions', Harvard University mimeo.
Alcala, F. and A. Ciccone (2004), 'Trade and productivity', *Quarterly Journal of Economics*, **119** (3), 613–646.
Axelrod, R. (1984), *The Evolution of Cooperation*, New York: Basic Books.
Brunetti, A., G. Kisunko and B. Weder (1997a), 'Institutional obstacles of doing business: region-by-region results from a world-wide survey of private sector', *World Bank Policy Research Working Papers*, **1759**.
Brunetti, A., G. Kisunko and B. Weder (1997b), 'Institutions in transition:

reliability of rules and economic performance in former socialist countries', *World Bank Policy Research Working Papers*, **1809**.

Buchanan, J. and G. Tullock (1962), *The Calculus of Consent, Logical Foundations of Constitutional Democracy*, Ann Arbor, MI: University of Michigan Press.

Clague, C., P. Keefer, S. Knack and M. Olson (1997), 'Institutions and economic performance: property rights and contract enforcement', in C. Clague (ed.), *Institutions and Economic Development: Growth and Governance in Less-Developed and Post-Socialist Countries*, Baltimore, MD and London: Johns Hopkins University Press, pp. 67–90.

Coase, R. (1937), 'The nature of the firm', *Economica*, **4**, 386–405.

Coase, R. (1992), 'The institutional structure of production', *American Economic Review*, **83** (4), 713–719.

Dixit, A. (2003), 'On modes of economic governance', *Econometrica*, **71** (2), 449–481.

Dixit, A. (2008), 'Economic governance', in S.N. Durlauf and L.E. Blume (eds), *The New Palgrave Dictionary of Economics*, 2nd edn, Palgrave Macmillan, available at: http://www.dictionaryofeconomics.com/article?id=pde2008_E000260& goto=economicgovernance&result_number=958 (accessed September 2010).

Djankov, S., E. Glaeser, R. La Porta, F. Lopez-de-Silanes and A. Shleifer (2003), 'The new comparative economics', *World Bank Policy Research Working Paper*, **3054** (May).

Dollar, D. and A. Kraay (2003), 'Institutions, trade and growth', *Journal of Monetary Economics*, **50** (1), 133–162.

Frankel, J. and D. Romer (1999), 'Does trade cause growth?', *American Economic Review*, **89** (3), 379–399.

Fukuyama, F. (1996), *Trust. The Social Virtues and Creation of Prosperity*, London: Penguin.

Gallup, J.L., J.D. Sachs and A.D. Mellinger (1998), 'Geography and economic development', *NBER Working Paper*, **w6849** (December).

Gintis, H. (2007), 'The evolution of private property', *Journal of Economic Behavior and Organization*, **64** (1), 1–16.

Hall, R.E. and C.I. Jones (1999), 'Why do countries produce so much more per worker than others', *Quarterly Journal of Economics*, **114** (1), 83–116.

Hayek, Friederich A. (1960), *The Constitution of Liberty*, South Bend, IN: Gateway Editions Ltd.

Kaufmann, D., A. Kraay and M. Mastruzzi (2007), 'The worldwide governance indicators project: answering the critics', *World Bank Policy Research Working Paper*, **4149**.

Kaufmann, D., A. Kraay and P. Zoido-Lopaton (1999), 'Governance matters', *World Bank Policy Research Working Papers*, **2196**.

Keefer, P. (2004), 'A review of the political economy of governance: from property rights to voice', *World Bank Policy Research Working Paper*, **3315** (May).

Knack, Stephen (2002), 'Social capital, growth, and poverty: a survey of cross-country evidence', in C. Grootaert and T. van Bastelaer (eds), *The Role of Social Capital in Development: An Empirical Assessment*, Cambridge: Cambridge University Press, Chapter 11.

Knack, S. and P. Keefer (1995), 'Institutions and economic performance: cross-country tests using alternative institutional measures', *Economics and Politics*, **7** (3), 207–227.

Knack, S. and P. Keefer (1997a), 'Does social capital have an economic payoff? A cross-country investigation', *Quarterly Journal of Economics*, **112** (4), 1251–1288.

Knack, S. and P. Keefer (1997b), 'Why don't poor countries catch up? A cross-national test of institutional explanation', *Economic Inquiry*, **35** (4), 590–602.

Kurtz, M.J. and A. Schrank (2007), 'Growth and governance: models, measures, and mechanisms', *Journal of Politics,* **69** (2), 538–554.

Lessnoff, M. (1990), *Social Contract Theory*, Oxford, UK: Blackwell.

Lin, Justin Yifu and Jeffrey B. Nugent (1995), 'Institutions and economic development', in J. Behrman and T.N. Srinivasan (eds), *Handbook of Development Economics*, vol. 3A, Amsterdam: North-Holland, Chapter 38.

Marx, Karl (1872[1974]), *Das Kapital*, London: Lawrence and Wishart.

Milgrom, P. and J. Roberts (1992), *Economics, Organisation and Management*, New York: Princeton University Press.

Nelson, R.R. and Winter, S.G. (1982), *An Evolutionary Theory of Economic Change*, London: Belknap.

North, Douglass (1990), *Institutions, Institutional Change, and Economic Performance*, Cambridge and London: Cambridge University Press.

North. D.C. (1994), 'Economic performance through time', *American Economic Review*, **84** (3), 359–368.

Nsouli, S.M., R Atoian and A. Mourmouras (2004), 'Institutions, program implementation, and macroeconomic performance', *IMF Working Papers*, **04/184**.

Olson, Mancur (1965), *The Logic of Collective Action*, Cambridge, MA: Harvard University Press.

Olson, Mancur (1982), *The Rise and Decline of Nations*, New Haven, CT: Yale University Press.

Olson, Mancur (1993), 'Dictatorship, democracy, and development', *American Political Science Review,* **87** (3), 567–575.

Ostrom, E. (1990), *Governing the Commons: The Evolution of Institutions for Collective Actions*, Cambridge: Cambridge University Press.

Rabin, M. (1998), 'Psychology and economics', *Journal of Economic Literature*, **36** (1), 11–46.

Rajan, Raghuram and Luigi Zingales (2000), 'The tyranny of inequality', *Journal of Public Economics,* **76** (3), 521–558.

Rodrik, D. (1999), 'Where did all growth go? External shocks, social conflict, and growth collapses', *Journal of Economic Growth*, **4** (4), 385–412.

Rodrik, D. (2000), 'Institutions and high-quality growth: what are they and how to get them', *Studies in Comparative International Development*, **35** (3), 3–31.

Rodrik, D., A. Subramanian and F. Trebbi (2004), 'Institutions rule: the primacy of institutions over geography and integration in economic development', *Journal of Economic Growth*, **9** (2), 131–165.

Sachs, J.D. (2001), 'Tropical underdevelopment', *NBER Working Paper*, **8119** (February).

Smith, A. (1976[1776]), *An Inquiry into the Nature and Causes of the Wealth of Nations*, edited by R.H. Campbell and A.S. Skinner, Oxford: Oxford University Press.

Stigler, George (1971), 'The theory of economic regulation', *Bell Journal of Economics and Management Science,* **2** (1), 3–21.

Taylor, K.W. and J. Frideres (1972), 'Issues versus controversies: substantive and statistical significance', *American Sociological Review*, **37** (4), 464–472.

von Mises, Ludwig (1949), *Human Action*, New Haven, CT: Yale University Press.

Wede, Janine R. (2009), *Shadow Elite: How the World's New Power Brokers Undermine Democracy, Government, and the Free Market*, New York: Basic Books.

Williamson, O.E. (1975), *Markets and Hierarchies: Analysis and Antitrust Implications*, New York: Free Press.

Williamson, O.E. (1985), *The Economic Institutions of Capitalism*, New York: Free Press.

World Bank (2002), *World Development Report 2002: Building Institutions for Markets*, Washington, DC. World Bank.

PART I

Governance institutions and micro-level
behaviour

2. Governance and asymmetric power[1]
Korkut Alp Ertürk

INTRODUCTION

Recent developments that broadly go under the heading 'Post Walrasian or neo-Institutionalist Economics' have carried contract and property right enforcement to the very centre of economic analysis. Enforcement issues that emanate from rational behaviour under less than ideal conditions, where the government can be counted on to enforce effectively neither property rights nor contractual obligations, have had increasing real-world relevance in recent decades as well. Think of issues that gained currency with globalization. Whether it is the much talked about weakening of the nation state, market reform chipping away at the developmental or welfare state as the case might be, or the shock therapy that transition economies had to go through, or, yet, the proliferation of failed states and the wars of pre-emption, in all, efficient government enforcement (along with provisioning of public goods) could hardly be taken for granted.

At the level of abstract theory, renewed interest in enforcement issues poses anew the intriguing question as to what would rational behaviour and market exchange entail in the absence of effective and costless enforcement of property rights and contractual obligations of individuals towards one another. What would give order to a Hobbesian 'state of nature' with a Leviathan who has fallen asleep? For instance, would peaceable exchange result from the interaction of self-seeking individuals who have to rely on their own devices to enforce contracts and protect their claims on property?[2] Under such conditions, how would market relations affect asymmetric power and be affected by it?

It is possible that older non-Walrasian economists' emphasis on power and power relations can make a contribution to our understanding of enforcement problems.[3] Think about what makes a mutually beneficial trade viable among drug dealers who by the very nature of their trade cannot rely on the legal enforcement of their property claims. Exchange between them is potentially peaceable and mutually beneficial only when both parties can deter each other effectively from predation. In such circumstances, agents respect each other's property claims to the extent they find each other's implicit threats of retaliation credible, and this often presupposes a rough balance of power.

The question has much broader import than hitherto thought for it involves how market exchange might work among agents with asymmetric power under conditions of less than effective exogenous enforcement. Consider an unskilled migrant labourer who is cheated of his daily wages by his employer. Stuck on the long side of the market, what is his rational course of action if seeking redress through the legal system is not realistic? One would think that his fortunes would rise or fall with his ability to project a perceived capability to retaliate that is credible enough to dissuade his employer from cheating by lowering his expected gain if he is so inclined. For instance, enlisting the support of others – whose allegiance he might have on the basis of primordial kinship ties – can possibly give our labourer a leg to stand on.

In this example, whether our labourer realizes the potential benefit from exchange depends on his success in deterring his employer from violating his contractual obligations. There is of course the other side of the trade as well. Once the employer finds it in his best interest to abide by his contractual obligations, it is not a foregone conclusion that he will benefit from exchange to its full potential unless he can see to it that the labourer does not shirk once gainfully employed. The challenge faced by the powerful agent is the well-known 'principal–agent' problem, while that of the weak agent is to redress the power imbalance so that the powerful side cannot 'take advantage' of his weakness. The important implication is that exchange is mutually beneficial only when both sides successfully deal with their respective challenge. While the 'principal–agent' problem has been explored in depth in its multifaceted manifestations, the same cannot be said for the problem that the weak agent faces. Nor is it often recognized that the failure of the weak agents to address the power imbalance can threaten the viability of and potential benefits from market exchange and thus have repercussions that go beyond their own wellbeing. More specifically, the chapter argues that the ability of the weak to redress the power imbalance they face in exchange makes it easier for the powerful agents to resist the temptation of short-term windfall profits at the expense of their long term interests.

The argument is laid out in a couple of stages because the game-theoretic nature of the problem the agents face on both side changes when the structure of interactions among them is transformed. Whether it is a pre-modern, traditional economy where the interacting agents as a rule are embedded within a given web of social ties or a modern economy where the norm becomes arms-length, anonymous exchange makes a difference.

The sections below discuss if and how endogenous enforcement might emerge and how asymmetric power is checked in the context of exchange that is, respectively, (1) among agents who repeatedly encounter each other and (2) those who are anonymous. The discussion then focuses on the commitment problem of the powerful in the latter, and ends with a few concluding remarks.

ENLIGHTENED SELF-INTEREST IN EMBEDDED MARKETS

Unlike many of his modern followers, Adam Smith was well aware that his invisible hand required individuals to show self-restraint in the pursuit of their self-interest. He knew that the invisible hand could not possibly work unless individuals restrained from theft, fraud or force – not just unlawful, but also what we would today call opportunistic behaviour – when they knew they could realistically expect to get away with it. He was well aware that legal sanctions and the threat of punishment could only go so far in dealing with the problem. Especially in a liberal society, he believed, individuals would need to refrain from opportunistic behaviour out of their own volition, and that required them to act on their enlightened rather than short term self-interest.

But, the problem is that awareness of enlightened self-interest in itself need not be sufficient for individuals to show self-restraint. For even all individuals fully realize that they benefit when everyone refrains from violating the rules and otherwise acting opportunistically, it still might not be rational for them to act on that realization. Behind this of course lurks a classic collective action problem. Everyone might realize quite well that it is in their enlightened self-interest to obey the rules and self-restrain, but whether it is actually rational for them to do so very much depends upon the extent to which they expect others will do the same. In other words, whether individuals act on their enlightened self-interest or not depends not just on their own commitment but also on their assessment of others' level of commitment as well.

We know well how the individual utility calculus can change in the repeated prisoners' dilemma. The gain from opportunistic behaviour (defection) in the current period is weighed against future benefits from continued cooperation. When the latter is high enough, mutually beneficial cooperation can emerge provided that agents have the ability to punish defectors by withholding future cooperation (Axelrod, 1984). The ability to punish defectors, in turn, rests on the ability to recognize defectors in repeated future encounters on the one hand, and on a symmetric capacity to punish, on the other. In other words, even if defectors are easily identifiable, a credible threat of punishment requires that transacting agents have a rough balance of power, that is, ability to punish the other.

In a similar vein, balance of power again plays a crucial role in Gintis' (2007) account of how de facto property rights might emerge in a game-theoretic context. Gintis shows how incumbency in some indivisible resource (or terrain) can translate to a de facto property right over it if agents value things more when they posses it (that is, the endowment effect) and are of roughly equal fighting ability. The intuition is that the incumbent is likely to fight much harder for the resource that his potential challengers are contesting. Clearly, the advantage incumbency confers would not amount to much if the power asymmetry is large enough.

It might not be too much of a stretch to suggest that in both the emergence of *cooperation* as well as de facto property rights, some spontaneous order can possibly emerge to underpin market exchange as long as interacting agents are not completely anonymous and symmetrically endowed in their capacity to retaliate against defection. In pre-modern, traditional economies where relations of kinship undergird at least some vital enforcement functions in market activity, in what Polanyi (2001[1944]) calls embedded markets, repeated encounters are of course the norm. In addition, the same kinship ties might also provide commonly shared notions of 'fairness' that can provide the weak with a mechanism of power balancing to prevent opportunistic behaviour on the part of the powerful.

Indeed, enforcement of property rights, rules and contracts in traditional societies seldom relies on legal sanctions enforced by formal institutions, but rather on informal networks whose members share common norms, values, and so on. Enforcement can take place at the level of the community because self-restraint derives either directly from a credible threat of ostracism or sanctions that are internalized by the individual. The norms that these sanctions are based on are often codified in religious/ethical values which the individual assumes are commonly shared by others in his community. To put it differently, such norms and sanctions function as commitment devices, enabling individuals to commit to acting on their enlightened self-interest on account of them because they can reasonably expect that others will do so as well.[4]

Of course, the broader question that is of interest here is: what happens when the common stock of shared conventions, values and norms dwindle in the course of social processes such as modernization and globalization, when the norm becomes exchange among individuals who are from diverse backgrounds with little in common? This is the world of what Polanyi calls disembedded markets, where transactions are arms-length and take place among anonymous others.[5] In this case, market exchange in large measure ceases to have the structure of repeated games, and comes to resemble a disconnected series of one-shot games. The worrisome implication is that a slippery slope can then emerge where self-restraint no longer pays off. Individuals become less likely to act on their enlightened self-interest when others begin to cheat when they can. Or, to put it the other way, it becomes increasingly costly to stick to one's enlightened self-interest.

This possibly explains why the free rider problem is much more pervasive in the anonymous world of modern economies. Likewise, it is no accident that many of the well-known information problems beset modern economies more, why our awareness of them is relatively recent and why reputational capital loses its bedrock quality as it comes to rest on the cash nexus of utility calculus rather than the individual's moral traits.

ENDOGENOUS ENFORCEMENT IN DISEMBEDDED MARKETS?

Above, I suggested that commonly shared norms and values in traditional societies can function as commitment devices, instilling in individuals the mutually reinforcing expectation that those acting opportunistically will be sanctioned and thus making it sensible to assume others will be self-restrained. It is also possible that the very notion of 'fairness' embedded in the same norms and values can be effective in constraining opportunistic behaviour on the part of the powerful. This of course brings up the question of if and how endogenous enforcement might be possible in modern economies, and what types of modern institutions and mechanisms might be effective in preventing the potentially adverse effect of asymmetric power on exchange.

It is clear that formal enforcement institutions are an essential prerequisite of a modern market economy – especially, given that no spontaneous order can be relied on. For a modern market system to be viable the whole battery of formal institutions – the most important of which are of course the courts and law enforcement – must be functional at least to a degree.[6] Moreover, as Russell Hardin (1995) has argued, we might expect that the very effectiveness of these institutions – or, rather their reputation that they are – can also work as a commitment device in the sense defined above. The expectation of swift justice against tax evaders and 'cheaters' one would think would enhance individuals' willingness to contribute to public goods, at least, in instances that involve a legal obligation.[7] The cost of enforcement would thereby be lowered as well, since the more credible the threat of punitive sanctions the lower is the need to actually mete out punishment. But if we do not already have efficient institutions of enforcement, how does one get there, or what happens when their effectiveness erodes over time for whatever reason, undermining their reputation?[8] It is possible that the answer depends on how asymmetric power is dealt with, or rather whether and how its potentially adverse effect on exchange is checked.

For our purposes here we can define minimally – along with Bowles and Gintis (1993) – whether agents are powerful or weak as to whether they happen to be on the long or short side of the market. Clearly, this presupposes that markets do not clear in equilibrium for all the reasons in efficiency wage type arguments (Shapiro and Stiglitz, 1984) and thus a segment of the agents on the long side of the market don't get to make a trade. Thus, those who are on the short side are in a powerful position in relation to the agents on the long side whose numbers well exceed what is in offer for exchange. They are powerful because they are in a position to pick and choose, while the others on the long side are *weak* because they have to compete among themselves to make a trade. Thus, the employer who is in a position to choose from a long list of applicants for hire, or the multinational corporation whose investment is sought by a large number of developing countries are typical examples of the powerful agents on the short side of the market.

An evocative example from Schelling (1960) captures well the essence of the problem the powerful agent has to deal with, which goes something like this. Think of a contrite kidnapper who would like to release his victim, but feels he cannot do so because his victim would have him arrested if let go. The victim's remonstrations that he would not go to the police are not credible because what is in his self-interest is patently time-variant. While still a captive he would want to be able to make a credible commitment not to go to the police when freed. But once he is free it would be a different story altogether, unless a way is found to make his prior commitment binding. The position of someone unemployed vying for a coveted job resembles that of the kidnapper's victim in Schelling's example. Before being hired, the prospective worker would want to commit to work hard if hired, while it would not necessarily be in his interest to do so if he actually gets the job. Thus, just like the kidnapper vis-à-vis his victim, the employer has to deal with the challenge posed by the predictable time-variance in the workers' self-interest and has to find a way that would make his employees stick to their commitment.

Thus the challenge the powerful agent faces is in essence the principal–agent problem tied to time-variance in the weak agent's self-interest. Though usually it comes up in different contexts, it is well recognized in the literature that contracting, even when enforceable at low cost, need not be sufficient to solve the problem the principal faces. The general challenge is to find a way to align the interests of the agent with that of the principal, whereby a generally workable strategy involves making the renewal of the employment contract contingent on the agent's performance. This obviously can only work if the wage exceeds what it would be under market clearing conditions. The worker must have something to lose, something better than what his second best alternative offers, for him to care about not losing his job and thus willing to perform well enough to renew his contract.

The issue can also be looked at from the point of view of globalization of investment where safeguarding of investors' property rights is a perennial issue. For just like the case with Schelling's kidnapping victim or the worker above, a similar kind of time-variance might characterize the shifting interests of host countries vis-à-vis foreign investors. A part of the foreign investors' (multinationals) challenge is to be prepared for the fact that the incentive structure can potentially shift drastically once they sink fixed costs in the country they invest in.[9] Again, contingent renewal can be seen to give the outline of a potentially workable strategy, which here takes the form of making continued foreign investment contingent on the 'good behaviour' of the host country. Obviously, this can work better if the country has only limited policy autonomy and is thus vulnerable to financial sentiment in international markets – the very attributes boosted by market reform and financial liberalization in recent decades. Moreover, if agents on the short side of the market are footloose and those on the long side footstuck, another salient characteristic of globalization in our era, then clearly the long side of the market gets much longer, increasing further the power asymmetry.

THE COMMITMENT PROBLEM OF THE POWERFUL

The problem with increasing power imbalance is that it makes it hard for the weaker agent to deal with his challenge. Moreover, if the weak agent cannot successfully redress the power asymmetry it is likely that the exchange will be short lived and its potential mutual benefit will go unrealized, adversely affecting the powerful agent as well. Put simply, what is involved here is not in essence very different from the plight of the store owner who charges extra for umbrellas during a rainstorm, only to find he has lost future customers. Though he makes windfall profits that day, he loses out in the long run. His long term interest might have been served better if the fear of a backlash from his customers deterred him from taking advantage of their temporary weakness. Thus, the powerful agent has his commitment problem as well. It might be in his long term interest to commit not to take advantage of the weakness of the weak, but that might be unlikely or more difficult to do when the weak agents are incapable of projecting a credible threat of retaliation.

Another example might help us think about how the weakness of the weak affects the powerful in a more general way. Think of Grief's (Grief et al., 1994) mediaeval sovereign who would like to attract long distance merchants to his territory. Initially, it would be in his interest to respect merchants' property and contractual rights and refrain from pilfering. But, once the trade becomes well-established, he might feel that he could maraud on individual merchants with impunity. The merchants might prevent this if they can credibly threaten a collective boycott. That requires them to be ready to act in tandem in the event the sovereign harms the property or person of any one of them. If their threat is credible enough everyone benefits, including the sovereign. The collective coordinated power of the merchants makes the sovereign stick to his commitment to refrain from acting opportunistically, which is in his own long term interest as well. But when the *weak* fail to redress the power imbalance by successfully coordinating among themselves, a slippery slope can potentially result, where exchange becomes increasingly lopsided and fails to flourish if it does not die out completely. Thus, the power that emanates from coalition formation among the weak agents can help ensure the powerful agent stick to his commitment and thus work as a commitment device. By preventing the powerful from 'taking advantage' of their weakness the weak not only help themselves but help trade remain mutually beneficial as well.[10]

But what about market competition? In the above example the sovereign clearly faces no competition from other rulers, and the question is, if he did, would that not be an equally effective commitment device as well? It appears that the answer depends on whether competition can be relied on to close the gap between the long and short sides of the market. Note that our initial assumption was that equilibrium did not entail market clearing, and that was in fact how we could define power asymmetry.

Until recently, it was generally thought that lack of market clearing could only be a shortlived disequilibrium situation, because the mutually beneficial trades that could be made between agents would propel the market towards clearing. For instance, many mainstream economists were never persuaded by Keynes' account of involuntary underemployment because they thought if each individual market except the labour market cleared, then the labour market would have to clear as well. The labour market would tend to clear because agents on both sides would exploit mutually beneficial trading opportunities.

It is now widely recognized that information problems, if nothing else, could prevent individual markets from clearing in equilibrium. While the potential for a mutually beneficial trade might exist, it need not be a viable option for the individual employer because of the collective action problem he faces when he does not know what other agents are likely to do. The potential benefit from hiring the unemployed worker might require that all other employers do so as well. Hiring when no one else does entails loss, and thus not hiring remains the preferred action when others cannot be counted on acting in tandem even though everyone would be better off if they did.

If no tendency exists for markets to clear in equilibrium – defined as position of rest – then competition is likely to have a pernicious effect as it would make it harder for powerful agents to act in their enlightened self-interest as a group. Note that it is in the collective interest of powerful agents not to take advantage of the weakness of the weak. But, the larger their population, the harder it is to supplant competition between them to secure a 'public good'. For each powerful agent is better off if everyone except them refrained from exploiting the opportunity offered by the weakness of the weak. Just as in any common resource problem, here, too, private gain is associated with collective cost. Those who behave opportunistically make it more costly for the others who exercise self-restraint.

Think of a group of cab drivers at some foreign tourist destination. The foreign tourists who do not know the area are easy pickings for the cab drivers as they come out of the airport. When drivers cheat by overcharging their passengers they might very well know that they are assailing their collective reputation which will eventually harm them all. Why do they do it? If they assume that other drivers are likely to cheat regardless of what they do they might conclude that self-restraint is pointless, making them think they might just as well cheat too. Those wavering might see their scruples vanish when competitive pressures intensify. In a similar vein, the financiers who engaged in the risky practices that eventually led to the financial crisis were probably not very different from the cab drivers in this example. The more scrupulous players who refrained from the riskiest practices often paid a price in terms of their competitive standing (Tett, 2009; Authers, 2010; Rajan, 2010). As self-restraint ceased to pay, few chose to exercise it.

Note that adding competition into the mix transforms the commitment problem of the powerful into something much more formidable than simple moral hazard. The latter is a failing of the individual while the former is a failing of the group. While both involve the short-sighted exploitation of an opportunity, the latter is caused when poor judgment is incentivized while with the former the failure to secure a common good makes individual good judgment and self-restraint unprofitable. This is because it becomes harder to assume that the next powerful agent will refrain from acting opportunistically once it is common knowledge that the weak can no longer deter. And this makes it harder for everyone to stick to their enlightened self-interest on the short side of the market. The fair-minded store owner who refuses to hike up the price of his umbrellas in a rainstorm, the honest cab driver who does not rip off tourists and the investment bank that shuns the subprime mortgages, all see their business suffer. Yet, the more likely the threat of a backlash, whether it is collective action on the part of customers, workers or tourists, the easier it might be for the enlightened powerful agents to deal with their commitment problem, while, by implication, anything that is detrimental to coalition-building on the part of the weak is liable to make it harder.

CONCLUSION

The foregoing raises the question whether governance institutions' effectiveness depends on the extent to which they make it easier for the weak to redress the power imbalance they face in exchange. The weak agents' ability to form coalitions, the main mechanism by which they can balance power asymmetries, depends in turn on how well they cope with two key challenges: (1) potential free riders in their midst and (2) competition from outside, that is, the other agents who have not made a trade on the long side of the market. In Grief's example above, the effectiveness of merchants depends on their ability to prevent their individual members from defecting on the embargo in the event of a boycott for extra reward. Moreover, in the event the boycott succeeds the merchants need to maintain their ability to act collectively over time, which means that in addition to thwarting free riders they need to be able to absorb and otherwise neutralize the competition of outside merchants who are bent on acting opportunistically. Arguably, a strong safety net and powerful closed-shop unions, both associated with the welfare state, were instrumental in easing both challenges, free riders and opportunistic competition from outside, and thus the types of institution that made historically collective action a more credible threat. Of course, as often remarked, neither institution – along with the welfare state – could resist the erosion caused by globalization, drastically reducing their effectiveness in bolstering the coalition-building ability of the weak. But, if the weak can no longer project a credible threat of collective action, this raises the question: what else can help the powerful solve their problem of commitment in the age of globalization? One also wonders if the rising importance of community around the world that is often found so baffling may be the last of refuge of the weak to protect themselves from 'opportunistic outside competition' in a world where they can no longer deter the powerful?

NOTES

1. I would like to thank Mehmet Ugur for his helpful comments and encouragement in writing this chapter.
2. A bourgeoning new literature that goes under the heading 'conflict economics' examines how peaceable exchange can emerge in a decentralized market economy in the absence of a government that can protect individuals' property rights. See, among others, Anderton (2000, 2003), Skaperdas (2002) and Rider (1999).
3. Albeit in other contexts, similar issues are taken up in the writings of earlier non-Walrasian economists at least since Marx, some of the insights of which the discussion in this chapter implicitly draws from.
4. In fact, a multitude of simple coordination problems are in practice solved by individuals drawing on what they assume are commonly shared practices, information and conventions with other individuals, what Schelling (1960) calls 'focal points'. For instance, when faced with a car coming from the opposite direction on a narrow countryside lane, we normally steer to the side of the road from which traffic flows in that particular country, assuming implicitly that the other driver will also do the same. We thus rely on a social convention and the expectation that it is commonly shared, rather than turning the occasion into a game of chicken. The latter would be more consistent with what economists call substantive or instrumental rationality, yet fail to solve our problem since postulates of rationality could only tell us what is the best thing to do respectively for the chicken and the hawk, but not who is to be which (Sugden, 1989).
5. Despite being very influential among other social scientists, Polanyi's influence among mainstream economists has been limited and thus his terminology remains little used. However, many economists draw a distinction between formal and informal governance in various different contexts that is similar to Polanyi's embedded/disembedded dichotomy. See, among others, Fafchamps (2004), Ensminger (1992), Li (2003) and Casella and Rauch (2002).
6. In fact, the rapid rise of governance as a separate sub-branch of study at a time of rapid 'modernization' around the world under the influence of globalization can be thought of a reflection of this salient fact. Again it might not be surprising that the World Bank became keenly interested in governance once it became obvious that market reform in many developing countries seriously weakened the institutions of enforcement that were frail to begin with. See Dixit (2008) for comprehensive overview of this bourgeoning literature and Dixit (2004) for a more extensive treatment.
7. Of course, civic obligations are yet another matter. As Adam Smith recognized, the credible threat of punitive sanctions might make law abiding agents, but not necessarily good citizens in a liberal society. Thus, one would think (and hope?) that institutions matter at yet a deeper level than the need to have an effective legal system in promoting endogenous forms of enforcement.
8. For instance, think of the recent literature on 'regulation capture' in advanced countries (Dal Bo, 2006; Mattli and Woods, 2009) and 'state capture' following market reform in transition and developing economies (Hellman and Kaufman, 2001; Hellman and Schankerman, 2000; Jensen, 2002).
9. See Grazia Ietto-Gillies' contribution in this volume for an insightful discussion of how transnational corporations strategize to cultivate and use 'asymmetric power' to their advantage.

10. See, Greif, Milgrom and Weingast (1994) for a discussion of how merchants used collective action to counter the rulers' tendency to violate their members' property rights in late medieval Europe. According to Acemoglu (2003) and Acemoglu and Robinson (2005) the rise of democracy can be traced to some ruling elite's recognition that making a credible commitment not to violate the property rights of their people is in their interest.

REFERENCES

Acemoglu, D. (2003), 'Why not a political Coase theorem? Social conflict, commitment and politics', *Journal of Comparative Economics*, **31**, 620–652.
Acemoglu, D. and J. Robinson (2005), *Economic Origins of Dictatorship and Democracy*, New York: Cambridge University Press.
Akerlof, G. and J. Yellen (1988), 'Fairness and unemployment', *American Economic Review, Papers and Proceedings,* **78** (2), 44–49.
Anderton, C. (2000), 'Exchange of goods or exchange of blows? New directions in conflict and exchange', *Defense and Peace Economics*, **7** (1), 83–102.
Anderton, C. (2003), 'Conflict and trade in a predator/prey economy', *Review of Development Economics*, **7** (1), 15–29.
Authers, J. (2010), *The Fearful Rise of Markets*, Upper Saddle River, NJ: FT Press.
Axelrod, R. (1984), *The Evolution of Cooperation*, New York: Basic Books.
Bowles, S. and H. Gintis (1993), 'The revenge of homo economicus: contested exchange and the revival of political economy', *Journal of Economic Perspectives*, **7** (1), 83–102.
Casella, A. and J. Rauch (2002), 'Anonymous market and group ties in international trade', *Journal of International Economics*, **58** (1), 19–47.
Dal Bo, E. (2006), 'Regulatory capture: a review', *Oxford Review of Economic Policy*, **22** (2), 203–225.
Dixit, A. (2004), *Lawlessness and Economics: Alternative Modes of Governance*, Princeton, NJ: Princeton University Press.
Dixit, A. (2008), 'Economic Governance. International Think-tank on Innovation and Competition', (INTERTIC) Lecture, University of Milan, 5 June.
Ensminger, J. (1992), *Making a Market: The Institutional Transformation of an African Society*, Cambridge: Cambridge University Press.
Fafchamps, M. (2004), *Market Institutions in Sub-Saharan Africa: Theory and Evidence*, Cambridge, MA: MIT Press.
Gintis, H. (2007), 'The evolution of private property', *Journal of Economic Behavior and Organization*, **64**, 1–16.
Greif, A., P. Milgrom and B. Weingast (1994), 'Coordination, commitment, and enforcement: the case of the merchant guild', *Journal of Political Economy*, **102** (41).
Hardin, R. (1995), *One for All. The Logic of Group Conflict*, Princeton, NJ: Princeton University Press.
Hellman, J. and D. Kaufman (2001), 'Confronting the challenge of State capture in transition economies', *Finance and Development*, **38** (3), 31–35.
Hellman, J. and M. Schankerman (2000), 'Intervention, corruption and capture: the nexus between enterprises and the State', *Economics of Transition*, **8** (3), 545–576.

Jensen, N. (2002), 'Economic reform, State capture, and international investment in transition economies', *Journal of International Development*, **14** (7), 973–977.

Li, J.S. (2003), 'Relation-based versus rule-based governance: an explanation of the East Asian miracle and Asian crisis', *Review of International Economics*, **11** (4), 651–673.

Mattli, W. and N. Woods (2009), *The Politics of Regulation*, Princeton, NJ: Princeton University Press.

Milanovic, B. (2003), 'The two faces of globalization: against globalization as we know it', *World Development*, **31** (4), 667–683.

North, D. (1981), *Structure and Change in Economic History*, New York: Norton.

Polanyi, K. (2001[1944]), *The Great Transformation*, 2nd edn, Boston, MA: Beacon Press.

Rajan, R. (2010), *Fault Lines. How Hidden Fractures Still Threaten the World Economy*, Princeton, NJ: Princeton University Press.

Rider, R. (1999), 'Conflict, the sire of exchange', *Journal of Economic Behavior and Organization*, **40**, 217–232.

Schelling, T. (1960), *The Strategy of Conflict*, Cambridge, MA: Harvard University Press.

Shapiro, C. and J. Stiglitz (1984), 'Equilibrium unemployment as a worker discipline device', *American Economic Review*, **74** (3), 433–444.

Skaperdas, S. (2002), 'Insecure property rights and efficiency of exchange', *Economics Journal*, **112** (476), 133–146.

Sugden, R. (1989), 'Spontaneous order', *Journal of Economic Perspectives*, **3** (4), 85–97.

Tett, G. (2009), *Fool's Gold*, New York: Free Press.

3. Norms, advice networks and joint economic governance: the case of conflicts among shareholders at the Commercial Court of Paris

Emmanuel Lazega, Lise Mounier and Paola Tubaro

INTRODUCTION

Businesses are usually very keen to participate in the governance of their markets (Lazega and Mounier, 2002, 2003; Falconi et al., 2005). In this chapter, we combine a sociological perspective on joint governance of markets with an economic perspective, such as that of Dixit (2009), that deals with issues of social optimality of private or public governance and enforcement institutions. Institutional and neo-institutional economic theory often separate official governance institutions from private self-governance (Greif, 1996; Ellickson, 1991; Milgrom et al., 1990; Williamson, 1985). At the inter-organizational level, at least two different sociological traditions also deal with the issue of self- and exogenous governance of markets, comparing the formal and often exogenous aspects with informal and endogenous ones.

In the socio-legal approach, exogenous governance (see for example Ayres and Braithwaite, 1992; Hawkins, 1984; Hawkins and Thomas, 1984; Shapiro, 1984; Weait, 1993; Weaver, 1977) is provided by government agencies backed up by courts. These studies focus, for example, on the decision by government agencies to prosecute deviant companies. Such decisions are not straightforward and may often be endogenous outcomes of the interaction between official inspectors and company managers. This is especially the case when strict enforcement of the law is associated with large risks emanating from large-scale losses and layoffs, and sometimes bankruptcy.

The second tradition focuses on self-governance mechanisms usually legitimated by state backing – that is, on inter-firm arrangements that provide self-governance and informal conflict-resolution mechanisms that govern inter-firm and firm-stakeholder transactions. Because litigation is costly, firms usually prefer unofficial dispute resolution whenever possible, especially when they have long-term continuing relationships (see for example Macaulay, 1963, 1986; Raub and Weesie, 1993, 2000; Rooks et al., 2000; Buskens et al., 2003); or as Dixit (2009) has indicated, when private-ordering governance institutions evolve to replace formal governance institutions that may sometimes be less efficient. Here the focus is on pressures to conform and the latter is shaped by resource dependencies, inter-dependence and reputation. Thus, these two traditions focus on different kinds of actors intervening in governance, the state and companies themselves – the latter sometimes through industry representatives.

In reality, the two forms of governance systems coalesce in various ways. One possible combination is Ayres and Braithwaite's 'responsive self-governance' (1992), acknowledging the existence of 'enforcement pyramids' that exist between governmental regulatory agencies and corporate actors and provide the opportunity to escalate from persuasion to warning letters to civil fines and criminal penalties to license suspension and revocation. Actors are aware of such enforcement pyramids, and know that an escalation can be triggered. This is why, in spite of costs, firms do use litigation both as plaintiffs and as defendants (Galanter and Epp, 1992; Dunworth and Rogers, 1996; Cheit and Gersen, 2000), and conflicts follow the disputing pyramid transforming informal complaints into court filings and formal judiciary decisions (Felstiner et al., 1980).

We further explore the idea that the two forms of governance are connected and that there can be 'joint' governance or a combined regime of endogenous and exogenous business conflict resolution. This can take many hybrid forms, and the joint element is defined as the coexistence of several sources of constraint, both external and internal, that weigh on the actors in charge of solving conflicts and enforcing rules. Specifically, we identify a form of joint governance in the case of a 'consular' court in which judges are business people elected by their peers, and serve as unpaid volunteers.

Courts are not static institutions making a-temporal and purely rational decisions (Heydebrand and Seron, 1990; Wheeler et al., 1988). Rather, they constitute a contested terrain, the prize or object of broader economic competition and conflict that occur outside them (Flemming, 1998). This is especially the case in consular courts, where judges can be regarded both as official third parties upholding legal rules and procedures in conflict resolution processes; and as unofficial and potential levers of influence representing their industry of origin, thereby possibly favouring outcomes that do not hurt the interests of this industry. As levers, they can sometimes weigh on judicial decisions directly, or do so indirectly by gaining other judges' consent on specific outcomes.

Thinking about joint governance in these terms follows both an organizational and a broadly conceived organizational and structural approach to economic institutions (Lazega and Mounier, 2002, 2003; Dixit, 2009) in which network analysis is used to study actors' resource interdependencies.[1] We use this twofold perspective to contribute to the study of economic and legal institutions that combine exogenous and self-governance of markets. On the basis of an empirical network survey combined with a jurisprudential study, we examine the first commercial court in France, a consular court to which the state delegates conflict-resolution powers with respect to inter-company disputes. This case provides insight into particular interests' efforts to shape the forum in which disputes between businesses are processed.

The remainder of this chapter is organized as follows. First, we describe the system of joint governance that French consular courts represent, outline the tension between particular interests and the general interest, and explain how advice network data can provide insight and present our fieldwork. We then provide details of our jurisprudential study, focusing on judges' attitudes in a case of conflict between minority shareholders and the board of a company, which we use to measure judges' degree of pro-interventionism in the internal affairs of a firm. The following section presents the stochastic actor-oriented model of network dynamics that we use and our results; the final section sums up and concludes.

THE COMMERCIAL COURT OF PARIS

For five centuries, the French solution to the problem of ensuring business conflict resolution and market discipline has consisted in the government sharing its judiciary power with the business community through consular commercial courts.[2] They represent a form of integration of business in the state apparatus in that judges are voluntary business people, elected for two to four years (for a maximum total of 14 years) by sitting judges and members of the Chamber of Commerce of their local jurisdiction.

Judges sit in judgment one day a week in matters of commercial litigation and bankruptcy.[3] As in any other court, their decisions can be challenged and brought to the Court of Appeal, where judges are career magistrates typically trained at *Ecole Nationale de la Magistrature*. That challenges are relatively infrequent (about five per cent of cases) allows these consular courts to claim that this combination of external and self-governance of local business communities is 'efficient'.

Judges include retired businesspeople[4] as well as more junior professionals, whether bankers, lawyers, or consultants, who seek experience, status and social contacts, sometimes on behalf of their employer – who keeps paying their salary one day a week while they are practicing at the court. Sitting as a lay judge helps younger members build their relational capital (as explicitly suggested in the flyers aiming to attract new candidacies) and opens doors for future positions in economic institutions namely the Chamber of Commerce, arbitration courts and the *Conseil économique et social*, an advisory board to the Prime Minister. Serving at the commercial court has traditionally been considered a 'chore' to be rewarded later on with such positions (Lemercier, 2003); further, lucrative contracts and missions are sometimes given on a discretionary basis by the acting president of the court to former judges to advise companies on a 'preventive' basis.

Consular courts are widely thought to be a cheaper and faster form of justice than a system with professional judges. Business bears more of the costs of its own governance, so that backlogs and waiting time are reduced relative to other courts; for example, there is neither jurisprudence, nor published cases. Another alleged advantage of this arrangement is that by their own business experience, lay judges are more likely than professional judges – who are civil servants – to understand the problems of entrepreneurs and to monitor satisfactorily the behaviour of company directors, particularly in cases of insolvency and bankruptcy (Carruthers and Halliday, 1998). Finally, lay judges are more likely to be familiar with idiosyncratic norms and customs (called *usages* in French commercial courts) based on traditional industry subcultures and contributing to organizing business practice, but often ignored in business law. Lay judges are thought to be in a better position to fine-tune norms and customs to unstable or changing business environments, and to foster regulatory innovations.

Thus French commercial courts have features that bring to light important aspects of the link between legal (exogenous) and social (endogenous) mechanisms in the governance of business. The state does not enforce and sanction alone, but requires the participation and adherence of individual and corporate actors. In effect in this case, elected representatives perform a function usually considered to be a state function, although they may also represent corporatist interests. This form of joint governance can be understood as industry self-governance with some oversight and ratification by the State (Grabosky and Braithwaite, 1986).

Consular Judges Between General and Particular Interests

The main challenge facing the system is the potentially difficult separation between general and particularistic interests. The institution officially assumes that judges will be entirely dedicated to their public mission; and judges themselves declare that once elected, they feel independent from their industry of origin and fully impartial. In principle, this is consistent with the business community's need for speed and decisiveness, a low number of appeals, sharp segregation of politics and personal patronage from judicial decision-making and as much neutrality as possible. However, the public has always suspected that elections of judges are politicized so that they then fail to distance themselves from their virtual 'constituency', the industry that endorsed their candidacy for the job. Especially in small towns, litigants' confidence in the impartiality of local commercial courts is often impaired.[5]

Indeed consular courts are sometimes thought to offer sectors of the business community, led by their *syndicats patronaux* (employers' associations), the opportunity to represent, or even to prevent damage to, the interests of their industry. Being at the court is a way of defending the customs of an occupation or profession. For example, the financial industry sees arrangements for corporate liquidation or administration as very important to its practice of commercial lending. Bankers could easily handle their affairs concerning corporate rehabilitation outside of courts if they perceive them as incompetent or opposed to their interests. Courts must often conform to the expectations of the financial industry or lose much of their business (Carruthers and Halliday, 1998: 488). The 'quality of justice' as defined by the financial industry (limiting risk and permitting failures, or extending credit and aid reconstruction) is a significant factor in its strategy. Representation at the court also signals to the constituency that the leaders of their *syndicat* are promoting the interests of the profession.

Thus from the perspective of each industry, consular judges are sometimes seen as judicial entrepreneurs (McIntosh and Cates, 1997) representing the sensitivity of the *syndicats patronaux* and organized interests that helped them into the courthouse in the first place by endorsing their candidacy. They are entrepreneurs because they are expected to identify problems and support solutions that make sense in their own business community – although judges themselves are often uncomfortable with the idea of being 'representatives' with a mandate from a specific industry.

Industry has attempted to influence courts in various ways. Flemming (1998) lists five such ways: jurisdiction (the range of disputes over which the court has authority), positions (actors formally authorized to participate in the disposition of cases), resources (the capacity to influence the decisions of other actors), discretion (the range of choices available to actors) and procedures (rules governing courtroom processes). Parties involved in that contest are not always directly involved in all the conflicts that are dealt with by the court, but they may have indirect concerns, material or symbolic, in the decisions of the court, which explains their efforts to influence.

Legal systems are often designed to protect judges from external influences, for instance through well-defined procedures and an appropriate system to manage conflicts of interest. However, these forms of protection are less likely to be effective in the case of elected judges than with career judges.

Over-representation of the banking and financial industry among the judges
In principle, this system of joint governance is more efficient when judges represent as many sectors as possible, so that they can bring in experience and expertise in various areas of economic activity. Indeed all the *syndicats patronaux* are allowed to present candidates to the elections of consular judges, but some sectors do so more systematically than others: the banking and financial industry is by far the most active, followed by services and construction.

These three industries are traditionally very litigious (Cheit and Gersen, 2000). The business docket in France is dominated by contract disputes and debt collection issues. A sizable portion of this docket involves the financial industry, for example in cases involving high levels of credit, thereby providing a strong incentive for it to invest in 'judicial entrepreneurship' (McIntosh and Cates, 1997). It also involves the construction industry which is structured as a cascade of subcontracting deals with strong incentives for conflict. These industries have high amounts of resources at stake in these conflicts. They are willing to play for the rules and endeavour to influence the court so as to impose their norms and practices over those of other industries. Their priorities can thus be defended in both the litigation and the bankruptcy benches.

The banking and financial industry is over-represented at the Commercial Court of Paris. When we conducted our fieldwork, from 2000 to 2005, it represented 3 per cent of the active population in France[6] and 5.1 per cent in Paris.[7] In terms of value added to the economy per branch (chained prices for previous year, 1995 basis), the share of the financial industry in the total value added to the French economy was 5.3 per cent.[8] However at the same time, about one third of judges at the Commercial Court of Paris were from the financial and banking industry. In addition, judges from the banking and financial sector often have a formal legal education: about 60 per cent of them had a law degree at the time of our fieldwork, a much higher percentage than representatives of other industries. This suggests that judges coming from the financial sector are potential levers of that industry and that their influence on others may threaten the court's independence.

Why do other industries fail to invest as much in judicial entrepreneurship? One reason is that some very large companies prefer arbitration which is more discreet and avoids publicity. Another reason is that smaller *syndicats*, such as retail, do not have the necessary clout, resources and organization to lobby effectively.

Advice networks of judges and decision-making

The fact that one-third of the judges come from the financial industry does not mean that they make one-third of the decisions in the court. Because most decisions are made by a collegial body of at least three members, bankers may participate either in much less or in much more than one-third of the decisions. An indirect way to capture their influence is through advice interactions between judges – that is, sets of relations through which they share knowledge, ideas, values and guidance – which can be taken to set the premises of judicial decisions.

Premise setting for judicial decision-making is at the core of our approach of micro-level knowledge sharing. Solutions to problems ultimately depend on how these problems are initially defined or framed, that is, how certain dimensions of a problem are highlighted while others are downplayed (Lindenberg, 1998; Lazega, 1992). Definitions of a problem that gain early acceptance among members of an organization, also including judges in a courthouse, are likely to subsequently dominate in the search of a solution. Indeed sentencing is often shaped by the kind of information that is included in pre-sentence reports, which cover precisely the definition of the situation and the framing of the problem. Some judges have the status and authority to have their views taken seriously from the very beginning, and they can be decisive with respect to who is likely to win. The extent to which they are in a position to exert such an influence depends on how they have carved out a place for themselves within the court. Theories of social exchange have stressed how the circulation of intangible or immaterial resources such as knowledge is closely tied to status games (Blau, 1964; Lazega, 1992): they thus suggest that reaching influential positions largely depends on judges' interactions with their colleagues, and thus on the functioning of the court as a community of members. In this perspective, patterns of advice seeking in the court show who is prepared to listen to whom when framing and defining problems in the judicial decision-making process.

Another way to see the importance of advice networks is to conceive of the court as a form of collective competence in which members, coming from diverse professional backgrounds, pool and share their experience and expertise in order to cope with a broad range of cases, some of them very complex. This is consistent with the sociological view of competence as a distributed, capitalized property in a process of collective learning, rather than as a purely individual capacity. Mutualization of competence can be seen as a form of corporate social capital (Leenders and Gabbay, 1999) and includes both formal and informal consultations among judges.[9] Formally, the deliberation procedure obviously provides opportunities to share knowledge; informally, judges also consult with one another intensely in areas of law and economics that they may not master equally well. While data about formal deliberations are not available, advice networks can still be mapped to provide insight into the informal component of this process.

The literature on advice networks has shown that especially within organizations, they are often shaped by a variety of influences, including the formal organizational chain or structure of the institution itself, and the normative orientation of members, to which we need to add in our case, pressures from corporate interests. Along these lines, our study of joint regulation focuses on how these three factors contribute to shaping the advice network at the court, with the idea that advice networks affect the normative orientation of the court and eventually its decisions.

Fieldwork at the Commercial Court of Paris

Fieldwork was conducted at the Commercial Court of Paris in 2000, 2002, and 2005. This court is one of the largest in France and handles around 12 per cent of all the commercial litigation in the country. It includes 21 chambers, some generalist and other specialized. The main distinction is between bankruptcy and litigation chambers, but many sub-specialties also exist (for example unfair competition, European law, multimedia and new technologies, and so on). Judges rotate yearly across chambers; each chamber has a president who reports to the president of the court.

Data on advice seeking among judges were collected at all three waves with the following name generator:

> Here is the list of all your colleagues at this Court, including the President and Vice-Presidents of the Court, the Presidents of the Chambers, the judges, and 'wisemen'. Using this list, could you check the names of colleagues whom you have asked for advice during the last two years concerning a complex case, or with whom you have had basic discussions, outside formal deliberations, in order to get a different point of view on this case.[10]

A very high response rate (over 80 per cent) enabled us to reconstitute the complete advice network among judges at this courthouse at each of the three waves. We also collected data about judges' attributes, most notably their professional and educational backgrounds as well as their formal position and tenure at the court.

In 2005, we included a set of new questions on how judges use their business experience to accomplish their tasks. Our goal was to identify some of the norms, customs and practices on which they rely on in order to make decisions, particularly when they can use their discretionary authority.[11] This is a difficult question because judges tend to say little about their work in order to protect their independence. To get around this difficulty, we used a jurisprudential method asking judges to comment on decisions made by other courts. These cases were deliberately chosen in areas where the law does not provide any clear-cut solution and judges must use their personal appreciation, a form of assessment that potentially calls upon norms and practices they may have learned in their industry of origin. In other words, we aimed to mobilize the judges' discretionary power in order to identify different collective tendencies.

Variation in responses is not surprising in itself since we intentionally chose cases allowing for a great deal of discretion. What interests us first and foremost is the extent to which variation in assessments drives the evolution of collective learning at this court, and thus indirectly influences decisions. We measure this effect by looking at the extent to which sharing assessments drive the evolution of the advice network among judges. We focus in this chapter on a specific case: that of litigation between majority shareholders represented by the board of a company and minority shareholders over the right of the latter to delay an Extraordinary General Assembly in which the board wanted to recapitalize the firm. The interest of this case is that, insofar as judges were asked to evaluate the decisions of a board, it measures their interventionism in the operations of a company, thereby capturing an important aspect of this form of joint governance of the economy. This case is presented below.

DEALING WITH CONFLICTS BETWEEN THE BOARD AND MINORITY SHAREHOLDERS

The case we used refers to specific clauses of the New Code of Civil Procedure (article 873, paragraph one, number 10), about judges' power to stop 'obviously illicit trouble'. The minority shareholders of a company asked a commercial court to postpone an Extraordinary General Assembly and to appoint an expert to check the refinancing operation decided by the board. Judges have discretionary power as two potentially conflicting principles inform French corporate law in this area: on the one hand, courts have the mission to protect the collective interest of the company (its survival) independently of the parties, but on the other hand, they should not interfere with its management. With this in mind, we asked Parisian commercial judges to comment on the following judgment (see Box 3.1), published by another French court.

BOX 3.1   WITH RESPECT TO MINORITY SHAREHOLDERS' RIGHT TO DELAY AN EXTRAORDINARY GENERAL ASSEMBLY

The shareholders in the minority group (from here on designated 'the Plaintiffs') of a company (from here on designated 'the Company') looking to decrease then reconstitute its own capital, which has become inferior to half its original amount, are suing the Company in emergency proceedings.

The Plaintiffs ask for an emergency ruling from the President of the Court, first that he postpone *sine die* the Extraordinary General Assembly meant to carry out this recapitalization, until an expert report is made available on why the capital of the firm has become inferior to half its original amount; and second that he designate an expert to investigate the financial situation of the Company, in particular:

- The state of its losses,
- The value of its assets and shares,
- The value of the Plaintiffs' participation in the Company.

The Plaintiffs also want the appointed expert to give his opinion about the appropriateness of the financial operations examined in the board's report and about the schedule proposed by board executives for these operations.

The President of the Court decides that the conditions required for designating a management expert are met because:

- The CEO of the Company had a personal interest in the operation and made a decision as an executive of the Company;
- The Company failed to communicate specific information to the Plaintiffs in response to their questions.

Furthermore, the Court states that bringing in an expert is in the interest of all shareholders, whether or not they belong to the majority. In addition, the Court considers that some of the claims that the Plaintiffs make against the Company are valid, in particular:

- The shareholder pact seems not to have been respected;
- The modalities of capital operations, notably the fact that the incorporation of reserves began after the reduction of capital, following an increase in capital in cash, seems not to have been clearly justified.

Taking all these elements into consideration, the President of the Court decides to postpone the Extraordinary General Assembly and selects an expert to report on the management of the Company.

Cases of this type are quite frequent at the Commercial Court of Paris every year, notably at the end of June, when companies must have their general assemblies. Postponement is risky for a company. In this case minority shareholders wonder if they will have to reach for their wallets even if they are not required to participate in the recapitalization operation, or see the value of their shares decrease. One judge speaks of the minority shareholders' worries vis-à-vis the majority:

> [I]t's also a matter of knowing whether the majority shareholders are suddenly reducing their capital in order to bring in new shareholders, if in reality there are ulterior motives behind the operation. The supposed increase of capital would be made to get rid of the minorities and to gain control without them. In this case, if the transaction only tries to exclude the minorities, it would be an abuse of power by the board. If it is not a hidden entrance of a third party, the case is then limited to a quieter hypothesis.

Three-quarters of the consular magistrates responded that they would have made the same decision as the president of this court concerning the designation of an expert. The same proportion would have postponed the general assembly. Here are excerpts of interviews justifying this decision:

> Minority shareholders have the right to ask questions, and we need to answer them in a very precise manner. If this isn't done, first of all it's a mistake. Secondly, a judge can't determine everything immediately. Why, because if you have to look at two years' worth of balance sheets . . . you need time. We can't rule with the few elements we have. So I'd almost say, at the beginning, you'd need to bring in a finance expert who could look at all of that, who'd analyze the reports of the Commissaire aux Comptes, to find out if the procedure was properly carried out, if management did everything that there is to do . . . So it's crucial to appoint an expert.

Business obeys a type of mathematical science: game theory. When the CEO of a company is attacked like that, he's got to know about it beforehand. Or he's a bad president. The judge knows that he knows. . . . [T]he judge says to himself: 'We know that you know, buddy. You took a risk.' He's the one who managed things badly, it's not our intervention of justice. The guy willingly made a mistake and the expert will make a decision about it.

The fact that most judges would have made the same decision and pushed back the Extraordinary General Assembly does not however constitute a systematic defence of minority groups:

There's an article in the Code that allows minorities to ask for what they call a minority assessment. And the Appeals Court is even more lax than we are. In one important case, an association of shareholders that was far from holding five per cent, asked for minority assessment. They based their demand on a very general article stating that one can ask for an assessment before attaining five per cent. We refused with the reasoning: we don't want to base our decision on a far-reaching general article that could end up short-circuiting a statute for a very unique case. But for us: 'you have the 5 per cent, you have precise questions, we accept the assessment'.

The minority of judges who would not have come to the same conclusion as the court do not distinguish themselves from the others in relation to their seniority in the institution, their type of activity, or their degrees. Their arguments reveal a relationship to the law and to judges' competences that deserves further analysis:

No, we would have said: did your assembly meet regularly? That's the only thing that we need to look at, and when it's been considered, if the elements that need to be provided are not the right ones, we'd have to take it back. But not before, we don't need to intervene in the management of a company, except to enforce procedural rules. . . . If the majority decides to make this transaction [re-capitalization], with the quorum and the conditions of validity, if the others suffer losses they can sue for damages. But we wouldn't say the Court has the power to postpone a general assembly. It's a big deal!

It's better to hold the EGA as soon as possible so that the capital itself can be reconstituted. If I'd been judge we would have demanded a written communication of the Commissaire aux Comptes' last two reports for the last two years . . . [D]oes he think it's useful and necessary to postpone? If not, we need to hold the EGA immediately. We're risking bankruptcy.

Luckily it's rare that just any small shareholder asks for an expert because he doesn't know what's happened in the company! Subject to all this, the demand seems excessive to me and even a little paralyzing. In any case you have to have an EGA . . . Maybe the small shareholders didn't want to follow the increase of capital and they decided to wage war against the big shareholders. But in this case you would sell your shares! It's the type of initiative that you definitely shouldn't encourage and multiply! At any moment, anyone can block the functioning of a company. In the case of embezzlement or fraud, we would understand. Is this really well founded or is it petty vengeance against a director with whom we can't sympathize coming from where, about what?

As soon as the magistrates leave the specific case to examine more general principles and to respond to the question of whether they should give preference to the common interest of a company, consensus disappears. Nearly the majority shares this opinion (46 per cent), while a quarter is hostile to it (22 per cent); the rest are hesitant (21 per cent) or refuse to answer (10 per cent). The fact that 22 per cent do not wish to give preference to the collective interest of the firm shows that the question of governance is very easily politicized.

The Court makes its verdicts based on the law. If the little guy's right, he gets the favourable solution. Survival of the company in itself is not a goal if it's at the expense of shareholders because by that logic it would be like favouring tenants over landlords, like in the USSR, where it was the State. We give verdicts to say who's wrong. If they come to the Court, it's because they already believe that in this conflict the survival of the company is at stake.

Notice that judges with a law degree and who belong to the banking and financial sector differ slightly from their colleagues in their appreciation of the decision of the court. They are more inclined to favour the collective interest of a company than the others, and less hostile to intervention in the management of a company, so that they tend to have a more 'pro-intervention' position than the rest of judges. We see the opposite for judges from the construction industry: they tend to adopt a less 'pro-intervention' attitude than the rest of the judges in litigation opposing the shareholders of a company.

MODEL FOR ANALYSIS

The outcome variable in our study is the selection of advice ties by judges, and we focus on the evolution over time of the network composed by these ties. We use the stochastic actor-oriented approach of Snijders (2001), with the software Siena version four, a package in the R statistical environment (Ripley and Snijders, 2010). The model postulates that the existing network structure has effects on changes in selection of advisors, specifies these effects, and takes into account interdependence between ties. (For a more extensive treatment, see Snijders 2001, 2005; Snijders et al., 2010.)

Model Specification

The model presents the evolution of the network from its state at the first observation to that observed at the second observation, and likewise the development from the second to the third observation, and so on. This evolution is presented as consecutive changes of advisor choice, which can be of three types: (1) creation of new ties (that is new advisor choices); (2) termination of existing ties (that is dropping advisors); or (3) maintenance of existing ties. These changes are assumed to occur sequentially between the observations, and actors are assumed to be aware of them and thus to have knowledge of the changing network. This first-order approximation is reasonable as the commercial court is a relatively small institution composed of about 150 members at each moment in time. Each of the changes of advisor is regarded as a choice made by the judge requesting advice. The probability distribution of these choices is modelled as being dependent on the so-called objective function, which is a function of the personal network of the member making the current choice.

Probabilities of change are higher toward network states having a higher value of the objective function; thus, the objective function can be loosely regarded as representing the attractiveness of the network, as seen from the viewpoint of the member concerned. The objective function is a linear combination of terms called 'effects', similar to the linear predictor in generalized linear modelling. The weights of these effects are the parameters in the statistical model, and are estimated from the data. Each effect represents a component potentially driving the network dynamics.

To state the model formally, suppose there are $i = 1, 2, \ldots, n$ actors and call X_{ij} the potential tie from actor i to actor j, which may have value 0 (absence) or 1 (presence). Assume that with a given frequency, actor i is given an opportunity to change from X_{ij} to $1 - X_{ij}$. Furthermore, assume that actor i makes changes that maximize its objective function $f_i(b, x(i \to j))$ (where x is a matrix representing the whole network of ties, b is a vector of statistical parameters, and $x(i \to j)$ is the state of the network when X_{ij} becomes $1 - X_{ij}$), plus a random disturbance with Gumbel distribution, as in random utility models. Under these conditions, the probability that such a change occurs is:

$$p_{ij}(\beta, x) = \frac{\exp(f_i(\beta, x(i \to j)))}{\sum_{h=1}^{n} \exp(f_i(\beta, x(i \to h)))}$$

This is the multinomial logit form of a random utility model. The statistical inference aims to estimate the parameters β, which indicate the preferred direction of changes, by a generalized method of moments.

Some of the parameters refer to endogenous effects that depend on the network itself: they represent dependency between network ties and account for path-dependency in network evolution. Others are related to exogenous effects and depend on the characteristics of the member making the choice and/or the member chosen. The model specification consists of specifying both the endogenous and the exogenous effects that are hypothesized to drive the dynamics of the network. This specification must include effects reflecting the hypotheses but also effects reflecting other mechanisms thought to drive network dynamics, in order to rule out alternative explanations (similar to control variables in regression models) and to provide a good model fit so that the standard errors of the parameter estimates are reliable.

Estimation Methodology

The effects included in the model are meant to explain network change, that is, the selection of advice ties by judges. Let us start with endogenous effects which, as mentioned earlier, account for path-dependency and can be regarded as controls, necessary to understand the dynamics of the network.

To begin with, we control for the effect of local sub-structures which are well known in the social networks literature to be likely drivers of the evolution of networks. Reciprocity captures the tendency for an actor to form an advice tie with those who seek advice from him or her, and is reflected in the objective function by the number of mutual ties of each given actor i. The transitive triplets effect refers to the propensity to seek advice from one's advisor's advisor, and is defined by the number of transitive patterns in actor i's relations, that is, ordered pairs of actors (j, h) to both of whom i is tied, while j is also tied to h. The three-cycle effect captures a tendency for the formation of short cycles of generalized exchange and depends on the number of three-cycles in i's personal advice relationships, that is, cycles in which i seeks advice from j, j from k, and k from i. The conjunction of a positive transitive triplets effect accompanied by a negative three-cycles effect may be regarded as a form of local hierarchy in advice.

In addition, we control for global structures depending on degrees. In social network analysis, in-degrees measure the number of incoming ties, and in-degree centrality captures the extent to which a judge is identified by others as one of their advisors; it can be interpreted as a form of popularity or status. Conversely, out-degrees measure the number of outgoing ties, and out-degree centrality is the number of advisors of a judge. These measures are relevant because the distribution of both in- and out-degrees is highly skewed in this particular network (Lazega et al., 2008, 2010a) and must be controlled adequately in order to obtain a good model fit. As proposed in Snijders et al. (2010), we include three degree-related effects relating to, respectively, the dispersion (variance) of in-degrees, the association (correlation) between in- and out-degrees and the dispersion (variance) of the out-degrees. First, in-degree popularity (sqrt) is defined as the sum of the square roots of in-degrees of a judge's advisors; a positive parameter for this effect indicates that judges with higher in-degrees are more attractive as advisors, and hence indicates a self-reinforcing effect leading to high dispersion of in-degrees. The square roots are used because we assume that a higher in-degree increases attractiveness of an advisor (monotonicity), but its impact becomes lower at higher values of the in-degree (decreasing marginal effect). Second, out-degree popularity (sqrt) is the sum of the square roots of out-degrees of a judge's advisors. When this effect is positive, judges with higher out-degrees are more attractive as advisors, resulting in a relatively high association between in-degrees and out-degrees. Again, the use of a square root measure presumes that differences between high out-degrees are relatively less important than the same differences between low out-degrees. Third, out-degree activity (sqrt) is defined as the out-degree of a judge times the square root of his/her own out-degree. If its parameter is positive, judges who currently ask many others for advice will have – compared to those who ask few others for advice – a relatively stronger tendency to add a new advisor rather than drop an old advisor. This is, again, a self-reinforcing effect: a positive parameter will lead to increased dispersion of out-degrees. In a previous paper (Lazega et al., 2010a) we interpreted degree-related effects as indicators of status that, over time, sustain the centrality of judges with high in-degrees and low out-degrees.

Notice that the in-degrees and out-degrees have the dual role of independent variables, and reflections of the dependent variables, that is the tie changes. This raises no logical issues because these two roles are separated in the dynamic model that we use: at any moment in time the current in-degrees are among the predictors for creation of new ties and maintenance of existing ties. Such a dual role is characteristic of models with feedback.

We also include exogenous variables, that is attributes of actors or pairs of actors. For the actor-level variables, we estimate the following basic three effects (see Snijders et al., 2010): *ego* effects to account for their advice-seeking behaviour, *alter* effects for being sought out for advice and similarity effects. A positive *ego* parameter would indicate that judges with these characteristics have a greater tendency to seek advice than others; a positive *alter* parameter would indicate that others have a greater tendency to seek advice from such judges; and a positive similarity effect would indicate that judges who are similar with respect to this attribute (both having it or both not having it) have a higher tendency to seek advice from each other.

The main variable of interest is judges' view of the case of shareholder conflict presented above, which we take as an indicator of their interventionism in boards; we represent it as a dummy variable. The other important variable of interest is the professional and educational background of judges. In line with the above discussion, we distinguish those from the banking and financial industry, and with legal education, from all others.

As a control, we also include judges' seniority, that is, number of years spent at the court, a proxy for position in the hierarchy: indeed some roles such as president of chamber can only be awarded to judges who have at least eight years of experience at the court. Another organizational aspect that we control for is chamber co-membership at the time of fieldwork and chamber co-membership during previous years, reflecting the division of labour in the court and the fact that two judges who are, or were in the past, in the same chamber are likely to have closer or more frequent contacts, and this may be reflected in their choice of advisors. Technically, chamber co-membership and previous chamber co-membership are changing dyadic variables, for which the changes keep track of new co-memberships between the first and the second periods of observation (2000–2002 and 2002–2005 respectively).

Parameter Estimates

Table 3.1 presents our results. We use a large dataset including all judges who were present at the court at least once in 2000, 2002 or 2005, plus those who were 'wisemen' in these years. This is a network with changing composition, whose members are partly renewed every year as judges who have finished their mandate leave and are replaced by newcomers, with a turnover of about 10 per cent. In this sense, this model is an extension of our previous work which only relied on the subset of judges who were present at all three waves (Lazega et al., 2008, 2010a). We fit the model separately for the two periods (2000–2002 and 2002–2005) to take into account differences in composition, average degree and other network characteristics over the waves, which might otherwise impair the quality of estimates (Lospinoso et al., 2010). This is needed all the more as the degree distribution in our dataset is much more skewed, thus leading to higher centralization, in Period One than in Period Two (Lazega et al., 2006; 2010b).

The rate parameter accounts for the amount of change between two subsequent observations of the network, that is, the speed at which the dependent variable (the network) changes. All other parameters are coefficients of the objective function or network evaluation function, used to compare different states of the network when the actor makes a choice to maintain present ties, to add a new tie, or to delete an existing tie. If

Table 3.1   *Bankers' norms drive the evolution of the advice network among lay judges at the Commercial Court of Paris (Siena model)*

	Period One (2000–2002)		Period Two (2002–2005)	
	Estimate	Standard error	Estimate	Standard error
Rate parameter	31.9	2.61	21.53	0.96
Out-degree (density)	−4.29*	0.28	−3.3*	0.25
Reciprocity	0.56*	0.16	0.36	0.22
Transitive triplets	0.14*	0.04	0.19*	0.03
Three-cycles	−0.19*	0.1	−0.03	0.05
In-degree – popularity (sqrt)	0.4*	0.02	0.34*	0.02
Out-degree – popularity (sqrt)	−0.19*	0.1	−0.19*	0.1
Out-degree – activity (sqrt)	0.38*	0.04	0.08*	0.04
Chamber co-membership	1.21*	0.08	1.68*	0.09
Previous chamber co-membership	0.8*	0.08	0.25*	0.1
Banker-Lawyer *alter*	0.14*	0.07	0.09	0.08
Banker-Lawyer *ego*	−0.18*	0.08	−0.25*	0.08
Banker-Lawyer similarity	0.07	0.07	0.09	0.08
Seniority *alter*	0.04*	0.01	−0.01	0.01
Seniority *ego*	0.01	0.01	−0.03*	0.01
Seniority similarity	0.12	0.23	−0.22	0.29
Interventionism in Boards *alter*	0.15*	0.06	0.13*	0.05
Interventionism in Boards *ego*	0.09	0.07	0.04	0.05
Interventionism in Boards similarity	0.01	0.09	0.03	0.07

Note: *statistically significant at 5 per cent level.

a parameter value is nil, the corresponding effect does not drive network dynamics; if it is positive, then there will be a higher probability of moving toward a personal network where the corresponding variable has a higher value; and the opposite if it is negative.

Among endogenous structural effects, the density effect is a basic indicator of network density and can be interpreted as an intercept. At local level the reciprocity effect is not always significant and does not allow concluding that judges tend to seek advice from those who themselves sought advice from them. The transitive triplets effect is positive and significant while the three-cycles effect is not consistently significant over time, so that we cannot conclude that there is local hierarchy in advice.

Endogenous feedback mechanisms at global rather than local level are captured through degree-related effects. We include in-degree popularity, out-degree popularity and out-degree activity, all in square root form. In-degree popularity is positive and statistically significant: it is evidence of a self-reinforcing process in which judges who are central at a given point in time see their centrality grow more strongly than others. Out-degree popularity is negative and suggests that judges with high out-degrees are less sought for advice, and the system moves towards a relatively low correlation between in- and out-degrees. Finally, out-degree activity is positive and significant (though more strongly so in the first than in the second period), suggesting that those who seek much advice remain in this role, and that the dispersion of out-degrees becomes or remains relatively high.

Regarding the exogenous variables, it is clear that chamber co-membership plays an important role in shaping the advice network, as already pointed out in our previous studies (Lazega et al., 2006, 2008). Previous chamber co-memberships also matter, even though their effect is smaller in size, indicating that some ties are lost with job rotation. Most of the other parameters exhibit time heterogeneity and do not display the same tendency over time. For instance, bankers with a law degree are particularly attractive as advisors in Period One (positive and statistically significant *alter* effect), but not in Period Two; their own advice-seeking behaviour is no different from that of other judges in Period One, but they tend to consult others less in Period Two (negative and significant *ego* effect). Likewise, more senior judges are attractive advisors in Period One but not afterwards, while the tendency of seniors not to seek advice from those more junior than themselves is only detectable in Period Two. These differences seem largely due to the changing composition of the network: indeed, senior judges and banker-lawyers appear to remain consistently differentially attractive as advisors over time when only the subset of judges who responded to the survey at all three waves is considered (Lazega et al., 2008, 2010a).

Interestingly, however, the 'Interventionism in Boards' *alter* parameter is positive and statistically significant over the two periods, thereby suggesting that judges who shared the decision to postpone the General Assembly and to appoint an expert have a consistently higher tendency to be consulted by others, so that their in-degree centrality becomes, or is, relatively high. Instead, the *ego* and similarity parameters are not significant. Hence, consensus on this choice contributes to driving the evolution of the advice network among judges at the Commercial Court of Paris and can be considered as a likely determinant of its final regulatory and judicial orientations. Since bankers with a law degree tend to be more interventionists in boards, on average, than the other judges, it is very likely that it is their influence that is being measured here with this effect. Thus the dominance of banker-lawyers – through their interventionist views with respect to boards, rather than through their sheer presence – extends to the court as a whole.

CONCLUSIONS

In this chapter, we have discussed a form of joint governance of the economy in which the government delegates important functions to civil society – here representatives of business acting as lay judges at a truly judicial commercial court. We outlined how this arrangement, despite its advantages in terms of effectiveness and efficiency of the conflict resolution process, entails the risk that particular industry interests prevail over the general interest. In particular it is known that the financial and banking sector as well as, to a lesser extent, the construction and services industries take strong action to ensure that their interests are taken into account.

Yet consular courts are complex structures in which sheer representation of the interests of specific sectors does not per se lead to dominance of these sectors. Final outcomes depend also upon the organizational features of the court, that is its structure in chambers and its internal hierarchy, and on the normative orientations of its members – in particular, we focused here on judges' pro-interventionist view in matters of company management at the board level. We investigated how these factors contribute to shaping the advice network at the court, that is the channels through which knowledge, norms, ideas and guidance circulate. The interest of this approach is that it confirms that advice networks affect the overall normative orientation of the court, and eventually its decisions.

Our Siena model provides evidence that adherence to a pro-interventionist (in boards) view is a driver of the evolution of the advice network. This is consistent with the observation that most judges agreed with the decision to accept the request of minority shareholders that they were asked to comment as a jurisprudential case. Despite variation in their answers, they find pro-interventionist colleagues more attractive as advisors, and do so consistently over time. The only other clear trend is, among organisational variables, chamber and previous chamber co-membership as a consistently strong driver of network dynamics.

However, the fieldwork suggests that differences in opinion remain strong and that, although judges agreed on the particular case they commented, they were not all ready to generalize it and protect minority shareholders in all circumstances. Further, there were nuances in judges' appreciation even of the most consensual answer, owing largely to the sector of activity of origin as bankers appeared more inclined to interventionism in boards than executives from the building industry.

These results support a sociological interpretation of joint governance as a multifaceted system, in which particular industries can have an influence not only by sending many judges in, but also more subtly by exerting persuasion through informal advice ties. They shed light on some of the risks of institutional capture (Lazega, 2009) attached to such an institutional design, but also on the complexity of the concept of joint governance of markets.

As underlined by Dixit (2009), governance equilibria identified in theory by many economists can fall short of social optimality for many reasons. Our findings show that 'joint governance', not to mention 'self-governance' or Dixit's 'private-ordering governance institutions', can also represent suboptimal solutions with respect to public interest. Even official governance institutions that are efficient in terms of speed can be suspected of harbouring conflicts of interests with private intermediaries. Our case study shows that, when contributing to official enforcement in governance, business relies on its most powerful segments (representatives of the banking industry for example) that act as a third party and distort such enforcement in invisible ways to suit its own interests rather than social welfare. Therefore, we conclude by pointing to the possibility that relation-based and rule-based modes of governance can be combined in suboptimal ways that allow certain parties to 'cheat' more easily, to protect their rent and power or to double-cross any other party in a conflict – simply by knowing that privately-selected officials acting as third parties are socially closer and intellectually more sensitive to these private interests.

NOTES

1. Since Max Weber's study of the German nineteenth century *Börse* (2000[1924]), organizational sociologists' works on economic institutions have greatly contributed to economic sociology. Some of them, such as Baker (1984) in his study of the Chicago Options Exchange, have added a structural spin to organizational approaches (White, 2002; Swedberg, 1994).
2. Arbitration also exists as a formal avenue of conflict resolution for businesses, but it is usually much more expensive and therefore limited to large and multinational companies.
3. For the characteristics of the French system of commercial courts as an institution of combined external and self-regulation, see Chaput (2002), Hirsch (1985), Ithurbide (1970), Jean (2000), Szramkiewicz (1989). There are 191 commercial courts in France, and around 3,000 consular judges making approximately 300,000 judicial decisions each year, of which 50,000 concern insolvency issues (Ministry of Justice figures for 1998; www.justice.gouv.fr/publicat/tc1807.htm (accessed 10 June 2010).
4. Two months after we began fieldwork, French commercial courts went on strike, for the first time in their history, against a proposed 2001 reform of their system. At the Commercial Court of Paris, we were surprised to see so many judges haunting the

corridors of the building during weeks of strike: many were retired, 'all dressed up with no place to go' as their younger colleagues said.

5. The state strives to increase its control. Since 1981, the attorney general has had an office at the court and is allowed to participate in deliberations, especially in bankruptcy proceedings. In 2001, a draft law was debated in the National Assembly and the Senate which aimed at introducing professional judges in the midst of consular judges, as a means to reassure businesses involved in court proceedings by improving 'control over the controllers'. The reform eventually failed but is indicative of a paradoxical situation. It was when the state began to withdraw from direct control of the economy in the 1980s that it started its attempts to increase its presence in commercial courts. The justification for this change in policy is to reassure European and global investors that they will receive a fair treatment in French commercial courts. This explanation, however, must be taken with caution: in spite of decades of selling its holdings, the French state's direct ownership in the economy remains strong.

6. Source: Labour force survey (Enquête Emploi) 2000, *Institut national de la statistique et des études économiques* (INSEE).

7. Source: *Institut national de la statistique et des études économiques* (INSEE), Mensuel no. 202, October 2001, Ile-de-France: 'Gros plan sur l'emploi francilien en 1999'.

8. Source: *Institut national de la statistique et des études économiques* (INSEE), National Accounts, 2001 (www.insee/fr/indicateur/cnat_annu/tableaux/t_1201_25_4.htm (accessed 20 June 2010).

9. The question is whether this represents social capital at the macro level, for society as a whole. One may argue that it is the case as with consular courts, civil society participates in the political process and in the life of institutions; the existence of virtuous knowledge-sharing processes would reinforce this view. However, others may contend that social capital in consular courts may in fact promote the particular interests of some industries and business organizations, rather than the general interest.

10. Wisemen are judges whose mandate has ended but remain available as advisors for other judges.

11. In the French legal system, this discretion is called *pouvoir souverain d'appréciation*.

REFERENCES

Ayres, Ian and John Braithwaite (1992), *Responsive Governance: Transcending the Degovernance Debate*, Oxford: Oxford University Press.

Baker, Wayne E. (1984), 'The social structure of a National Securities Market', *American Journal of Sociology*, **89**, 775–811.

Blau, Peter (1964), *Exchange and Power in Social Life*, New York: John Wiley and Sons.

Buskens, Vincent, Werner Raub and Chris Snijders (2003), 'Theoretical and empirical perspectives on the governance of relations in markets and organizations', *Research in the Sociology of Organizations*, **20**, 1–18.

Carruthers, Bruce G. and Terence Halliday (1998), *Rescuing Business: The Making of Corporate Bankruptcy Law in England and the United States*, Oxford: Oxford University Press.

Chaput, Yves (2002), 'L'indépendance renforcée du juge économique', *Revue de Jurisprudence Commerciale, Special issue: Colloque de La Baule: Le Juge de l'économie*, **46**, 74–94.

Cheit, Ross E. and Jacob E. Gersen (2000), 'When businesses sue each other: an empirical study of State Court litigation', *Law and Social Inquiry*, **25**, 789–816.

Dixit, Avinash (2009), 'Governance institutions and economic activity', *American Economic Review*, **99**, 5–24.

Dunworth, Terence and Joel Rogers (1996), 'Corporations in court: Big Business litigation in US federal courts, 1971–1991', *Law and Social Inquiry*, **21**, 497–592.

Ellickson, Robert C. (1991), *Order Without Law: How Neighbors Settle Disputes*, Cambridge, MA: Harvard University Press.

Falconi, Ana Maria, Karima Guenfoud, Emmanuel Lazega, Claire Lemercier and Lise Mounier (2005), 'Le Contrôle social du monde des affaires: une étude institutionnelle', *L'Année sociologique*, **55** (2), 451–484.

Felstiner, William L.F., Richard L. Abel and Austin Sarat (1980), 'The emergence and transformation of disputes: naming, blaming, claiming', *Law and Social Inquiry*, **15**, 631–654.

Flemming, Roy B. (1998), 'Contested terrains and regime politics: thinking about America's trial courts and institutional change', *Law and Social Inquiry*, **23**, 941–965.

Galanter, Marc and Charles E. Epp (1992), 'A beginner's guide to the litigation maze', *Business Economics*, **27**, 33–38.

Grabosky, Peter and John Braithwaite (1986), *Of Manners Gentle: Enforcement Strategies of Australian Business Regulatory Agencies*, Oxford: Oxford University Press.

Greif, Avner (1996), 'Contracting, enforcement, and efficiency: economics beyond the law', *Annual World Bank Conference on Development Economics*, 1996, 239–265.

Hawkins, Keith O. (1984), *Environment and Enforcement*, Oxford: Oxford University Press.

Hawkins. Keith O. and John M. Thomas (eds) (1984), *Enforcing Governance*, Boston, MA: Kluwer-Nijhof.

Heydebrand, Wolf V. and Carroll Seron (1990), *Rationalizing Justice: The Political Economy of Federal District Courts*, Albany, NY: SUNY Press.

Hirsch, Jean-Pierre (1985), *Les deux rêves du commerce. Entreprise et institution dans la région lilloise (1780–1860)*, Paris: Editions de l'EHESS.

Ithurbide, René (1970), *Histoire critique des tribunaux de commerce*, Paris: LCDG.

Jean, Jean-Paul (2000), *La réforme des tribunaux de commerce, Regards sur l'actualité*, Paris: La documentation française.

Lazega, Emmanuel (1992), *Micropolitics of Knowledge. Communication and Indirect Control in Workgroups*, New York: Aldine-de Gruyter.

Lazega, Emmanuel (2009), 'Quatre siècles et demi de New (New) Law & Economics: du pragmatisme juridique dans le régime consulaire de contrôle social des marchés', *Revue Française de Socio-Economie*, **3**, 97–120.

Lazega, Emmanuel and Lise Mounier (2002), 'Interdependent entrepreneurs and the social discipline of their cooperation: the research program of structural economic sociology for a society of organizations', in Olivier Favereau and Emmanuel Lazega (eds), *Conventions and Structures in Economic Organization: Markets, Networks, and Hierarchies*, Cheltenham, UK and Northampton, MA, USA: Edward Elgar, pp. 147–199

Lazega, Emmanuel and Lise Mounier (2003), 'Interlocking judges: on joint external and self-governance of markets', *Research in the Sociology of Organizations*, **20**, 267–296.

Lazega, Emmanuel, Claire Lemercier and Lise Mounier (2006), 'A spinning top model of formal structure and informal behaviour: dynamics of advice networks in a Commercial Court', *European Management Review*, **3**, 113–122.

Lazega, Emmanuel, Lise Mounier, Tom A.B. Snijders and Paola Tubaro (2008), 'Réseaux et controverses: de l'effet des normes sur la dynamique des structures', *Revue française de sociologie*, **49**, 467–498.

Lazega, Emmanuel, Lise Mounier, Tom A.B. Snijders and Paola Tubaro (2010a), 'Norms, status and the dynamics of advice networks', in press, *Social Networks*, available at http://dx.doi.org/10.1016/j.socnet.2009.12.001 (accessed 1 December 2010).

Lazega, Emmanuel, Saraï Sapulete and Lise Mounier (2010b), 'Structural stability regardless of membership turnover? The added value of blockmodelling in the analysis of network evolution', in press, *Quality and Quantity*, electronic version published, DOI 10.1007/s11135-009-9295-y.

Leenders, Roger and Shaul Gabbay (eds) (1999), *Corporate Social Capital and Liabilities*, Boston, MA: Kluwer.

Lemercier, Claire (2003), *Un si discret pouvoir. Aux origines de la Chambre de commerce de Paris, 1803–1853*, Paris: La Découverte.

Lindenberg, Siegwart (1998), 'Solidarity: its microfoundations and macro dependence, a framing approach', in Patrick Doreian and Thomas J. Fararo (eds), *The Problem of Solidarity: Theories and Models,* New York: Gordon & Breach.

Lospinoso, Joshua A., Michael Schweinberger, Tom A.B. Snijders and Ruth M. Ripley (2010), 'Assessing and accounting for time heterogeneity in stochastic actor oriented models', *Advances in Data Analysis and Computation*, forthcoming.

Macaulay, Stewart (1963), 'Non-contractual relations in business: a preliminary study', *American Sociological Review*, **28**, 55–67.

Macaulay, Stewart (1986), 'Private government', in Leon Lipson and Stanley Wheeler (eds), *Law and the Social Sciences*, New York: Russell Sage.

McIntosh, Wayne V. and Cynthia L. Cates (1997), *Judicial Entrepreneurship: The Role of the Judge in the Marketplace of Ideas*, Westport, CT: Greenwood Press.

Milgrom, Paul R., Douglass C. North and Barry R. Weingast (1990), 'The role of institutions in the revival of trade: the law merchant, private judges, and the champagne fairs', *Economics and Politics*, **2** (1), March, 1–23.

Raub, Werner and Jeroen Weesie (1993), 'Symbiotic arrangements: a sociological perspective', *Journal of Institutional and Theoretical Economics*, **149**, 716–724.

Raub, Werner and Jeroen Weesie (eds) (2000), *The Management of Durable Relations: Theoretical and Empirical Models for Households and Organizations*, Amsterdam: Thela Publishers.

Ripley, Ruth M. and Tom A.B. Snijders (2010), *Manual for Siena version 4*, available at http://www.stats.ox.ac.uk/~snijders/siena/ (accessed 1 December 2010).

Rooks, Gerrit, Werner Raub, Robert Selten and Frits Tazelaar (2000), 'How inter-firm cooperation depends on social embeddedness: a vignette study', *Acta Sociologica*, **43**, 123–137.

Shapiro, Susan P. (1984), *Wayward Capitalists: Target of the Securities and Exchange Commission*, New Haven, CT: Yale University Press.

Snijders, Tom A.B. (2001), 'The statistical evaluation of social network dynamics', in Michael E. Sobel and Mark P. Becker (eds), *Sociological Methodology*, Boston, MA and London: Basil Blackwell, pp. 361–395.

Snijders, Tom A.B. (2005), 'Models for longitudinal network data', in Peter J. Carrington, John Scott and Stanley Wasserman (eds), *Models and Methods in Social Network Analysis*, New York: Cambridge University Press, Chapter 11.

Snijders, Tom A.B., Gerhard G. van de Bunt and Christian E.G. Steglich (2010), 'Introduction to stochastic actor-based models for network dynamics', *Social Networks*, **32**, 44–60.

Swedberg, Richard (1994), 'Markets as social structures', in Neil Smelser and Richard Swedberg (eds), *Handbook of Economic Sociology*, Princeton, NJ: Princeton University Press; and New York: Russell Sage Foundation.

Szramkiewicz, Romuald (1989), *Histoire du droit des affaires*, Paris: Montchrestien.

Weait, Matthew (1993), 'Icing on the cake: the contribution of the compliance function to effective financial services regulation', *Journal of Asset Protection and Financial Crime*, **1**, 83–90.

Weaver, Suzanne (1977), *Decision to Prosecute: Organization and Public Policy in the Antitrust Division*, Cambridge, MA: The MIT Press.

Weber, Max (2000[1924]), 'Die Börse', *Theory and Society*, **29**, 303–337.

Wheeler, Stanton, Kenneth Mann and Austin Sarat (1988), *Sitting in Judgment: The Sentencing of White Collar Criminals*, New Haven, CT: Yale University Press.

White, Harrison C. (2002), *Markets from Networks: Socioeconomic Models of Production*, Princeton, NJ: Princeton University Press.

Williamson, Oliver E. (1985), *The Economic Institutions of Capitalism*, New York: Free Press.

4. Legal versus reputational penalties in deterring corporate misconduct

Peter-Jan Engelen

INTRODUCTION

Traditionally, most countries rely heavily on public law enforcement through court-imposed or supervisory-imposed legal sanctions to insure corporations to comply with the law. Most regulators ignore financial markets as one of the channels to induce companies to behave responsibly. This chapter examines the relationship between formal legal governance institutions and the role of market-imposed reputational penalties. Its aim is to establish the relative effectiveness of both types of institutions in encouraging responsible corporate behaviour. As the field of economic governance compares the performance of different institutions under different conditions (Dixit, 2009), this chapter contributes to the literature on market-induced versus public enforcement mechanisms.

Specifically, we focus on the effectiveness of public versus market-induced enforcement efforts of illegal insider trading by corporate insiders. We test whether there is any interaction between a country's public enforcement power and the magnitude of reputational penalties companies experience for the illegal insider trading of their managers. The analysis combines two recent datasets on the United States and six European countries covering illegal insider trading practices by the company's CEO and other executives. This is the first cross-country study which links the magnitude of reputational penalties to differences in the country's level of law enforcement. As law enforcement varies significantly cross-country, one can postulate to observe different reputational penalties for our set of seven countries. We test the hypothesis of any substitution effect between legal penalties and reputational penalties. If this is the case, our results can have important consequences for a country's sentencing guidelines and for supervisors' enforcement heuristics.

Market-induced enforcement strategies are important in cases where

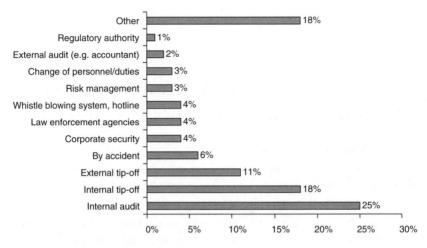

Source: Bussmann and Werle (2006).

Figure 4.1   Distribution of the detection mechanisms of corporate crimes

reputational loss matters and public law enforcement is expensive or ineffective. A recent global survey of more than 5,500 companies about their experience with economic crimes showed that only 28 per cent of the managers had trust in law enforcement agencies and only 30 per cent of the detected perpetrators were actually sentenced (Bussmann and Werle, 2006). Moreover, in most of the cases companies themselves detected the perpetrators, while only in 4 per cent of the cases were they detected by law enforcement agencies (see Figure 4.1). The study showed a clear preference to settle cases internally when companies were subject to economic crime by their managers. As companies are sensitive to bad publicity, reputational penalties through the stock market can be an effective alternative for ineffective public law enforcement.

The chapter is organized as follows. After the introduction, the traditional law enforcement channels and market-induced enforcement channels through reputational penalties are discussed.

The next section elaborates on insider trading rules and enforcement in the USA and in Europe. Then we test the interaction between a country's public enforcement powers and the magnitude of reputational penalties companies experience for the illegal insider trading of their managers. The final section concludes.

DIFFERENT ENFORCEMENT CHANNELS OF SECURITIES LAWS

After raising some concerns with respect to the traditional law enforcement channels through formal governance institutions, we elaborate on market-based reputational mechanisms as an alternative governance mechanism.

Traditional Law Enforcement

Traditionally, the law and finance literature has focused on the importance of public and private law enforcement as means to promote the development of financial markets around the world (La Porta et al., 2006). This chapter does not aim to provide a full overview of these formal legal governance institutions. We only observe that the debate on whether public enforcement or private enforcement is preferred to develop strong capital markets is still not settled (Jackson and Roe, 2009). In some areas, public enforcement seems to be the most effective, while in other areas this is the case for private law enforcement. The interaction between both levels of enforcement is still not well understood.

In the law and finance literature private law enforcement, especially through collective remedies likes class actions, is said to be an effective alternative for failing public law enforcement (Jackson and Roe, 2009). Others stress the fact that class actions do not really contribute much to shareholders and often assume concurrent public law enforcement (Coffee, 2006; Romano, 2005). Cox and Thomas (2003) examine 248 securities violation class actions settled between 1997 and 2002. They compare class action with and without parallel Securities and Exchange Commission (SEC) enforcement. Their data shows that private enforcement efforts result in a larger settlement when the SEC has a concurrent enforcement action: on average, a private action with parallel SEC action settles for US$11.2 million, while a similar case without SEC action settles for only US$9.5 million (US$7.2 and US$4.8 million, respectively, for the median – see Panel A in Table 4.1). This dataset also shows that the SEC targets smaller companies than pure private class actions (market capitalization of US$471.8 versus US$1206.8 millions – see Panel B in Table 4.1). Finally, private actions with parallel SEC enforcement reach settlement quicker than pure private actions (see Panel C in Table 4.1).

Cox and Thomas (2005) revisit their earlier study and split their sample into pre- and post-Enron subsamples. The total sample includes 389 class actions and covers the period between 1990 and 2003, of which 300 are in the pre-Enron and 89 in the post-Enron time frame. The pre-Enron data in Panel A of Table 4.2 are similar to the results presented in Table 4.1.

Table 4.1   Settlements of private actions for securities violations between 1997 and 2002

	Mean	Median	Number of observations
Panel A. Settlement amount (US$ millions)			
Without a parallel SEC action	9.5	4.8	211
With a parallel SEC action	11.2	7.2	37
Panel B. Market capitalization of defendant companies (US$ millions)			
Without a parallel SEC action	1206.8	128.4	186
With a parallel SEC action	471.8	75.7	30
Panel C. Time to reach settlement (in months)			
Without a parallel SEC action	26.8	23.8	152
With a parallel SEC action	20.8	16.6	26

Source: Cox and Thomas (2003).

Table 4.2   Settlement amounts of private actions for securities violations pre- and post-Enron

	Mean	Median	Number of observations
Panel A. Settlements prior to 1 January 2002 (US$ millions)			
Without a parallel SEC action	10.1	5.0	248
With a parallel SEC action	11.5	6.6	52
Panel B. Settlements after 1 January 2002 (US$ millions)			
Without a parallel SEC action	16.6	5.6	68
With a parallel SEC action	53.7	16.0	21

Source: Cox and Thomas (2005).

However, we observe a significant increase in the settlement amount of private actions with parallel SEC actions after 1 January 2002. The data for the post-Enron time frame reveal an average settlement amount of US$53.7 versus US$16.6 million in pure private actions (US$16.0 versus US$5.6 million for the median – see Panel B in Table 4.2). Apparently the SEC focuses on larger companies in the post-Enron period.

The results from Cox and Thomas (2003, 2005) show that private class actions are more effective with a parallel public enforcement action. Their data does not answer the question on the effectiveness of pure public law enforcement actions. Jackson and Roe (2009) argue that public law enforcement is at least as important as private enforcement in explaining the development of capital markets around the world. This chapter does not try to take a stand in the choice between public and private law enforcement; it merely makes the case for a third enforcement channel which is currently largely ignored in the law and finance literature: market-induced enforcement through financial markets. This chapter is a first step in examining the interaction and coordination between public and private law enforcement and market-induced law enforcement. The next section addresses the question of this third enforcement channel.

Market-induced Enforcement

After introducing the concept of market-induced reputational penalties, this section gives an overview of the empirical literature on measuring the reputational losses companies experience for corporate malfeasance.

The concept of reputational penalties

The reputational literature starts with the models of Klein and Leffler (1981), Shapiro (1982, 1983) and Lott (1988) and defines reputation in terms of customer expectations about product quality. In those models atomistic customers update their expectations about product quality of a seller when they receive news about product defects or product unsafety. They will switch to another seller with higher quality products or they will keep buying products from the same seller at a lower price. The loss of cash flows that occurs due to changing customer behaviour is called a reputational penalty. It therefore reflects the lower expected quasi-rents from future sales since customers are no longer willing to pay a premium price for superior product quality. This mechanism induces companies to maintain product quality at a high level because the market mechanism internalizes the cost of corporate misconduct in repeating business transactions.

To understand why a firm experiences a stock price decline upon the discovery of corporate malfeasance, we zoom in on the pricing mechanism of the stock exchange. In an efficient stock market, any stock price decline upon the announcement of corporate misconduct reflects the expected legal penalties and reputational penalties the firm will incur. Legal penalties include fines, damage payments and compliance costs, while reputational penalties might reflect lower company profits due to lower expected future cash flows or a higher cost of capital.

Figure 4.2 shows the channels of the stock price decline in more detail. The market price of a share on the stock exchange is actually an

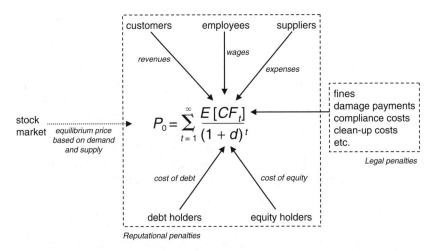

Stock price = present value of all future expected cash flows

Notes: P_0 = current stock price; CF_t = cash flows at time t; d = discount factor; $E[.]$ = expected value operator; t = time parameter.

Source: Engelen and van Essen (2011).

Figure 4.2   Channels of stock market penalization

equilibrium price of the expectations of investors about the value of the company through the mechanism of supply and demand. The reputational penalty is actually an aggregation of the penalties stakeholders impose on the company through different channels. Customers will impose a reputational penalty on the company by buying fewer products (or even boycotting products) leading to lower expected cash flows, which in turn leads to a lower stock price (Posnikoff, 1997). In a similar way, suppliers can become more expensive because they are only willing to do business with the company with stricter conditions or because they are more reluctant to provide trade credit. The labour force may become more expensive because of lower job satisfaction, higher absenteeism, lower job performance or higher job turnover of employees (Viswesvaran et al., 1998; Vitell and Davis, 1990). This will lead to increased costs and thus to a lower stock price. Reputational penalties might also show up in the discount rate through higher costs of capital from debt holders (Graham et al., 2008) as well as equity holders (Hribar and Jenkins, 2004; Palmrose et al., 2004). The latter means that stock market investors might demand a higher required rate of return (cost of equity) to reflect a higher company risk.

Empirical studies on reputational penalties

The early reputational penalties literature focused on product recalls. One would expect to see a negative stock price reaction upon the announcement of product recalls or the disclosure of unsafe products or service practices. The empirical results from the product recall and product safety literature indeed suggest that stock markets react negatively to news that affects a firm's reputation. This early strand of literature examines drug recalls, air crashes, automobile recalls and other recalls. Jarrell and Peltzman (1985) find considerable stock market losses for producers of recalled pharmaceutical products. Since the stock market imposes a substantial loss of firm value over and above the product-specific recall costs, they interpret their results as a reputational penalty imposed by the stock market. Examining the 1982 Tylenol product recall Mitchell (1989) and Dowdell et al. (1992) confirm that the negative stock price impact exceeds the direct costs and is largely due to the loss of brand-name capital.

Chalk (1986, 1987) shows that the stock market losses suffered by shareholders upon the announcement of air crashes largely exceeds any estimates of regulatory and liability costs. The difference is again attributed to a reputational penalty. Mitchell and Maloney (1989) compare a sample of at-fault crashes with a sample of no-fault crashes. The former includes crashes due to pilot error and improper maintenance and signal airline negligence, while the latter category includes crashes due to manufacturer error or miscellaneous causes not controlled by the airline (bad weather, air traffic control error). The empirical results show no stock price reaction for no-fault crashes and a clear negative stock price impact for at-fault crashes. Taking into account increases in insurance premium, about 42 per cent of this stock market decline can be attributed to a reputational loss.

Studies on automobile recalls mostly find stock markets react negatively to the recall announcements. Again the stock price decline is not in line with the costs of the product recalls, leading Jarrell and Peltzman (1985), Barber and Darrough (1996) and Rupp (2001, 2004) to conclude that the reputational penalty is substantial. It 'documents . . . a direct link between product reliability and shareholder wealth. The stock market imposes a penalty on a manufacturer that produces defective vehicles' (Barber and Darrough, 1996: 1098). Govindaraj and Jaggi (2004) estimate about 21 per cent of the negative stock price reaction is associated with a reputational cost, although it might be a conservative estimate.

Alexander (1999) points out that this reputation mechanism is not limited to a seller–customer framework but can be applied to a wide range of settings of repeated transactions. Besides customers, other related parties such as suppliers, employees and external financiers can change their implicit and explicit contracts with the company. Reputational losses are actually the downward revised present values of lower future net sales or higher future costs of capital. In an efficient capital market, this will be translated in a lower stock price. While legal penalties include fines, damage payments and compliance costs, reputational penalties might include lower company's profits due to lost customers, suppliers or employees, or it might lead to a higher cost of capital, due to a higher cost of equity or an increased cost of bank debt (see Figure 4.2).

The empirical studies on corporate malfeasance indeed show that the reputation mechanism is observed in a wide range of types of corporate misconduct. Aggregate studies including types of misconduct such as bribery, tax evasion, illegal political contributions, employee discrimination and criminal antitrust violations exhibit a strong negative stock price decline. Davidson and Worrell (1988) examine the daily returns of a wide sample of illegal business practices and find a significant negative abnormal return of –1.08 per cent. Similar results are reported by Reichert et al. (1996) examining a sample of 83 announcements of filing of formal indictments against companies for corporate illegalities at firm level during the 1980s.

Rao and Hamilton (1996) examine a sample of 58 events on bribery, employee discrimination, environmental pollution, insider trading and business ethics. They find a monthly abnormal return of –5.67 per cent for the full sample on the announcement moment of the publication in financial press. Gunthorpe (1997) shows a negative abnormal return of –1.33 per cent on the announcement date of 69 cases of formal investigations into fraud, bribery, price fixing and the breach of contract.

Using a dataset on criminal offenses by 78 USA corporations, Alexander (1999) finds a stock market penalty for a wide range of illegalities such as contract violations, bribes, fraudulent bids, FDA violations, safety violations, illegal antitrust practices, export violations and environmental and wildlife offenses. Over a two-day period around the announcement in press she measures a significant –2.84 per cent abnormal return. Correcting for legal penalties, she attributes the difference to a reputation penalty.

However, pooling all types of corporate malfeasance in one sample as is the case in the above aggregate studies makes the results difficult to interpret. Markets might react differently to various types of corporate misconduct. For instance, financial markets might react negatively to accounting fraud, but positively to bribery. Accounting fraud could be considered as bad business practice (decrease of cash flows), while bribery might be considered as an acceptable business practice to obtain important business contracts in certain countries (increase of cash flows). Moreover, financial markets might react more strongly to certain types of corporate misconduct than to others (for example fraud versus environmental violations).

Any aggregation across all types of malfeasance could make the results difficult to interpret since the price impacts of different illegal categories might offset each other, and thus, a smaller overall abnormal return is observed.

While the above studies use an aggregate sample of a diverse range of corporate misconduct, the scope of the following studies is more focused by examining a specific type of corporate malfeasance. Peltzman (1981) examines the impact of FTC charges on false and misleading advertising on companies' stock prices and observes a negative abnormal return of 3.12 per cent.

Over the period 1981–1987 Karpoff and Lott (1993) examine 132 cases of fraud of customers, suppliers, employees, government and investors and find that public announcements of corporate fraud in press leads to an average decline of 1.34 per cent of the stock price. On a subsample of 15 companies they collect information on the level of the legal penalties and find that the stock market loss is in no relation to the expected penalties. They interpret the stock price decline therefore as a reputational penalty imposed on the financial market.

Estimates of reputational penalties for environmental violations do not seem to be significantly different from zero. Karpoff et al. (2005) examine 478 USA environmental violations over the period 1980–2000 to determine to what extent reputational penalties impose a significant cost on violating firms. For the full sample they find a stock market loss of 1 per cent over a two-day period and for the allegations subsample a two-day abnormal return of –1.69 per cent. Using detailed information on a subsample of 148 violations with respect to fines, damage awards, compliance and cleanup costs, they find that the equity loss constitutes only of expected legal penalties. This implies that 'firms do not on average experience reputational loss when they violate environmental regulations' (Karpoff et al., 2005: 668).

Karpoff et al. (2008) examine 585 USA firms for financial misrepresentation between 1978 and 2002. Financial accounting misconduct is penalized by a very heavily equity loss. Companies thus pay substantial reputational penalties for cooking the books. According to their measurement 24.5 per cent of the equity loss can be attributed to market adjustment to reflect the correct fundamental value of the company's financial situation, 8.8 per cent can be associated with expected legal penalties and no less than 67 per cent is due to a reputational penalty. Or in absolute dollars terms: 'For every dollar of inflated value when a firm's books are cooked, firm value decreases by that dollar when the misrepresentation is revealed; in addition, firm value declines an additional 36 dollar cents due to fines and class action settlements and $2.71 due to lost reputation' (Karpoff et al.,

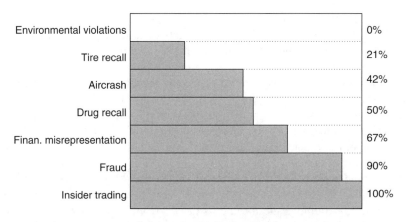

Note: Information on environmental violations is obtained from Karpoff et al. (2005), on tire recalls from Govindaraj and Jaggi (2004), on drug recalls from Mitchell (1989), on airline crashes from Mitchell and Maloney (1989), on financial misrepresentation from Karpoff et al. (2008), on fraud from Karpoff and Lott (1993) and on illegal insider trading from Engelen (2009).

Figure 4.3   Reputational penalty as percentage of equity loss for different types of corporate misconduct

2008: 606). Karpoff et al. clearly show that legal penalties are only a small part of the total losses suffered by these firms. The reputational penalty is far more important.

Finally, Engelen (2009) shows that companies experience a reputational penalty for illegal insider trading by their managers. The study observes a clear negative abnormal return on the day of the newspaper announcement of the illegal insider trading practice of 1.5 per cent. These results indicate that the rotten apple (in the otherwise clean barrel) theory of no stock price reaction to the press announcement of illegal insider trading by top managers is not supported by the data. On the contrary, the heavy stock price drop suggests that financial markets perceive the illegality as a systemic problem.

Figure 4.3 gives an overview of the magnitude of the reputational penalties reported in the literature. It shows that we find percentages between 21 per cent and 42 per cent for product recalls and 67 per cent for financial misrepresentation. Compared to other forms of corporate misconduct the reputational penalty for illegal insider trading is at one end of the spectrum (100 per cent reputational penalty), while environmental violations imposing no reputational penalty on companies are at the other end (Karpoff et al., 2005). This is in line with the theoretical literature which predicts that a reputational penalty will work effectively in case the damaged party is a related party, such as customers, suppliers, employees and external financiers, but will not work well in case of unrelated or third parties. For instance, Karpoff and Lott (1993) find a reputational penalty of 90 per cent of the equity loss for party-related misconduct such as fraud of stakeholders, fraud of the government and financial reporting fraud. As predicted by theory, they do not find any reputational penalty for regulatory violations without direct involvement of related parties (for example check-kiting scheme).

ILLEGAL INSIDER TRADING IN THE USA AND EUROPE

Most countries established insider trading rules to curtail earning excess returns by trading on privileged information (Bhattacharya and Daouk, 2002). Table 4.3 gives an overview of the year of introduction of insider trading laws in the USA and the six European Union (EU) countries included in this study.

The USA insider trading rules are governed by the statutory authority from Section 10b of the Securities Exchange Act of 1934. Based on this authority, the SEC enacted rules 10b-5 and 14e-3 and it applied to impersonal stock exchange transaction beginning in 1961 (Bainbridge, 2005). Moreover, milestone USA Supreme Court rulings (*Dirks v. SEC*, *Chiarella v. United States*, *United States v. O'Hagan*) further determined the scope of application of those rules. In *Chiarella v. United States*, the USA Supreme Court rejected the SEC's equal access to information policy. Insiders are only liable if they breach a fiduciary duty to the source of the information. In *Dirks v. SEC* the USA Supreme Court extended this view to tippees, requiring a breach of the tipper's fiduciary duty before the tippee becomes liable.[1] In *United States v. O'Hagan*, the USA Supreme Court accepted the misappropriation theory, which bases insider trading liability on 'a breach of a duty owed to the source of the information'. A misappropriator is thus liable if he fails to disclose to his principal the use of confidential information for his personal gain while having a duty of loyalty or a duty of confidentiality. The USA regulation shows that legal prohibition is an evolving field developed by court decisions (Bainbridge, 2005).

Before 1984 illegal insider trading was sanctioned in the USA with a maximum criminal penalty of US$10,000 or an imprisonment of maximum two years, although jail sentences were nonexistent before 1980 (Seyhun, 1992). The sanctions were seriously aggravated in the USA during the 1980s. First, the Insider Trading Sanctions Act (ITSA) of 1984

Table 4.3   *Comparative overview of insider trading rules and enforcement in Europe and the US*

Country	Year of introduction	Scope	Sanction	IT law	Actual enforcement	Year of first enforcement
Belgium	1989	2.00	1.00	3.00	1.00	1994
France	1970	2.00	2.00	4.00	1.00	1972
Germany	1994*	2.00	1.00	3.00	1.00	1995
Luxembourg	1991	2.00	1.00	3.00	1.00	1999
Netherlands	1989	2.00	1.00	3.00	1.00	1994
UK	1980	2.00	1.00	3.00	1.00	1981
US	1934	2.00	2.00	4.00	1.00	1961
World	1991	1.76	0.97	2.73	0.48	1994

Notes:
*   Before 1994 Germany had a voluntary code on insider trading (introduced in 1970, amended in 1976 and 1988).

Year of introduction: indicates in which year insider trading laws have been introduced in a country. *Source:* Bhattacharya and Daouk (2002), corrected where necessary.

Scope: measures the breadth of the insider trading prohibition. Scope ranges from 0 to 2, with 0 representing the most permissive insider trading prohibition and 2 representing the most restrictive insider trading prohibition. *Source:* Beny (2005).

Sanction is a proxy for the expected criminal and monetary sanctions for violating a country's insider trading laws. Sanction ranges from 0 to 2, with 0 representing the lowest expected sanctions and 2 representing the highest expected sanctions. *Source:* Beny (2005).

IT Law: An aggregate index equals the sum of Scope and Sanction. IT Law ranges from 0 to 4, with 0 representing the most lax insider trading legal regime and 4 representing the most restrictive insider trading legal regime. *Source:* Beny (2005).

Actual enforcement: indicates whether insider trading laws are enforced in reality. *Source:* Bhattacharya and Daouk (2002) [updated for recent years].

Year of first enforcement: indicates the year in which the insider trading laws have been enforced for the first time. *Source:* Bhattacharya and Daouk (2002) [updated for recent years].

raised the maximum criminal fine tenfold to US$100,000. Moreover, up to 1984 only criminal sanctions were possible. The SEC had to refer the case to the Public Prosecutor for criminal prosecution. Only after a criminal conviction was disgorgement possible. The ITSA gave the SEC the authority to impose civil sanctions for insider trading cases, up to three times the obtained profit. Second, the Insider Trading and Securities Fraud Enforcement Act of 1988 (ITSFEA) again increased the criminal fines tenfold to a maximum US$1,000,000 for individuals, and imprisonment fivefold to a maximum ten years. Over a period of five years the maximum criminal penalty thereby increased 100 times (Engelen,

2007). The maximum fine is now US$1,000,000, while imprisonment is a maximum of ten years. Moreover, the SEC can ask for disgorgement of the profit and can impose treble civil damage sanctions as well.

With the exception of France and the UK, most of the EU countries introduced insider trading laws in the 1990s (Bhattacharya and Daouk, 2002). Since insider trading rules in the EU were introduced by means of a directive which requires its member states to achieve a particular result, the insider trading laws in the different member states are largely harmonized.[2] Member states which had insider trading rules before the introduction of the Insider Trading Directive had to adjust their laws in line with the directive (as was the case with France and the UK). Table 4.3 shows that the insider trading laws in the six EU countries are therefore very comparable in the breadth of the insider trading prohibition (Scope) and in the potential criminal and monetary sanctions (Sanction). Table 4.3 also demonstrates that the EU regulation is better in scope and sanction than the world average (Beny, 2005). The scope of the regulation in the EU is similar to that of the USA. Overall, one can conclude that the insider trading rules (law in the books) of the USA and the six EU countries are similar.

Even when the insider trading laws in the books seem quite good, the enforcement (law in action) of insider trading regulation is even more important (Bhattacharya and Daouk, 2009). To gain more insight into the enforcement in the USA and the six European countries, Tables 4.3 and 4.4 present data along two dimensions: (1) actual enforcement and (2) enforcement potential or power (Beny, 2005). Actual enforcement measures whether the insider trading rules were enforced in reality in a country. Columns 6 and 7 in Table 4.3 above showed that insider trading rules were enforced in all countries by the mid 1990s or earlier. Although this rough proxy shows actual enforcement effort, it hides the real enforcement record.

In Table 4.4, enforcement power measures the potential impact of supervisors enforcing insider trading rules. We document this by reporting three proxies from the literature. First, investigative powers is an index developed by La Porta et al. (2006) to measure the mean of the securities market supervisor's power to command documents during an investigation of securities laws violations and to subpoena the testimony of witnesses. Second, public enforcement power is a wider index which indicates the enforcement of the supervisor of securities markets and equals the mean of 5 indices as defined in Table 4.4 above.[3] Third, Beny (2005) also uses private enforcement power to indicate whether investors can bring private law suits against violators of securities laws in a given country.

We see that only France and the UK have investigative powers and

Table 4.4   Comparative overview of enforcement in Europe and the US

Country	Investigative power	Public enforcement power	Private enforcement power
Belgium	0.25	0.15	0.00
France	1.00	0.77	0.00
Germany	0.25	0.22	0.00
Luxembourg	NA	NA	NA
Netherlands	0.50	0.47	0.00
UK	1.00	0.68	0.00
US	1.00	0.90	10.00
World	0.60	0.52	2.91

Notes:
Investigative power: the index of investigative powers equals the arithmetic mean of (1) document and (2) witness. Document is an index of the power of the supervisor to command documents when investigating a violation of securities laws. Equals one if the supervisor can generally issue an administrative order commanding all persons to turn over documents; equals one half if the supervisor can generally issue an administrative order commanding publicly traded corporations and/or their directors to turn over documents; and equals zero otherwise. Witness is an index of the power of the supervisor to subpoena the testimony of witnesses when investigating a violation of securities laws. Equals one if the supervisor can generally subpoena all persons to give testimony; equals one half if the supervisor can generally subpoena the directors of publicly traded corporations to give testimony; and equals zero otherwise. *Source:* La Porta et al. (2006).

Public enforcement power: the index of public enforcement indicates the enforcement of the supervisor of securities markets. It equals the arithmetic mean of (1) supervisor characteristics index; (2) rule-making power index; (4) investigative powers index; (5) orders index; and (5) criminal index. *Source:* La Porta et al. (2006).

Private enforcement power: indicates if private parties have a private right of action against parties who have violated the country's insider trading laws, multiplied with the efficiency of the judiciary. *Source:* Beny (2005).

public enforcement power of similar level as the USA. Other EU countries have much lower scores than the USA and even below the world average. None of the six EU countries has private enforcement possibilities. Although the European Commission considers the enforcement of insider trading rules of crucial importance to ensure the integrity of European financial markets, EU countries have not been very successful in curtailing illegal insider trading (Hostetter, 1999). EU public law enforcement seems to be ineffective in deterring corporate insiders from exploiting their informational advantage.

However, there is a third alternative for curtailing illegal insider trading by corporate insiders. Instead of a public law enforcement mechanism, financial markets can function as a market-induced enforcement mechanism by imposing a reputational penalty on companies whose agents trade on privileged information. Such a market discipline might serve as a substitute for poor public law enforcement in order to ban illegal insider trading.

TRADE-OFF BETWEEN LEGAL AND REPUTATIONAL PENALTIES?

This section analyzes whether there is any interaction between legal penalties and reputational penalties. The empirical literature shows that the level of reputational penalties varies over different types of corporate misconduct. Reputational penalties are large and a multiple of legal penalties in cases of fraud, financial misrepresentation and illegal insider trading, but are non-existent in case of environmental violations or human rights violations (see supra). Karpoff et al. (2005:655) therefore conclude that 'legal penalties, and not reputational penalties, are the primary deterrents to environmental violations'. In contrast, Karpoff et al. (2008:606) document a reputational penalty which is over 7.5 times the legal penalties, leading the authors to conclude that 'a focus on purely legal penalties would miss the point [that] most of the penalty comes from lost reputation'. When regulators 'ignore the importance of reputational penalties, they will establish suboptimal legal rules and penalties for financial misconduct'.

Karpoff and Lott (1993) argue the case that reputational penalties and legal penalties can be substituted to deter illegal behaviour for the subset of corporate misconduct for which reputation effects matter. This is consistent with the theory of the economics of crime that argues that the expected total penalty for a crime should be equal to the crime's social cost (Becker, 1968). As the expected total penalties incorporate both legal penalties and reputational penalties, low legal penalties can be compensated by a reputational penalty. If reputational penalties are very large, regulators can rely more on market-induced penalties and legal penalties should be kept small to reach optimal deterrence (Karpoff et al., 2005). Regulators should focus on corporate malfeasance with low or even zero reputational penalties and use legal penalties for optimal deterrence. If reputational penalties are high and regulators choose to increase legal penalties as well, the level of the expected total penalties might be too high and overdeterrence will be achieved (Alexander, 1999). This is especially the case when detection and enforcement is not free, as is the case with public enforcement through administrative and criminal procedures. Financial market discipline might thus serve as a substitute for expensive legal penalties by imposing a market-induced reputational penalty. If legal and reputational penalties are substitutes, regulators might coordinate both penalties through sentencing guidelines in order to reach optimal deterrence (Alexander, 1999).

We test the hypothesis of the substitution effect between legal penalties and reputational penalties by focusing on one type of corporate misconduct, namely illegal insider trading. Illegal insider trading is an interesting category of corporate malfeasance since it allows for an unbiased estimate of the reputational penalty. Engelen (2009) shows that, unlike other types of corporate misconduct, illegal insider trading by corporate insiders does not occur at the company level, but at the individual level. Therefore, any legal penalties for getting caught for illegal insider trading are attributed to those individuals and not to the company. Any financial market discipline occurs at the company level by driving down the stock price. This market-induced penalization is therefore not an anticipation of any expected legal penalties at the corporate level, but can be interpreted as a pure reputational penalty.

We examine differences in reputational penalties for illegal insider trading across seven countries. By combining two recent datasets, one on six European countries (Engelen, 2009) and another on the USA (Engelen, 2010), we test whether reputational penalties vary with differences in public and private law enforcement. As law enforcement varies significantly cross-country, one can postulate to observe different reputational penalties. This is the first cross-country study which links the magnitude of reputational penalties to differences in the country's level of law enforcement.

Abnormal returns are measured through the standard market model event study methodology. Individual stock abnormal returns ($AR_{i,t}$) are measured as the difference between the actual return on the event day ($R_{i,t}$) and the expected return according to the market model $R_{i,t} = a_i + b_i \cdot R_{m,t} + e_{i,t}$, with $R_{i,t}$ = the return of stock i in period t; $R_{m,t}$ = the market index return in period t; a_i, b_i = intercept and slope coefficient of the market model (stock-*i*-specific and time-independent parameters); $e_{i,t}$ = random disturbance term of the market model for stock i in period t. The parameters of the market model are estimated over a period from (−140) to (−21) trading days before the event day. The average abnormal return on the event day is the aggregation of the individual stock abnormal returns aligned in event time. The significance of average abnormal returns is tested using the standard test statistic assuming cross-sectional independence, which standardizes abnormal returns for each stock by its standard deviation calculated from the estimation period.

Table 4.5 presents the finding from the full European sample of Engelen (2009), where he had analyzed the abnormal return behaviour around the announcement of illegal insider trading practices by the CEO and other

Table 4.5   Abnormal return behaviour around the news of illegal insider trading in press

Days	European sample		USA sample	
	AAR	t-test	AAR	t-test
–2	–0.0028	0.830	–0.0058	–2.378
–1	–0.0095	–1.499	0.0052	0.886
0	–0.0153	–9.531***	–0.0217	–4.331***
1	–0.0009	–0.378	–0.006	0.343
2	–0.0014	–2.175	–0.0021	0.917

Note: The table reports daily mean market model abnormal returns for a five day event window [–2,+2] for two samples of announcements of illegal insider trading by corporate insiders (CEOs and other executives) reported in financial press. The European sample includes 101 announcements during the period 1995–2005, while the USA sample includes 100 announcements during the period 1993–2008. The significance of the mean abnormal returns is tested using the standard parametric test statistic assuming cross-sectional independence. As such, ***denotes statistical significance at the 0.1 per cent level for a one-tailed test, **denotes statistical significance at the 1 per cent level for a one-tailed test, *denotes statistical significance at the 5 per cent level for a one-tailed test.

Source: Engelen (2009, 2010).

executive managers reported in press in six European countries (Belgium, Germany, France, Luxembourg, the Netherlands and the UK) for the period 1995–2005. This sample includes 101 events.[4] The results are presented in Table 4.5, which shows a market model average abnormal return on the news of illegal insider trading of –1.53 per cent, significant at the 0.1 per cent level.[5] Table 4.5 supplements the finding from the European dataset with 100 events from the USA dataset (Engelen, 2010), which shows a market model average abnormal return on the news of illegal insider trading of about –2.17 per cent, significant at the 0.1 per cent level.[6]

Earlier, in Tables 4.3 and 4.4, we discussed the countries' insider trading rules and the countries' public and private law enforcement. We will now use the data of both studies to calculate the average abnormal returns for three subsamples: Investigative Power, Public Enforcement Power and Private Enforcement Power. We use the market model abnormal returns from both studies as input for each subsample.[7] The 'Investigative Power' subsample analyzes the level of reputational penalty for different country-level scores on the investigative powers index developed by La Porta et al. (2006) measuring the mean of the supervisor's power to command documents during an investigation of securities laws violations and to subpoena the testimony of witnesses. The 'Public Enforcement Power' subsample performs an analogous analysis for scores on an index which indicates the

Does economic governance matter?

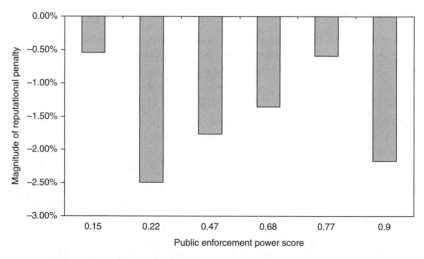

Note: Public enforcement power: the index of public enforcement indicates the enforcement of the Supervisor of securities markets. It equals the arithmetic mean of (1) supervisor characteristics index; (2) rule-making power index; (3) investigative powers index; (4) orders index; and (5) criminal index. See detailed definitions in La Porta et al. (2003). Index takes values of 0.15, 0.22, 0.47, 0.55, 0.77 and 0.90 (scale between 0 and 1; higher is more powers). *Source:* La Porta et al. (2006)

The abnormal returns are average market model abnormal returns. *Source:* Engelen (2009, 2010)

Figure 4.4   Abnormal return behaviour around the news of illegal insider trading according to the Public Powers Index

enforcement of the supervisor of securities markets and equals the mean of (1) supervisor characteristics index, (2) rule-making power index, (3) investigative powers index, (4) orders index and (5) criminal index (La Porta et al., 2006). The third subsample 'Private Enforcement Power' (Beny, 2005) uses scores on the private enforcement power index measuring whether investors can bring private law suits against violators of securities laws in a given country.

Figure 4.4 reports the average reputational penalties for different levels of the Public Enforcement Power Score. This index varies between 0 and 1, with higher scores indicating more powers. There appears to be some connection between the level of the public enforcement index and the magnitude of the reputational penalty. If the public enforcement index goes down from 0.77 (France) to 0.68 (UK), 0.47 (Netherlands) and 0.22 (Germany), the reputational penalty goes up from –0.60 per cent to –1.36 per cent, –1.77 per cent and –2.49 per cent, respectively. However, the lower and upper ends of the public enforcement index deviate from this pattern.

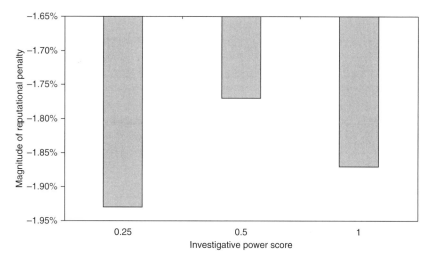

Note: The index of investigative powers equals the arithmetic mean of (1) document; and (2) witness. Document is an index of the power of the supervisor to command documents when investigating a violation of securities laws. Equals one if the supervisor can generally issue an administrative order commanding all persons to turn over documents; equals one half if the supervisor can generally issue an administrative order commanding publicly traded corporations and/or their directors to turn over documents; and equals zero otherwise. Witness is an index of the power of the supervisor to subpoena the testimony of witnesses when investigating a violation of securities laws. Equals one if the supervisor can generally subpoena all persons to give testimony; equals one half if the supervisor can generally subpoena the directors of publicly traded corporations to give testimony; and equals zero otherwise. Index takes values of 0.25, 0.50 and 1 (scale between 0 and 1; higher is more powers). *Source:* La Porta et al. (2006).

The abnormal returns are average market model abnormal returns. *Source:* Engelen (2009, 2010)

Figure 4.5   Abnormal return behaviour around the news of illegal insider trading according to the Investigative Powers Index

At the lowest public enforcement level of 0.15 (Belgium) the reputational penalty is only –0.54 per cent, which is of similar magnitude to France with a high public enforcement score of 0.77. At the highest public enforcement score of 0.90 (USA), the reputational penalty is –2.17 per cent, which is of similar size to Germany with an enforcement score of only 0.22.

When we proxy enforcement quality by the investigative powers index we see no clear pattern (see Figure 4.5). Although the lowest score of 0.25 on the investigative powers index exhibits the largest reputational penalty of –1.93 per cent and the reputational penalty decrease with an increase of the index (–1.77 per cent for a score of 0.50), the reputational penalty goes up again for the highest score of 1 on the investigative powers index.

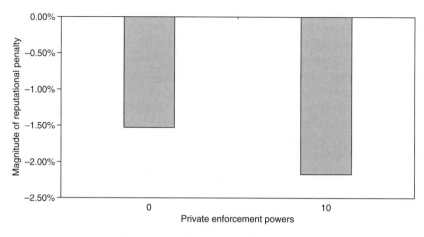

Note: Private enforcement power: indicates if private parties have a private right of action against parties who have violated the country's insider trading laws, multiplied with the efficiency of the judiciary. Index takes values of 0 and 10 (scale between 0 and 10; higher is more powers). See detailed definitions in Beny (2005).

The abnormal returns are average market model abnormal returns. *Source:* Engelen (2009, 2010)

Figure 4.6   *Abnormal return behaviour around the news of illegal insider trading according to the Private Powers Index*

Finally, we compute the reputational penalty for the private powers index. Contrary to our expectations, the results show the biggest reputational penalty for the subsample with the highest score of the private powers index (–2.17 per cent), while the subsample with no private powers exhibits a reputational penalty of only –1.59 per cent (see Figure 4.6).

To test more formally whether there is any correlation between enforcement quality and reputational penalty, we calculate the Pearson's correlation between the magnitude of the reputational penalty and the public enforcement power index, the investigative powers index and the private enforcement index. The correlation coefficient between reputational penalty and public enforcement power is only –1.22 per cent, between the reputational penalty and private enforcement index only –3.80 per cent and between the reputational penalty and the investigative powers index only 0.12 per cent, none of which is statistically significant. Based on these correlations, we find no evidence that reputational penalties for illegal insider trading by managers substitute public or private law enforcement of illegal insider trading. Both types of penalties function independently from each other. As one can argue that our dataset exhibits polyserial correlation, we also compute polyserial correlation coefficients as robustness check (Olsson et al., 1982; Drasgow, 1986).[8] The polyserial correlation coefficient between the size of reputational penalty and the public enforcement power, the private enforcement power and the investigative powers index are –4.1 per cent, –4.9 per cent and 0.21 per cent, respectively. This confirms the conclusion of no substitution between reputational penalties and legal penalties.

CONCLUSIONS

This chapter examines the relationship between formal legal governance institutions and the role of market-imposed reputational penalties. Its aim is to establish the relative effectiveness of both types of institutions in encouraging responsible corporate behaviour and to contribute to the literature on market-induced versus public enforcement mechanisms. Market-based reputation penalties can supplement with formal legal penalties in order to address a wide range of corporate malfeasance and a wide range of actors involved. The empirical reputational penalties literature shows that companies experience significant equity losses upon the discovery of corporate malfeasance. For various types of corporate misconduct the magnitude of the reputational penalty exceeds the size of the legal penalties. This reputation mechanism works well for misconduct where customers, suppliers, employees and external financiers can change their implicit and explicit contracts through repeated transactions with the company. Examples include fraud, financial misrepresentations and illegal insider trading. Reputational penalties do not seem to work for misconduct involving third parties such as environmental violations and human rights violations.

The analysis is illustrated by one type of corporate malfeasance: illegal insider trading. The data show that both USA and European companies experience market-based reputational penalties for illegal insider trading practices of their CEO and executive managers. The penalty is in the range of between one and half and two per cent abnormal stock return. Furthermore we tested whether there is any interaction between a country's public and private enforcement power and the magnitude of reputational penalties companies experience for the illegal insider trading of their managers. This is the first cross-country study which links the magnitude of reputational penalties to differences in the country's level of law enforcement. Our results can have important consequences for a country's sentencing guidelines and for supervisors' enforcement heuristics. We test whether reputational penalties substitute poor public or private law enforcement. If reputational penalties are very large, regulators can rely more on market-induced penalties and legal penalties should be kept small to reach optimal deterrence. If legal penalties are low due to lax public law enforcement, we expect reputational penalties to be higher.

We use a rich dataset of 201 announcements by combining a sample of listed USA companies and a sample of six European countries and test whether there is any substitution between reputational penalties and formal legal penalties. The analysis reports no correlation between the size of the reputational penalty and the country's level of public and private law enforcement. The results offer no evidence that reputational penalties for illegal insider trading by the company's CEO and executive managers vary with the level of public and private law enforcement in a given country. This does not imply that reputational penalties do not supplement with formal legal penalties in order to address corporate malfeasance. Expanding the dataset to a wider range of countries and to a wider range of corporate misconduct should shed more light on this issue. Future research should analyze in more detail whether coordination between market-induced, public and private law enforcement is possible in order to deter corporate crime. Even if financial markets do not adjust the reputational penalty to the level of the legal penalties, regulators can use the existence and magnitude of reputational loss as guidance for their enforcement heuristics.

NOTES

1. In the context of takeover bids, Rule 14e-3 prohibits insiders of the bidder and target to tip inside information to persons likely to buy shares of the target for their own account (Bainbridge, 2005).
2. The EU introduced insider trading regulations in 1989 by means of the European Directive (89/592/EEC) of 13 November 1989 for the Coordination of the Regulations of Insider Trading, *O.J.*, L334/30, 18 November 1989 [in short: the Insider Trading Directive].
3. For detailed definitions, see La Porta et al. (2006).
4. More details on the data collection, the sample cleaning and sample description can be found in Engelen (2009).
5. Other benchmark models renders similar results. See Table 3 in Engelen (2009).
6. The full sample in Engelen (2010) contains 222 events and also includes lower level employees and outsiders. These two categories are not relevant for the current study as we want to match two datasets on similar types of traders.
7. Using the other benchmark models of both studies renders similar results. These results are available from the author upon request.
8. Polyserial correlation occurs when one variable is continuous and another variable is ordinally defined.

REFERENCES

Alexander, C. (1999), 'On the nature of the reputational penalty for corporate crime: evidence', *Journal of Law and Economics*, **42**, 489–526.

Bainbridge, S. (2005), 'An overview of USA insider trading law: lessons for the EU?', *European Company Law*, **1**, 22–26.

Barber, B.M. and M.N. Darrough (1996), 'Product reliability and firm value: the experience of American and Japanese automakers, 1973–1992', *Journal of Political Economy*, **104** (5), 1084–1099.

Becker, G. (1968), 'Crime and punishment: an economic approach', *Journal of Political Economy*, **76** (2), 169–217.

Beny, L.N. (2005), 'Do insider trading laws matter? Some preliminary comparative evidence', *American Law and Economics Review*, **7** (1), 144–183.

Bhattacharya, U. and H. Daouk (2002), 'The world price of insider trading', *Journal of Finance*, **57**, 75–108.

Bhattacharya, U. and H. Daouk (2009), 'When no law is better than a good law', *Review of Finance*, **13**, 577–627.

Bussmann, K.D. and M.M. Werle (2006), 'Addressing crime in companies', *British Journal of Criminology*, **46**, 1128–1144.

Chalk, A. (1986), 'Market forces and aircraft safety: the case of the DC-10', *Economic Inquiry*, **24** (1), 43–60.

Chalk, A. (1987), 'Market forces and commercial aircraft safety', *Journal of Industrial Economics*, **36** (1), 61–81.

Coffee, J. (2006), 'Reforming the securities class action: an essay on deterrence and its implementation', *Columbia Law Review*, **106**, 1534–1586.

Cox, J. and R. Thomas (2003), 'SEC enforcement heuristics: an empirical inquiry', *Duke Law Journal*, **53**, 737–779.

Cox, J. and R. Thomas (2005), 'Public and private enforcement of the securities laws: have things changed since Enron?', *Notre Dame Law Review*, **80**, 893–908.

Davidson, W.N. and D.L. Worrell (1988), 'The impact of announcements of corporate illegalities on shareholder returns', *Academy of Management Journal*, **31** (1), 195–200.

Dixit, A. (2009), 'Governance institutions and economic activity', *American Economic Review*, **99**, 5–24.

Dowdell, T., S. Govindaraj and P.C. Jain (1992), 'The Tylenol incident, ensuing regulation, and stock prices', *Journal of Financial and Quantitative Analysis*, **27** (2), 283–301.

Drasgow, F. (1986), 'Polychoric and polyserial correlations', in S. Kotz and N. Johnson (eds), *The Encyclopedia of Statistics*, Vol. 7, London: Wiley, pp. 68–74.

Engelen, P.J. (2006), 'Difficulties in the criminal prosecution of insider trading. A clinical study of the Bekaert case', *European Journal of Law & Economics*, **22** (2), 121–141.

Engelen, P.J. (2007), 'Structural problems in the design of market abuse regulations in the EU', *Journal of Interdisciplinary Economics*, **19**, 57–82.

Engelen, P.J. (2009), 'The reputational penalty for illegal insider trading by European managers', *27th Annual EALE Conference*, Roma, Italia, 17–19 September and *2009 Academy of Management Annual Meeting*, Chicago, USA, 7–11 August.

Engelen, P.J. (2010), 'Measuring reputational penalties. The case of USA illegal insider trading', 5th Annual Conference on Empirical Legal Studies (CELS), Yale Law School, New Haven, CT, 4–5 November.

Engelen, P.J. and M. van Essen (2011), 'Reputational penalties on financial markets to induce corporate responsibility', in W. Vandekerkhove, J. Leys, B. Scholtens, S. Signori and H. Schaefer (eds), *Responsible Investment in Times of Turmoil* (Issues in Business Ethics Series), Berlin: Springer Publishers, forthcoming.

Gerety, M. and K. Lehn (1997), 'The causes and consequences of accounting fraud', *Managerial and Decision Economics*, **18**, 587–599.

Govindaraj, S. and B. Jaggi (2004), 'Market overreaction to product recall revisited. The case of Firestone Tires and the Ford Explorer', *Review of Quantitative Finance and Accounting*, **23**, 31–54.

Graham, J.R., S. Li and J. Qiu (2008), 'Corporate misreporting and bank loan contracting', *Journal of Financial Economics*, **89**, 44–61.

Gunthorpe, D.L. (1997), 'Business ethics: a quantitative analysis of the impact of unethical behaviour by publicly traded corporations', *Journal of Business Ethics*, **16**, 537–543.

Hostetter, V. (1999), 'Turning insider trading inside out in the European Union', *California Western International Law Journal*, **30**, 175–208.

Hribar, P. and N.T. Jenkins (2004), 'The effect of accounting restatements on earnings revisions and the estimated cost of capital', *Review of Accounting Studies*, **9**, 337–356.

Jackson, H. and M. Roe (2009), 'Public and private enforcement of securities laws: resource-based evidence', *Journal of Financial Economics*, **93**, 207–238.

Jarrell, G. and S. Peltzman (1985), 'The impact of product recalls on the wealth of sellers', *Journal of Political Economy*, **93** (3), 512–536.

Karpoff, J.M. and J.R. Lott Jr (1993), 'The reputational penalty firms bear from committing criminal fraud', *Journal of Law and Economics*, **26**, 757–802.

Karpoff, J.M., D.S. Lee and G.S. Martin (2008), 'The cost to firms of cooking the books', *Journal of Financial and Quantitative Analysis*, **43** (3), 581–611.

Karpoff, J.M., J.R. Lott Jr and E.W. Wehrly (2005), 'The reputational penalties for environmental violations. Empirical evidence', *Journal of Law and Economics*, **48**, 653–675.

Klein, B. and K. Leffler (1981), 'The role of market forces in assuring contractual performance', *Journal of Political Economy*, **89**, 615–641.

La Porta, R., F. Lopez-De-Silanes and A. Shleifer (2006), 'What works in securities laws?', *Journal of Finance*, **61**, 1–32.

Lott Jr, J.R. (1988), 'Brand names, ignorance, and quality guaranteeing premiums', *Applied Economics*, **20**, 165–176.

Mitchell, M. (1989), 'The impact of external parties on brand-name capital: the 1982 Tylenol poisonings and subsequent cases', *Economic Inquiry*, **27** (4), 601–618.

Mitchell, M. and M. Maloney (1989), 'Crisis in the cockpit? The role of market forces in promoting air travel safety', *Journal of Law and Economics*, **32**, 329–355.

Olsson, U., F. Drasgow and N. Dorans (1982), 'The polyserial correlation coefficient', *Psychometrika*, **47**, 337–347.

Palmrose, Z., V.J. Richardson and S. Scholz (2004), 'Determinants of market reactions to restatement announcements', *Journal of Accounting and Economics*, **37**, 59–89.

Peltzman, S. (1981), 'The effects of FTC advertising regulation', *Journal of Law and Economics*, **24**, 403–448.

Posnikoff, J. (1997), 'Disinvestment from South Africa: they did well by doing good', *Contemporary Economic Policy*, **15**, 76–86.

Rao, S.M. and J.B. Hamilton III (1996), 'The effect of published reports of unethical conduct on stock prices', *Journal of Business Ethics*, **15**, 1321–1330.

Reichert, A.K., M. Lockett and R.P. Rao (1996), 'The impact of illegal business practice on shareholder returns', *The Financial Review*, **31** (1), 67–85.

Romano, R. (2005), 'The Sarbanes-Oxley Act and the making of quack corporate governance', *Yale Law Journal*, **114**, 1521–1611.

Rupp, N. (2001), 'Are government initiated recalls more damaging for shareholders? Evidence from automotive recalls, 1973–1998', *Economics Letters*, **71** (2), 265–270.

Rupp, N. (2004), 'The attributes of a costly recall. Evidence from the automotive industry', *Review of Industrial Organization*, **25**, 21–44.

Seyhun, H.N. (1992), 'The effectiveness of insider-trading sanctions', *Journal of Law and Economics*, **35** (1), 149–182.

Shapiro, C. (1982), 'Consumer information, product quality, and seller reputation', *The Bell Journal of Economics*, **13** (1), 20–35.

Shapiro, C. (1983), 'Premiums for high quality products as returns to reputations', *The Quarterly Journal of Economics*, **98** (4), 659–679.

Viswesvaran, C., S. Deshpande and J. Joseph (1998), 'Job satisfaction as a function of top management support for ethical behaviour', *Journal of Business Ethics*, **17**, 365–371.

Vitell, S. and D. Davis (1990), 'The relationship between ethics and job satisfaction', *Journal of Business Ethics*, **9**, 489–494.

5. Strategies of transnational companies in the context of the governance systems of nation-states[1]

Grazia Ietto-Gillies

INTRODUCTION

The transnational or multinational companies (TNCs or MNCs) are much talked about as if they were a totally different type of institution from the normal company or firm.[2] Are they? And if they are, what makes them so? The distant antecedents of the transnational company can be dated back centuries to the Medici Bank in Renaissance Florence or to the trading companies from Northern Europe in the seventeenth and nineteenth centuries. Many business historians (Cox, 1997; Jones, 2002) agree that the main factor that led to the development of the TNC was the formation of joint stock companies.

Nonetheless a TNC is not just another joint stock company. What are the key elements that make a company a TNC? The defining element is operations across frontiers. But not just any type of cross-border operations. Imports and exports on their own are not operations that identify a company as a TNC. The specific characteristics that identify the TNC are: (1) ownership of assets abroad leading to (2) direct business operations; and (3) the ability to control those operations.

Control has two main connotations in the context of a TNC. The first connotation is the equity stake in the foreign enterprise. What percentage of the foreign assets must be owned by the main company for the latter to have control? The International Monetary Fund (1977) guidelines set a minimum of 10 per cent. Equity control is a necessary condition but not a sufficient condition to ensure control of operations and directions of the foreign concern. Equity control by itself does not lead to strategic managerial control if the means of exercising such control are not available. In particular, if the system of communications and the organization of the business across countries are not suitable for the exercise of such managerial control. This was indeed the case of much foreign business prior to the First World War when there was a considerable amount of foreign investment. There were, in fact, many enterprises whose assets were owned wholly or in large part by person or groups or companies in foreign countries (such as Britain or Holland). However, though the owners had controlling stakes in the businesses, they were not in a position to exercise managerial control because of the large distance between home and host countries and the poor transportation and communication systems. Wilkins (1988) has termed these businesses as 'free-standing enterprises' to highlight the fact that, though they were owned wholly or partially by foreign nationals (whether individuals or groups or companies), they were managed and developed as independent concerns.

The modern transnational corporation is characterized by having both equity control and the ability to manage the foreign affiliates at a distance. In the last few decades the latter ability has been greatly enhanced by the following two key developments: (1) improvement in the systems of transportation and communications; and (2) improvement in the system of internal organization of companies. These two developments are interlinked: easier transportation and communication – particularly via the Information and Communication Technologies (ICTs) – led to changes in the internal organization of companies and the latter affected the increase in ICT intensity of companies.

The relevant type of management in our context is the one related to the setting of strategic goals and the monitoring of performance, rather than the day-to-day operational management. The issue of strategies and strategic behaviour by TNCs is key to the approach taken in this chapter. It is argued that the existence of different governance systems in different countries allows companies with operations across different nation-states to develop strategies that enhance the asymmetry of power between them and other actors with which they interact in the course of their business.

This chapter is organized as follows. First, we shall consider issues of transnationality, power and strategic behaviour. Next, three key dimensions of nation-states are identified. One of them is of particular relevance for the strategies of TNCs. The following section analyses how TNCs may exploit the differences in governance/regulatory regimes to develop specific strategies for enhancing their asymmetry of power in relation to other actors such as labour, governments and suppliers. Next we discuss some of the advantages towards rival companies given by transnationality and specifically: acquisition and diffusion of knowledge and innovation and risk spreading. Then we consider the wider context and boundaries of the theory put forward in previous sections. The last section summarizes and concludes.

TRANSNATIONALITY, POWER AND STRATEGIC BEHAVIOUR[3]

In the first section, we mentioned how developments in the internal organization of companies contributed to their ability to grow and international-ize. In the relevant literature, developments in the internal organization of companies have been analysed under several paradigms and particularly: the 'strategy', the 'efficiency' and the 'institutionalist' paradigms. Penrose (1959) sees the boundaries of the firm and its internal organization chang-ing as the firm grows. Growth and growth strategies lead to changes in the internal organization and the latter facilitates further growth. In a similar vein, Chandler's (1962) historical narrative sees the internal organization of corporations evolving mainly in response to strategic objectives, in par-ticular growth strategies. Chandler's line is taken up by Stephen Hymer, the pioneer of the theory of international firms. Hymer (1970) analyses the relationship between the evolution in the internal structure of the firm and multinationality, in particular, how the former facilitated the latter.

Williamson (1975, 1981, 1984) sees changes in the internal organization as driven by efficiency objectives; specifically, by the desire to economize on transactions costs, as well as to minimize the pursuit of individual goals and opportunistic behaviour within the organization.

The institutionalist school sees the internal structure of companies – and of organizations in general – as evolving in response to the institutional environment in which they operate. The relevant institutional environ-ment is delimited by the organizational field(s) of the company. The organization field of reference is loosely defined to include all agents who have some form of business interaction with the company, from suppliers to consumers to rival firms to regulatory agencies (DiMaggio and Powell, 1983). Companies may straddle different organizational fields (Westney, 2005). This is the case with diversified as well as with transnational com-panies. The former straddle several fields because of the different products they are involved in; the latter straddle different fields in relation to the dif-ferent countries in which they operate. Diversified TNCs will have scope for interaction with a variety of fields connected with both their different products and the different countries in which they operate.

Operating across different organizational fields generates conflicts. Of particular relevance are the ones between a given subsidiary and the head-quarters of the company to which it belongs and/or the same subsidiary and other units of the company located in various countries.

The management literature has dealt with the impact of institutional environments and organizational fields on the internal structure of firms including multinational companies (Westney, 2005). What has received less attention is the impact of the institutional environment and related governance systems on companies' strategic behaviour. The latter topic is the subject of this chapter particularly with reference to the locational strategies of TNCs.

Strategic behaviour has many connotations and can be analysed in relation to two specific dimensions: strategies towards 'what' (1) and towards 'whom' (2). Regarding (1), the 'what' is seen in relation to the activities of the firm such as: its products' range, the markets it seeks to penetrate, its production processes, the technology used, the organization of the production process and the geographical configuration of its production activities. As regards (2), the analysis of strategic behaviour is in relation to specific actors such as: rival companies, consumers, suppliers, distributors, sub-contractors, the labour force and governments.

Closely linked to the latter issue is the relationship between strategic behaviour and power. Zetlin (1974: 1090) argues that power '. . . is essentially relative and relational: how much power, with respect to whom?'. Following Fred Hirsch, Pagano (2003) sees power and prestige as positional goods, a view that echoes Zetlin's characterization. It follows from this view that: '. . . power and status are zero-sum goods and the increase in the positive consumption of positional goods by some individuals brings about an increase in negative consumption by some other individuals' (Pagano, 2003: 641).

In the economics/business literature, companies' power has usually been analysed mainly in relation to market power and therefore with respect to rival firms. However, power may also relate to other players in the economic system and specifically to labour, governments, suppliers/distributors, subcontractors or buyers/consumers.

A strategic use of power can aid the resolution of conflicts between the specific company under analysis and other agents. The conflicts are usually over distributional issues arising from production or market conditions. In the case of conflicts with rivals, the distribution relates to market shares; in the case of labour, the conflict is over distribution between profits and wages; in the case of conflicts with governments the issue is distribution over the overall surplus and how much should go to the private or public sphere (via taxation or financial incentives or subsidies).

In the next three sections we shall analyse how transnationality generates opportunities for strategic behaviour by firms operating across nation-states. The strategic behaviour considered will focus on labour, governments and suppliers and, to a lesser extent, on rival companies. This is not because the latter is not considered important but mainly because many aspects of it have been well covered in the literature. In fact, in the international business literature the strategic behaviour towards rivals has been considered by many authors in the context of developing theories of why companies operate across frontiers and which modalities they employ. The strategic behaviour towards rivals is considered in Hymer (1960), Vernon (1966), Knickerbocker (1973) and Cowling and Sugden (1987).

Sugden (1991) and Ietto-Gillies (2002, 2005) stress strategic behaviour towards labour. Other authors have followed the 'efficiency' route and developed theories that explain internationalization activities and modalities in term of cost efficiency and, specifically, minimization of transaction costs (McManus, 1972; Buckley and Casson, 1976; Helpman, 1984, 1985; Markusen, 1984, 1995; Helpman and Krugman, 1985). Dunning's well known eclectic framework has elements of both efficiency and strategic behaviour (1977, 1980).[4]

TNCs AND THE NATION-STATES

In this section we shall consider the relevance of national frontiers and their different dimensions for the strategic behaviour of companies. At the semantic level trans-nationalization implies the existence of national borders. In this sense we can say that in a world with no nation-states there would be no TNCs, meaning that we would not characterize a company as a TNC just as we do not currently attach a special label (such as 'trans-regional') to companies that operate in many regions of the same country.

But the issue is much deeper than the attribution of labels. We do specific studies of companies that invest across nation-states but not of companies that invest across regions of the same nation-state. In other words we attach relevance to the origin/nationality/identity of the investor in the case of trans-national operations but not in the case of trans-regional operations. There is one area of economics, within the confines of the nation-state, in which, traditionally, the identity of the investor has been considered important: the case of public versus private sector investment. The main reason for this is the fact that public sector investors are supposed to have different aims from the private sector ones: social aims versus profits aims. However, this does not apply to investment across frontiers versus investment within the same nation-state. In both cases we are talking of private companies motivated by profits. The objectives remain the same whether the company invests within a single nation-state or across several of them. What differs is not the aim but the strategies and opportunities for strategies. Operations across nation-states give opportunities for specific additional strategies that do not exist – or not to the same extent – within the confines of a single nation-state. These opportunities arise from the specific governance systems of nation-states.

This raises the wider issue of the relationship between nation-states and companies and of the importance of the nation-state for companies. Is there something specific to the nation-state (and of relevance to corporations) which is not to be found at the level of regions within a country?

In order to tackle these issues it is helpful to consider the key dimensions of nation-states and of operating across national frontiers. These are: spatial or geographic; cultural and regulatory dimensions.

The spatial/geographic dimension has to do with distance between locations and its relevance is largely linked to transportation and transaction costs. The distance between locations in different nation-states is often greater than the distance between locations within the same nation-state. But this is not always the case. For example, the spatial distance between Turin and Palermo is greater than the one between Turin and Geneva. Similarly, the distance between New York and Montreal is less than the one between New York and San Francisco.

The linguistic/cultural dimension – particularly the business culture element – affects the operations of companies in terms of transaction, organizational and managerial costs. The cultural distance is usually greater between nation-states than between regions of the same nation-state. But again, this is not always the case. Regions close to the border of two nation-states often have more similar business cultures than distant regions within the same nation-state.

The regulatory regimes dimension encompasses the sets of laws, regulations and customs governing the economic, social and political life of a country. It includes the regulations governing production, markets and the movement of resources across countries. These regulations stem directly from a country's system of economic governance[5] and related institutions. Countries differ in their system of governance and specifically with regard to the sets of regulations just mentioned. These differences often have historical as well as political roots. Regulatory regimes tend to differ – sometimes substantially – between different nation-states. However, they tend to be more homogeneous and consistent within each nation-state.

In this perspective the nation-state can be seen as the locus of a set of 'regulatory regimes'. These comprise the set of specific rules and regulations – emerging from the overall governance system and related institutions – which affect people, firms and wider organizations directly and in terms of their business relationships. Some of these rules and regulations stem from the legal or institutional system, some from government policies; several have more than one connotation, that is they incorporate legal, institutional and/or policy elements. In relation to the business world, the following nation-states' regulatory regimes are of particular relevance: (1) rules and regulations regarding the social security system and in particular different regimes regarding labour and its organization; (2) fiscal regimes; (3) regime of industrial policy with regard financial and other incentives to business; (4) currency regimes; and (5) rules and regulations regarding environmental and safety standards.[6] In the next section we shall concentrate on the first three only of these regimes.

All three dimensions (geographical, cultural and regulatory) discussed here have cost implications. A company operating across frontiers may face additional costs and risks ranging from transportation and transactions costs to managerial and organization costs. They include also costs specific to the third dimension such as: costs of insurance against risks of currency fluctuations; additional costs of acquiring information about fiscal, social security and environmental standards regulations in other countries as well as information about their labour market conditions; costs of mastering – and managing in the context of – different laws, regulations, customs and their institutions.

However, there are also advantages of operating across frontiers and these advantages can – to a large extent – explain the huge increase in FDI since the Second World War. Ertürk (Chapter 2, this volume) points out how globalization increases the asymmetry in power relations. The TNCs are in such a position because they can truly plan, organize and control across frontiers. They can also develop strategies to take advantage of differences in regulatory regimes across frontiers. The asymmetry of power emerges because many of the agents with which they interact cannot plan and organize across national frontiers, or not to the same extent as the TNCs. These agents at the other end of the TNCs' asymmetric power relation are: labour, governmental agencies, suppliers and rival firms. The asymmetry derives from the advantages that transnationality gives them in terms of bargaining with labour, in negotiations with suppliers and in dealings with national and regional governments.

In addition to these, transnationality can also give companies advantages with regard to the following: acquisition of knowledge and innovation, and risk spreading. These advantages can lead to – or further enhance – the asymmetry of power towards rival firms.

TRANSNATIONALITY INCREASES THE ASYMMETRY OF POWER

As already mentioned most international business literature on companies' strategic behaviour has concentrated on strategies towards rivals rather than on strategic behaviour towards other actors. Yet companies face other relevant actors in connection with their business activities, particularly labour, governments and suppliers. From the perspective of the company and its profitability the best position to be in is one in which it has power over its rivals as well as other actors.

Transnationality and Power Towards Labour

The power relations of companies towards rivals and towards labour are affected by two different aspects of the organization of production: specifically, the market concentration and the internationalization of production activities. Both market concentration and internationalization have increased in the decades immediately after the Second World War. However, the last quarter of the twentieth century saw considerable changes in companies' strategic behaviour with respect to the organization of production and the production process. Specifically, changes in the organization of the production process within and between firms and changes in companies' strategies towards the geographical location of their activities. In the late 1970s, 1980s and to some extent also the 1990s, many large companies have been downsizing, that is outsourcing the production of part of their activities, usually the non-core part but, at times, some core activities as well. This means that, whereas the decades following the Second World War saw an increase in the internalization of production activities, the following decades saw the opposite process: many large firms subcontracted part of their activities to smaller firms who were usually independent in terms of ownership though, often, dependent in terms of strategic control of their activities (Cowling and Sugden, 1987). The last 35 years have seen acceleration in the expansion of activities abroad by large companies, some on an internalized basis and some outsourced to smaller firms in foreign countries.

The explanation of these historical patterns can be aided if we see them in the context of possible strategies of companies towards labour. The concentration of production leads to oligopolies and thus to market power. However, it may – at the same time – strengthen the power of labour because labour employed within the same ownership unit – that is within business enterprises all belonging to the same company – may find it easier to organize and take action compared to a situation in which it is dispersed across units belonging to different owners.

As regards the international location of production, labour has, traditionally, found it easier to organize and resist when working within the same country. Spatial proximity, shared condition of labour and shared contractual obligations lay the foundations for easier organization and resistance. Moreover, shared historical, cultural and social environments give labour a stronger feeling of solidarity. On the whole, the differentials in the actual and potential for labour organization and for bargaining power are higher between countries separated by institutional, political, cultural, legal and governance borders than within each border. We can characterize areas of 'labour organization regimes' as those geographical areas within which – ceteris paribus – labour finds it easy to organize itself effectively due to shared cultures, institutions, legal framework and working conditions.

This discussion leads to the identification of two main dimensions in the organization of production: (1) an ownership dimension by which we mean to capture whether or to what extent the firm internalizes its production activities or uses external, arm's length transactions with other firms for part of its value chain activities; and (2) a geographic dimension which captures the extent to which production activities take place within the same (or nearby) locations or the extent to which they are dispersed in several locations. In the latter context, of particularly relevance is whether the activities are located in different nation-states for the reason explained below; or (3) a mixture of ownership and geographic dimension. The latter is a combination of dimensions (1) and (2).

Companies within a sector may – ceteris paribus – face a more powerful labour force when the same is employed: (1) within the same company/ institution rather than being dispersed into many; and (2) within the same country. It is in the interest of companies to develop strategies that increase their power towards labour while not diminishing – and possibly increasing – their power over rivals. Possible strategies in this direction involve the segmentation/fragmentation of labour while retaining their market power. Two specific types of fragmentation strategies are possible and have been followed: (1) organizational fragmentation through the externalization of some activities; and (2) geographical (by nation-state) fragmentation through the location of production in various countries characterized by different regulatory regimes.

The organizational fragmentation can involve various degrees of externalization of production: from full outsourcing and use of market transactions to varying degrees of control through sub-contracting and similar arrangements; from the employment of labour full time and on permanent contracts to the casualization of labour (Ietto-Gillies, 2002). Some of the externalization routes – such as sub-contracting – allow the company considerable control of production without the added responsibility for the labour employed.

The second strategy involves the spread of production in countries/ areas not linked by common labour organization regimes, that is areas that have different trade unions and/or different labour and social security laws, regulations and standards. These elements make the organization of labour and its resistance to the demands of capital more difficult. In this case fragmentation takes a geographical (by nation-states) route. This involves the dispersion of production over many nation-states, albeit within the internal, hierarchical organization route. Some degree of both geographical and organizational dispersion and fragmentation is also possible, for example through cross-countries externalization such as international sub-contracting. The two fragmentation strategies reinforce each other in the labour fragmentation potential and therefore in the difficulties they generate for the organization and resistance of labour in its bargaining with capital.

Two consequences derive from this analysis, both relevant for TNCs' strategic decision in terms of the location of international production. First, that – ceteris paribus – companies may seek to locate in areas of weak labour organization regimes; thus foreign direct investment would flow from areas of strong labour organization regimes towards areas of weak regimes (that is areas where labour is in a weak position).

Second, even if the differentials in labour organization regimes across nation-states are not high, the dispersion of employment across many countries – though within the same company – fragments/segments the employed labour force and thus makes its organization more difficult and its bargaining position weaker. Such dispersion gives a stronger position to companies vis-à-vis labour compared to a situation in which the growth of production within the same company were to occur all or most within a single country. Thus, we have a situation in which the internationalization of production per se may give companies advantages towards its labour force.

The organizational pattern of production that arose from the late 1970s onwards – outsourcing and increased international location – can be seen, partly, as a strategic reaction by companies to the increased power of labour in the decades after the Second World War, the latter being aided by the concentration of production into large units (often developed in the same site or in spatially close sites).

Our analysis goes some way towards explaining why (1) the largest share (69.6 per cent) of the stock of inward FDI is directed towards developed countries as well as originating in the same group of countries (84.3 per cent) and (2) large amounts of FDI are horizontal.[7] Companies keen to source foreign markets can produce most of their output in the home country and source foreign markets via exports, or they can produce directly abroad near their foreign markets. In the first case they would be likely to face a stronger workforce – ceteris paribus – than in the second case, for the reasons explained above. The large amounts of horizontal

FDI in countries with large markets – other developed countries – are therefore taken as a sign of a possible geographic fragmentation strategy.

Strategies that are successful in enhancing the bargaining power of companies towards labour are likely to affect the distribution between wages and profits.

Transnationality and Power Towards Suppliers

Let us now consider the issue of asymmetry of power towards other actors. Operations across different nation-states can enhance the bargaining power of companies towards suppliers and governments. The existence of multiple sourcing channels (whether actual or potential) in the various countries gives the TNCs a powerful bargaining position towards suppliers. This is particularly the case because many suppliers have specific characteristics which make them liable to low bargaining power with large TNCs. In particular: (1) suppliers are often smaller companies operating in a more competitive environment than their customer; (2) they are often located in developing countries; (3) they cannot easily develop alternative international networks. In this situation it is not difficult to see how a big TNC with a large transnational network and which can rely on several actual or potential suppliers will use its international position to enhance its bargaining power towards specific suppliers.

Transnationality and Power Towards Governments

Having production locations and business activities in several nation-states can also give the company a strong bargaining position towards governments of the nation-states and their regions. Transnational companies can – and do – play governments of different countries or regions against each other with the objective of raising the offer of incentives for the location of inward FDI (Oman, 2000; Phelps and Raines, 2002). For example, the lack of fiscal harmonization within the EU has led to competition by governments for attracting foreign companies – sometimes only nominally rather than with jobs and capital relocation – via lower and lower rates of corporation tax.[8] Moreover, if a company has production facilities in many countries its threat of relocation becomes very credible (Kogut, 1983) and can be used as bargaining power with governments to gain high incentives.

There are further advantages to be gained by a company with direct business activities in different nation-states. The latter, as loci of different governance systems and regulatory regimes are also loci of specific taxation regimes. Operating across several such regimes puts the company in a position to be able to minimize its worldwide tax liability via the manipulation of transfer prices, that is prices charged for the exchange of goods and services within the firm but across national frontiers (Ietto-Gillies, 2005).[9]

In the last analysis all these strategies aim to shift the distribution of the surplus from the social sphere (of government and taxpayers) to the private sphere of companies.

ADVANTAGES OF TRANSNATIONALITY TOWARDS RIVALS

The various types of strategic behaviour we have discussed in the previous section increase power in bargaining with labour or governments or suppliers. Are there also advantages to be gained towards rivals? A better bargaining position towards these actors puts the company in a stronger position also vis-à-vis rival companies. Any advantages towards labour and/or governments deriving from location strategies and leading to higher profits can be turned into indirect advantages towards rivals as it increases the potential for higher market shares.

There are, however, other specific elements of transnationality that may enhance the TNC's power towards rivals, particularly in terms of innovation acquisition and development and of risk spreading. The locational diversification of technological and production activities allows the company to learn from its environment and thus to increase its overall ownership advantages (Cantwell, 1989; Castellani and Zanfei, 2006). Various units within the company – be they the headquarters or subsidiaries – form an internal network within which there is exchange of knowledge, innovation and technology (Hedlund, 1986; Hedlund and Rolander, 1990; Zanfei, 2000; Castellani and Zanfei, 2002; Frenz and Ietto-Gillies, 2007; Filippetti et al., 2011). The exchanges are often facilitated by movements of highly-skilled personnel whose flows have been increasing worldwide (Salt, 1997; OECD, 2002).

Moreover, each company unit will be in contact with the innovation context and system of the country in which it operates. The unit learns from these locational contexts and then transmits the acquired knowledge to other parts of the company via the latter's internal network. Often the learning from the locational context and system is heightened by formal innovation-based collaborative agreements leading to external networks (Frenz and Ietto-Gillies, 2009). Other external networks can also lead to learning and acquisition of knowledge such as the networks linking subsidiaries to their local suppliers and customers. The two types of networks, internal to the company and external to it, operate together to facilitate the diffusion of knowledge and innovation, with significant effects for the local businesses, the TNCs and the various countries (home and hosts) in which they operate. Thus the geographically-fragmented configuration of production activities increases the scope for diffusion of knowledge and innovation. This advantage in knowledge acquisition can be turned into a competitive advantage towards companies which are less internationalized and, therefore, less able to tap into international sources of knowledge and innovation.

A further advantage is connected with risk spreading. A strategy of dispersion of production and multiple sourcing can also be a diversification strategy which allows the spread of the risks of disruptions to production due, for example, to political upheavals or industrial disputes in any one country. Disruptions to production can come about also through other problems such as natural disasters. Most risks linked to the latter are not nation-specific but are more likely to be specific to the physical and geographical environment. However, the ability of countries to cope with them and to minimize risks and costs for business is, to a large extent, nation-specific and thus specific to the social, economic and governance environment and not just to the physical environment. Thus a strategy of fragmentation by nation-states may become also a strategy of geographical diversification in order to spread risks deriving from the social and political, as well as the physical, environment.[10] This enhances the TNC's advantages towards those rival firms which are not internationalized or not to the same extent.

WIDER CONTEXT AND BOUNDARIES

The previous two sections developed a theory of the TNC that emphasizes the advantages that transnationality confers to companies in terms of enhancement of power towards labour, suppliers and governments as well as rival companies. From a simple reading of such a theory one might conclude that transnationality is all a bed of roses. In other words, the higher the level of internationalization the higher the advantages for companies. I would now like to discuss the boundaries and limitations of such an extreme conclusion.

In general, do companies derive only advantages from a strategy of fragmentation of production across different nation-states? The answer is certainly negative, first of all, because the fragmentation strategy may lead to higher unit costs if it requires operating below the most efficient size in some, if not all, the locations. Moreover, the diversity of regulatory regimes across which TNCs operate may, in itself, generate extra costs and uncertainties. For example, different currencies generate transaction costs; exchange rates fluctuations may bring losses as well as gains; operating across different cultures, governance and institutional contexts may result in higher transaction, organizational and managerial costs.

But there are wider caveats and limitations. First with regards to labour: are outsourcing strategies and international location of production to be interpreted only in terms of strategic behaviour towards labour? The answer is emphatically: no. There are many other reasons why companies want to outsource (such as the achievement of more flexibility of supply to demand conditions or the lowering of fixed costs) and want to locate abroad (such as proximity to markets or sources of materials or of labour). However, whatever the reasons – and there are likely to be several – one of the outcomes is that both outsourcing strategies and international location of production lead to a weakening of the employed labour; it therefore increases the asymmetry of power between the company and its workforce.

Another caveat arises from the assumptions related to the social security regimes or the tax regime or that of incentives towards inward FDI. In the real world some countries are fully centralized and their governance system with respect to social security, fiscal regimes and industrial policy apply throughout. In others there is regional decentralization and the regulatory regimes differ from region to region of the same country, such as regions of the UK or states within the US. This is sometimes the case with regard to fiscal regimes and with regard the possibility of specific regional development institutions offering attractive packages for inward investment. However, the degree to which regions' regulatory regimes differ tends to be not as high as that between nation-states. To the extent that they differ, TNCs can bargain with regional governments – and play one against the other – as well as with national governments.

In the last couple of decades we have seen increasing calls for decentralization and more fiscal and labour market autonomy for the regions. This has been – and is – very much in evidence at the political level, for example in Italy. But similar sentiments have also been voiced in more academic circles. Ohmae (1995) strongly argues for the formation of strong regions free to bargain with TNCs directly without having to go via the institutions of the nation-state of which they are part. He advocates the formation of region-states oriented towards the global economy rather than the national economy. He writes:

> Region states . . . are economic not political units, and they are anything but local in focus. They may lie within the border of an established nation state, but

they are such powerful engine of development because their primary orientation is toward – and their primary linkage is with – the global economy. They
are, in fact, among the most reliable ports of entry. (Ohmae, 1995: 88–89)

According to my analysis the region-states advocated by Ohmae would
lead to competition between different regions of the same nation-state for
the attraction of inward investment. This is a situation which favours the
TNCs in their bargaining for special concessions. Reliable ports of entry
yes, but for whom and in whose interest?

A last point to make is that there have been attempts at forging cross-
country links between trade unions (Guardian, 2007). However, the
aftermath of the 2008 financial crisis is not likely to foster cross-country
solidarity of the workforce. Quite the contrary, as each labourer, union
and indeed government wants to protect jobs in their own country.

The latter point is illustrated by the case of Fiat, the Italian motor
car manufacturer, in its bargaining with the workforce in Pomigliano,
Southern Italy in the winter and spring 2010. The company management had put two alternatives for their investment strategies: investing
in Pomigliano or in Poland. The first alternative was conditional on the
Italian workforce accepting a new contract which offered much worse conditions than the existing one, including clauses deemed unconstitutional
by some lawyers. In this case asymmetric power towards Polish and Italian
workers was being used to further the asymmetry of power towards the
Pomigliano workforce. The Italian trade unions negotiated to secure the
investment in Pomigliano at the cost of jobs in Poland. They could hardly
do anything else. Their bargaining power was reduced by competing with
the Polish workers as well as by division within the three main negotiating
unions, allied to different political parties.

SUMMARY AND CONCLUSIONS

This chapter starts with a discussion of ownership and organizational
control within companies. This leads to a discussion of organizational
structures. The focus then moves on the links between governance, institutions and strategic behaviour of companies. A discussion of different
dimensions of nation-states leads to an analysis of the opportunities and
scope generated by nation-states for companies that can plan, organize,
manage and control across frontiers. The nation-states are considered in
terms of spatial, cultural/linguistic and regulatory regimes dimensions.

It is argued that differentials in regulatory regimes between different
countries create scope for advantages and for strategic behaviour by

TNCs. The strategic behaviour is seen in relation to other actors: labour, suppliers, governments as well as rival firms in relation to elements such as knowledge acquisition and risk spreading.

Why do we need a special study of the TNCs? Because nation-states differ in their governance, institutions and specific regulatory regimes. These differences allow companies operating across different nation-states to take advantage by developing specific strategies. Assume for a moment a hypothetical world in which nation-states did not exist and the whole world was governed from one centre with the same type of institutions and governance system. In such a world we would not need to develop special studies and theories of the transnational corporations. We would, instead, operate within the parameters of location theory and economic geography to explain why firms invest in a specific locality.

In our real world we have nation-states characterized by different dimensions – as argued above – and, in particular, by different governance systems, institutions and related regulatory regimes. I refer in particular to systems of governance and institutions regarding taxation or labour markets. In relation to the latter a big role is played by the governance system related to trade unions, by those that regulate the social security system in a country and by the wider governance that affects the labour market such as immigration controls or obstacles to the emigration of skilled labour.

Different regulatory regimes in different nation-states put the TNCs in advantageous positions in their bargaining with other actors such as labour, suppliers and governments. Moreover, transnationalism gives companies additional advantages in terms of acquisition of knowledge and of risk spreading. These overall advantages can be used to develop strategies that further widen the asymmetry of power between TNCs and other actors who do not have transnational power – or not to the same extent – such as labour, governments and uninational (or not very inter-nationalized) companies. The boundaries and wider context of the theory are discussed above.

The enhanced asymmetry of power, derived from strategies linked to transnationality, has distributional implications with regard the distribution between wages and profits and the distribution of the economic surplus between the social and private sphere. Our analysis has also strategy and policy implications for other actors. In general, labour and governments should avoid strategies that generate scope for further fragmentation such as collision between trade unions and/or workers in different sectors or countries. There should be caution in embracing political moves towards regional fragmentation of regulatory regimes. Though decentralization of power to the regions does bring some benefits, it may also result in stronger bargaining power for TNCs in their dealings with local or regional governments. At the level of the EU, harmonization of social security and fiscal regimes would strengthen the power of labour and governments. In general, labour and governments should work towards strategies leading to the development of what Galbraith (1957) labelled 'countervailing power'.

NOTES

1. I am grateful to Mehmet Ugur and David Sunderland for useful comments on an earlier draft of this chapter.
2. The term transnational is used by the UNCTAD who had a specialized department/division dealing with TNCs since 1972. I prefer this term because it best conveys the fact that these companies plan, control and manage *across* several countries and not independently in each of them.
3. Many of the issues considered in the second to fifth section are developed in greater details in Ietto-Gillies (2011), Chapters 1 and 14.
4. All the theories cited in this chapter – as well as others – are summarized and critically analysed in Ietto-Gillies (2011), Part III.
5. The term and concept of governance are rather fuzzy and wide-ranging (Dixit, 2008) and the Oxford English Dictionary gives several definitions. The ones relevant to this chapter relate to governance as: 'the manner in which something is governed or regulated; . . . system of regulations; . . .'.
6. On the latter issue the *Guardian* (2010) reports that Transocean, the owner of the rig leased by BP in Gulf of Mexico disastrous oil exploration, was registered in The Marshall Islands and possibly responsible to their governmental institutions for environmental and safety standards.
7. Data refer to 2009 and are from UNCTAD (2010), Annex Table 2, p. 172. There is also a large amount of intra-industry FDI worldwide (Dunning and Norman, 1986; Alfaro and Charlton, 2009). However, it should be noted that intra-industry FDI is connected to both vertical and horizontal FDI.
8. See the case of Ireland where very low rates of corporation tax have upset other European governments while not being of much benefit in her unfolding (as I write) economic and political crisis.
9. OECD (2010) gives detailed guidelines on how to detect transfer prices manipulation.
10. Rugman (1979) suggests that the international spread of activities may be a risk diversification strategy on the part of the company.

REFERENCES

Alfaro, L. and A. Charlton (2009), 'Intra-Industry foreign direct investment', *The American Economic Review*, **99** (5), 2096–2119.

Buckley, P.J. and M.C. Casson (1976), 'A long-run theory of the multinational enterprise', in P.J. Buckley and M.C. Casson (eds), *The Future of the Multinational Enterprise*, London: Macmillan, pp. 32–65.

Cantwell, J. (1989), *Technological Innovation and Multinational Corporations*, Oxford: Blackwell.

Castellani, D. and A. Zanfei (2002), 'Multinational experience and the creation of linkages with local firms: evidence from the electronic industry', *Cambridge Journal of Economics*, **26** (1), 1–25.

Castellani, D. and A. Zanfei (2006), *Multinational Firms, Innovation and Productivity*, Cheltenham, UK and Northampton, MA, USA: Edward Elgar.

Chandler, A.D. (1962), *Strategy and Structure: Chapters in the History of the Industrial Enterprise,* Cambridge, MA: MIT Press.

Cowling, K. and R. Sugden (1987), *Transnational Monopoly Capitalism*, Brighton: Wheatsheaf.

Cowling, K. and R. Sugden (1998), 'The essence of the modern corporation: markets, strategic decision-making and the theory of the firm', *The Manchester School*, **66** (1), 59–86.

Cox, H. (1997), 'The evolution of international business enterprise', in R. John, G. Ietto-Gillies, H. Cox and N. Grimwade, *Global Business Strategy*, London: International Thomson Business Press, pp. 9–46.

DiMaggio, P.J. and W. Powell (1983), 'The iron cage revisited. Institutional isomorphism and collective rationality in organizational fields', *American Sociological Review*, **48**, 147–160.

Dixit, A.K. (2008), 'Economic Governance', in S.N. Durlauf and L.E. Blume (eds), *The New Palgrave Dictionary of Economics, Second Edition,* London: Palgrave Macmillan.

Driffield, N. and J.H. Love (2003), 'FDI, technology sourcing and reverse spill-overs', *The Manchester School*, **71** (6), 659–672.

Dunning, J.H. (1977), 'Trade, location of economic activity and the MNE: a search for an eclectic approach', in B. Ohlin, P.O. Hesselborn and P.M. Wijkman (eds), *The International Allocation of Economic Activity*, London: Macmillan, pp. 395–431.

Dunning, J.H. (1980), 'Explaining changing patterns of international production: in defense of the eclectic theory', *Oxford Bulletin of Economics and Statistics*, **41** (4), 269–295.

Dunning, J.H. and G. Norman (1986), 'Intra-industry investment', in H.P. Gray (ed.), *Uncle Sam as Host,* Greenwich, CT: JAI Press, pp. 73–94.

Filippetti, A., M. Frenz and G. Ietto-Gillies (2011), 'Are innovation and inter-nationalization related? An analysis of European countries', *Industry and Innovation*, **18** (5), July.

Frenz, M. and G. Ietto-Gillies (2007), 'Does multinationality affect the propensity to innovate? An analysis of the third UK Community Innovation Survey', *International Review of Applied Economics*, **21** (1), 99–117.

Frenz, M. and G. Ietto-Gillies (2009), 'The impact on innovation performance of different sources of knowledge. Evidence from the UK Community Innovation Survey', *Research Policy*, **38**, 1125–1135.

Galbraith, J.K. (1957), *American Capitalism. The Concept of Countervailing Power*, London: Penguin Books.

Guardian, The (2007), 'Amicus moves to create multinational "super-union"', 2 January.

Guardian, The (2010), 'Congress raises safety concerns over rig's Marshall Islands flag', 31 May.

Hedlund, G. (1986), 'The hypermodern MNC – a heterarchy?', *Human Resource Management*, **25** (1), 9–35.

Hedlund, G. and D. Rolander (1990), 'Action in heterarchies: new approaches to managing the MNC', in C.A. Bartlett, Y. Doz and G. Hedlund (eds), *Managing the Global Firm*, London: Routledge, pp. 15–46.

Helpman, E. (1984), 'A simple theory of international trade with multinational corporations', *Journal of Political Economy*, **92** (3), 451–471.

Helpman, E. (1985), 'Multinational corporations and trade structure', *Review of Economic Studies*, July, 443–458.

Helpman, E. and P. Krugman (1985), *Market Structures and Foreign Trade. Increasing Returns, Imperfect Competition and the International Economy*, Cambridge, MA: MIT Press.

Hymer, S.H. (1970), 'The efficiency (contradictions) of multinational corporations', *American Economic Review*, **60** (2), 411–418.

Hymer, S.H. (1960, published 1976), *The International Operations of National Firms: A Study of Direct Foreign Investment*, Cambridge, MA: MIT Press.

Ietto-Gillies, G. (2002), *Transnational Corporations. Fragmentation amidst Integration*, London: Routledge.

Ietto-Gillies, G. (2011), *Transnational Corporations and International Production: Concepts, Theories and Effects*, 2nd revised edn, Cheltenham, UK and Northampton, MA, USA: Edward Elgar (forthcoming).

IMF (1977), *Balance of Payments Manual*, 4th edn, Washington, DC: IMF.

Jones, G. (2002), *Merchants to Multinationals – British Trading Companies in the Nineteenth and Twentieth Centuries*, Oxford: Oxford University Press.

Knickerbocker, F.T. (1973), *Oligopolistic Reaction and Multinational Enterprise*, Cambridge, MA: Division of Research, Graduate School of Business Administration, Harvard University.

Kogut, B. (1983), 'Foreign Direct Investment as a sequential process', in C. Kindleberger and D. Andretsh (eds), *The Multinational Corporation in the 1980s*, Cambridge, MA: The MIT Press.

McManus, J. (1972), 'The theory of the international firm', in G. Paquet (ed.), *The Multinational Firm and the Nation State*, Don Mills, Ontario, Canada: Collier-Macmillan, pp. 66–93.

Markusen, J.R. (1984), 'Multinationals, multiplant economies and the gains from trade', *Journal of International Economics*, **16** (3/4), 205–224.

Markusen, J.R. (1995), 'The boundaries of multinational enterprises, and the theory of international trade', *Journal of Economic Perspectives*, **9** (2), 169–189.

OECD (2002), *International Mobility of the Highly Skilled*, Paris: OECD Publishing.

OECD (2010), *Transfer Pricing Guidelines for Multinational Enterprises and Tax Administrations 2010*, Paris: OECD Publishing.

Ohmae, K. (1996), *The End of the Nation State. The Rise of Regional Economies*, London: Harper Collins.

Oman, C.P. (2000), 'Policy Competition for Foreign Direct Investment. A Study of Competition among Governments to Attract FDI', OECD Development Center, Paris: OECD Publishing.

Pagano, U. (2003), 'Nationalism, development and integration: the political economy of Ernest Gellner', *Cambridge Journal of Economics*, **27**, 623–646.

Penrose, E. (1959), *The Theory of the Growth of the Firm*, Oxford: Blackwell.

Phelps, N. and P. Raines (eds) (2002), *The New Competition for Inward Investment*, Cheltenham, UK and Brookfield, VT, USA: Edward Elgar.

Rugman, A.M. (1979), *International Diversification and the Multinational Enterprise*, Lexington, MA: Lexington Books.

Salt, J. (1997), 'International movements of the highly skilled', *International Migration Unit: Occasional Papers,* **3**, OECD/GD (97), 169.

Sugden, R. (1991), 'The importance of distributional considerations', in C.N. Pitelis and R. Sugden, *The Nature of the Transnational Firm*, London: Routledge, pp. 168–193.

UNCTAD (United Nations Conference on Trade and Development) (1996), 'World Investment Report 1996. Investment, Trade and International Policy Arrangements', Geneva, Switzerland: United Nations.

UNCTAD (United Nations Conference on Trade and Development) (2008), 'World Investment Report 2008. Transnational Corporations and the Infrastructure Challenge', Geneva, Switzerland: United Nations.

UNCTAD (United Nations Conference on Trade and Development) (2010), 'World Investment Report 2010. Investing in a Low-Carbon Economy', Geneva, Switzerland: United Nations.

Vernon, R. (1966), 'International investment and international trade in the product cycle', *Quarterly Journal of Economics*, **80**, 190–207.

Westney, D.E. (2005), 'Organization theory and the multinational corporations', in S. Ghoshal and D.E. Westney (eds), *Organization Theory and the Multinational Corporation*, New York: Palgrave Macmillan, pp. 47–67.

Wilkins, M. (1988), 'The freestanding company, 1817–1914', *Economic History Review*, **61** (2), 259–282.

Williamson, O. (1975), *Markets and Hierarchies: Analysis and Anti-trust Implications*, New York: Free Press.

Williamson, O.E. (1981), 'The modern corporation: origins, evolution, attributes', *Journal of Economic Literature*, **19**, 1537–1568.

Williamson, O.E. (1984), 'Efficient labour organization', in F.H. Stephens (ed.), *Firms, Organization and Labour: Approaches to the Economics of Work Organization*, London: Macmillan, pp. 87–118.

Zanfei, A. (2000), 'Transnational firms and the changing organisation of innovative activities', *Cambridge Journal of Economics*, **24** (5), 515–542.

Zetlin, M. (1974), 'Corporate ownership and control: the large corporation and the capitalist class', *American Journal of Sociology*, **79** (5), 1073–1119.

PART II

Governance institutions and macroeconomic
outcomes

6. The effects of convergence in governance on capital accumulation in the Black Sea Economic Cooperation countries

Ahmet Faruk Aysan, Ömer Faruk Baykal and Marie-Ange Véganzonès-Varoudakis

INTRODUCTION

In an increasingly interdependent world, regionalization is considered as a means of collaboration and integration among member states. The Black Sea Economic Cooperation (BSEC) project is a regional economic co-operation arrangement established on 25 June 1992 by 11 countries: Albania, Armenia, Azerbaijan, Bulgaria, Georgia, Greece, Moldova, Romania, the Russian Federation, Turkey and Ukraine. The region constitutes a sizeable market with a population of over 350 million people. The main aim of BSEC is to develop and diversify existing economic relations among its members, by making efficient use of the advantages arising from their geographical proximity. At the same time, BSEC is expected to help transform the centrally planned economies and improve economic and social integration through intra-regional convergence of governance institutions and inter-regional convergence with the European Union (EU).

Good governance institutions help guarantee property rights and minimize transaction costs, thus creating an environment conducive to investment and growth. Since the establishment of BSEC, member countries have gone through a transition process and, to a large extent, this has been about institutional transformation. Although this transformation had a significant impact on economies of the member states, the convergence of the institutions in the region has not been widely studied in the literature. This chapter attempts to fill this gap.

To fulfill this objective, we first investigated the relation between governance institutions and investment for a sample of 43 developing countries through using dynamic system GMM (generalized method-of-moments) estimations. Our approach has not been just to focus on specific institutions, but to be as exhaustive as possible in considering the institutional variables. To this end, we have categorized the various types of governance indicators widely used in the literature and grouped them into three categories: administrative quality (AQ), political stability (PS) and democratic accountability (PA), through principal component analysis. We have also formed two more general governance indexes (GOV1 and GOV2), using most of the information contained in these governance indicators, to check the overall effect of institutions on investment decisions. This categorization has enabled us to estimate the impact of a significant number of governance institutions. In fact, instead of putting highly correlated variables into the final regressions, or just picking up certain indicators, this chapter utilizes all the available information in explaining the investment decisions.

Our empirical results reveal the importance of institutional variables for capital accumulation. This is true for administrative quality (AQ), political stability (PS) and democratic accountability (PA), as well as for the general indices of governance (GOV1 and GOV2). This outcome indicates that governance institutions are a significant determinant of growth through their impact on investment and confirms that institutions are part of convergence between economies. This result is all the more important in the context of the BSEC countries, where the scope for enhancement of governance institutions is still significant.

This result has been related to the second objective of this chapter, which is to investigate the impact of BSEC on the convergence of governance in the region. We observe two types of convergence: the convergence within the BSEC region and the convergence toward the EU-12. With respect to the latter, and considering the possible accession of some BSEC countries to the EU in the future, we simulate how much capital accumulation would be enhanced if governance institutions reached the standards of EU-12 average. The simulations indicate a large gain of such an institutional convergence and reveal in which fields BSEC countries have more scope for improvement. Overall, to the best of our knowledge, this chapter is the first attempt in the literature to investigate the link between regionalization, institutional convergence and economic convergence in the BSEC region.

The chapter is organized as follows. The next section gives a brief account of BSEC countries in recent years. The following section explains the rationale behind categorization of governance institutions into three headings. Next we present other determinants of investment. We then lay down the econometric model and give the regression results. The following section illustrates the institutional convergence within BSEC countries, as well as with the EU-12 region and simulates the possible investment gains from convergence of their governance institutions to EU-12 average. Finally, we provide the concluding remarks.

OUTLOOK OF BLACK SEA ECONOMIC COOPERATION COUNTRIES

BSEC countries showed strong real GDP growth from 2002–2008 with 6.6 per cent average annual growth, that is growth has been sustained at high levels over an extended period of time (Figure 6.1). The rate more than tripled the average annual rate of growth of the Euro zone economies and almost doubled the rate of the world economy during the same period. Considering also that the growth rate in the second half of the 1990s up to 2001 was a mere 0.34 per cent, the remarkable growth performance of the eleven-country economic block can be easily seen. In spite of the recent decline during the global recession, the outlook of the region remains optimistic.

At the same time, improvements in the business environment in the BSEC region have lowered country risk, leading to a positive trend in foreign direct investment (FDI) in the region. Once attracting only US$8 billion in 2000, the region recorded a volume of FDI inflows of US$131 billion in 2008 (Figure 6.2). The highest annual jump in FDI flows has been also witnessed in recent years, as volume of FDI that flew into the region in 2006 hit US$83 billion, compared to US$47 billion in 2005, up by more than 75 per cent. Similarly, the share of foreign investment attracted displayed a constant rise in the 2000s. However, regional development

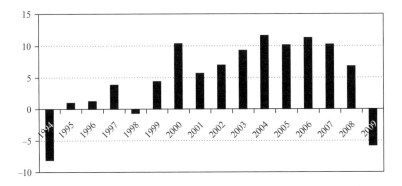

Source: IMF.

Figure 6.1   BSEC growth rates: 1994–2009

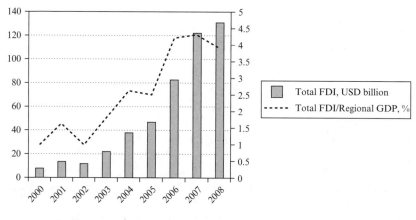

Source: BSTDB.

Figure 6.2   Total FDI inflows into BSEC: 2000–2008

must be backed up by structural reforms in order to attain sustainable
economic growth and faster economic convergence with the EU members.

GOVERNANCE INDICATORS

In order to establish the connection between governance and investment,
we need to identify the governance indicators and group them with respect
to their functionality in affecting investment. Various authors have aggregated certain indices to better capture the common features of the existing
data. Kaufmann et al. (2003) categorize governance institutions under six
broad groups; and The World Bank (2004) uses two governance indicators by aggregating the relevant data for these features of governance. We
categorize governance indicators following Aysan et al. (2007) and distinguish three broad categories of governance institutions, 'Administrative
Quality' (AQ), 'Public Accountability' (PA) and 'Political Stability' (PS).
This has also helped in addressing the multi-collinearity problem that
arises when using several highly-correlated variables in the same equation.

The first governance index, administrative quality (AQ), aims to reflect
the ability of the government in preparing a business-friendly environment for investors. This variable incorporates three indicators from
the International Country Risk Guide (ICRG, 1999): (1) 'Control over
Corruption', (2) 'Quality of Bureaucracy' and (3) 'Law and Order'.
Corruption, which is usually defined as the abuse of public office for

private gains, is documented to affect economic activities adversely more in developing countries, though developed countries are not immune to it. Mo (2001) links corruption to low growth through reduced human and physical capital. Also, Akai et al. (2005) show that the effect of corruption on economic growth is negative and significant in the medium and long term. The ICRG index of 'Quality of Bureaucracy' measures the ability of the government to put into effect sound policies. Rauch and Evans (2000) examine the direct impact of bureaucratic quality on economic growth. A higher 'quality of bureaucracy' index indicates that the government has the expertise to govern without drastic policy changes. In the 'Law and Order' index, 'law' reflects the perceived assessment of the durability and impartiality of the legal system, while 'order' measures perceptions of the extent to which constituents observe and comply with existing legislation. A reliable judiciary system reduces transaction costs for enterprises and sends positive signals to investors that rules of law are equitably and consistently protected and enforced.

The second governance indicator 'political stability' (PS) includes three variables from ICRG: 'government stability', 'internal conflict' and 'ethnic tensions'. Absence of political stability increases the vulnerability of an economy in the eyes of both its citizens and foreign investors. Several authors, using different indicators of political uncertainties, have provided empirical evidence that weak institutions associated with political instability hamper aggregate investment (Rodrik, 1991; Alesina and Perotti, 1996; Le, 2004).

The third governance indicator 'public accountability' (PA) consists of two indicators from Freedom House: 'civil liberties, and 'political rights', and one from International Country Risk Guide (ICRG): 'democratic accountability'. Public accountability is an integral part of the investment climate of an economy since investment decisions are highly sensitive to perceptions concerning the credibility of the political regime and policies. Public accountability, by leading to better economic performances, lowers the discontent of the population and produces a more stable political environment in which investors carry out their business. A participatory political system shows the stability of social institutions and entails more support of the public for the political system. The more open and participatory the political system is, the higher the likelihood that the government may be induced to develop and implement sound economic and social policies. Empirical evidence on the impact of democracy on economic growth is mixed (see Doucouliagos and Ulubaşoğlu, 2008), but the evidence does usually indicate a positive effect of various indicators of democratic institutions on investment in the developing world (Pastor and Sung, 1995).

In addition to these three governance indicators, we have generated two global indexes of governance: (GOV1) which summarizes the information contained in all nine initial indicators participating in (AQ), (PA) and (PS); and (GOV2) which excludes 'civil liberties' and 'political rights' from the main list. All the political and governance indicators have been aggregated by using principal component analysis (PCA) methodology. PCA is mathematically defined as an orthogonal linear transformation that transforms the data to a new coordinate system. PCA can be used for dimensionality reduction in a data set by retaining those characteristics of the data set that contribute most to its variance. Results of PCA are given in the Appendix (Tables 6A.2–6A.6).

OTHER DETERMINANTS OF INVESTMENT

The neoclassical flexible accelerator model is the most widely accepted model of investment. It is based on the idea that enterprises invest more if their profits are higher. The determinants of investment in the neoclassical accelerator model are the expected aggregate demand (the accelerator), the user cost of capital, the wage rate and the initial capital stock. We chose the real interest rate in the year (t) to capture the user cost of capital and the GDP growth rate in year (t–1) to account for the accelerator effect.

The role of human capital, together with physical capital, is also considered in growth models, especially after the advent of endogenous (or new) growth theory (Pritchett, 1996; Barro, 2001). In the neoclassical model, there is no explicit role for education and no externalities. Moreover, human capital enhances better governance institutions. More educated people become more competent bureaucrats (Galor et al., 2005). Therefore human capital is likely to affect investment through its impact on the quality of governance institutions. Recent growth theories have attempted to model these processes, both by introducing human capital explicitly into production functions and by allowing for the possibility of externalities (Lucas, 1988). Our indicator of human capital includes life expectancy at birth, and average years of primary, secondary and higher schooling in the total population over 15 years old.

Macroeconomic stability is likely to affect investment positively. The macroeconomic stability indicator (MS) was obtained by using inflation and the ratio of external debt to GDP. External debt represents the risk to an economy of encountering difficulties in reimbursing its debt and facing a financial crisis. Inflation can be disruptive to investment if it leads to unsustainable macroeconomic imbalances (see Fischer, 1993; De Gregorio, 1992).

The effect of structural reforms is reflected by trade policy and financial development. The financial development provides more opportunities and incentives for firms to invest. There has also been a tendency to underline the role of the economic policies, especially of foreign trade openness on economic growth (Sachs and Warner, 1997; Rodrik, 1999). These studies link trade policy and economic growth, where more openness brings higher economic results. Estimations usually include the rate of growth of exports and the summation of exports and imports as a percentage to GDP as a proxy of trade openness. We chose the private credit by banks and other depository institutions to proxy financial development and the ratio of export and import in total GDP to capture trade policy. As for the governance indicators, all structural and policy indicators have been calculated by using the principal component analysis (PCA) methodology shown in the Appendix (Tables 6A.7–6A.9). In terms of the source of the data, all variables come from the WDI database of the World Bank.

ECONOMETRIC ANALYSIS

Our empirical model explains the share of investment in GDP. In order to account for the persistency in investment, we control for the lag of the dependent variable, which is consistent with the fact that investment decisions take time to materialize. First we introduce the three measures of governance separately, namely 'administrative quality' (AQ), 'public accountability' (PA) and 'political stability' (PS). We then use the two global measures of governance (GOV1) and (GOV2). Since the lag dependent variable is among the control variables, we estimate the model by using Arellano-Bover/Blundell-Bond linear dynamic panel-data estimation. The model is as follows:

$$inv_{it} = \alpha_0 inv_{it-1} + \alpha_1 GI_{it} + \alpha_2 X_{1it} + n_i + v_{it} \tag{1}$$

where inv_{it} is the share of investment in GDP, inv_{it-1} is the lag of the dependant variable, GI_{it} represents the indexes of governance (AQ, PA, PS, GOV1 and GOV2), X_{1it} is the vector of other control variables (including GDP growth, real interest rates, per-capita, GDP, human capital, structural reform indicators, macroeconomic stability indicators and lagged investment) and n_i and v_{it} are the fixed effects and the idiosyncratic error terms respectively. As usual, i indicates the country and t represents the time of the variable.

As explained in above, the real interest rate (in year t) and the GDP growth rate (in year t–1) account for the neoclassical flexible accelerator representation. These variables are anticipated to have respectively a negative and positive impact on investment. The model also takes into account the GDP per capita to capture the convergence effect of the Solow growth model. Countries with lower GDP per capita are presumed to catch up gradually with the more developed counterparts, by having more capital accumulation over the time. A negative sign on the coefficient of GDP per capita is thus expected. Structural reform (SR), human capital (Hum) and macroeconomic stability (MS) are anticipated to play a positive role on capital accumulation. However, the sign of the coefficient for MS is expected to be negative due to the fact that the MS indicator is constructed to increase as inflation and/or the debt ratio increases.

As for the estimation method, we used the Arellano-Bover/Blundell-Bond linear dynamic panel-data estimation technique. There are several advantages in doing so. When OLS, or regular panel data models, are used to estimate equation (1), the results are biased due to the inclusion of the lagged dependent variable, inv_{it-1}. The lagged dependent variable is correlated with the unobserved panel-level effects, and therefore it is not exogenous as assumed by the OLS or some other panel estimations. The Arellano-Bover/Blundell-Bond linear dynamic panel-data model includes p lags of the dependent variable as covariates and contains unobserved panel-level effects.

Since the unobserved panel-level effects are correlated with the lagged dependent variables, other standard estimators are inconsistent. To account for this problem, Arellano and Bond (1991) derived a consistent generalized method-of-moments (GMM) estimator for this model. However, this estimator has certain deficiencies when the autoregressive parameters are too large, or when the ratio of the variance of the panel-level effect to the variance of idiosyncratic error is too large. An improvement came from Blundell and Bond (1997) who developed a system estimator that uses additional moment conditions. With their contribution, deeper lags of the lagged dependent variable become uncorrelated with the transformed error term and remain as instruments for the transformed lagged dependent variable. We employed this improved dynamic panel system when estimating our model and used the Arellano-Bond robust VCE estimator in all the specifications.

Equation (1) has been estimated on an unbalanced panel of 43 developing countries 1985–2005 (see Appendix, Table 6A.1 for the list of countries). Table 6.1 presents the estimation results for the three governance indicators taken separately (AQ, PS and PA, columns 1 to 3), as well as for the more aggregated ones (GOV1 and GOV2, columns 4 and 5).

Estimations confirm the importance of governance institutions for investment decisions. This is true for all measures of governance. A high rank of 'administrative quality' in the sense of a low level of corruption, a good quality of bureaucracy and better law and order, leads to more capital accumulation. This result holds for political stability (as

Table 6.1 Governance institutions and other determinants of investment: estimation results

	AQ	PS	PA	GOV1	GOV2
GDP growth (*t*–1)	0.35	0.35	0.36	0.35	0.35
	(8.21)***	(8.32)***	(8.87)***	(8.10)***	(8.08)***
Real interest	0.0007	0.0007	0.0007	0.0007	0.0007
	(1.86)*	(1.90)*	(2.03)**	(2.03)**	(2.00)**
GDP per capita	–0.0003	–0.0003	–0.0002	–0.0003	–0.0003
	(–4.64)***	(–4.94)***	(–4.26)***	(–5.01)***	(–4.89)***
Human capital	0.56	0.57	0.43	0.51	0.51
	(2.57)***	(2.79)***	(1.91)*	(2.40)**	(2.44)**
Structural reform	2.51	2.62	2.78	2.49	2.52
	(10.18)***	(11.42)***	(13.19)***	(10.30)***	(10.39)***
Macroeconomic	–0.14	–0.12	–0.18	–0.95	–0.99
stability	(–0.64)	(–0.55)	(–0.83)	(–0.43)	(–0.44)
Administrative	0.72				
quality (AQ)	(2.92)***				
Political stability		0.56			
(PS)		(1.74)*			
Political			0.34		
accountability			(1.84)*		
(PA)					
GOV1				1.05	
				(3.05)***	
GOV2					0.93
					(2.73)***
Trend	0.5	0.46	0.47	0.45	0.45
	(2.14)**	(2.06)**	(2.07)**	(1.95)*	(1.97)**
Investment (*t*–1)	0.15	0.16	0.17	0.15	0.15
	(5.60)***	(5.79)***	(6.72)***	(5.73)***	(5.84)***
Constant	10.5	10.6	10.1	10.9	10.8
	(3.72)***	(3.92)***	(3.88)***	(3.90)***	(3.90)***
Number of	844	844	844	844	844
observations					

Note: Dependent variable is share of investment in GDP; *t*-values are in parentheses; (***), (**), (*) indicate significance at 1 per cent, 5 per cent and 10 per cent respectively.

government stability, ethnic tensions and internal tensions), as well as public accountability, although with a lower level of significance in both cases (10 per cent level). These results are confirmed with a high level of significance (1 per cent) when introducing the more global indicators of governance (GOV1) and (GOV2).

As far as other results are concerned, our estimations verify partially the neoclassical theory of the firm in the case of developing countries. In all specifications, the accelerator variable (GDP growth) has the expected positive sign and is highly significant (at the 1 per cent level). This implies that anticipations of economic growth induce more investment. On the other hand, the real interest rate turns out to be positive and significant (at the 10 per cent level in the first two estimations, 5 per cent otherwise), which is contrary to the user cost of capital argument. This finding indicates that investors continue capital accumulation in spite of increasing interest rates. It looks however quite reasonable considering the fact that, in developing countries, the returns from investment are rather high when the business cycles are favourable to the investors (and vice versa). In addition, estimations confirm the Solow's convergence argument that countries with lower GDP per capita accumulate more capital in transition. The GDP per capita variable turns out to be highly significant (at the 1 per cent level) with an expected negative coefficient.

Other interesting outcomes concern structural reforms and human capital, which stand as significant positive factors on investment decisions (at 1 per cent, and 1 to 10 per cent levels depending of the specification, respectively). Macroeconomic stability, however, does not appear as a significant factor in capital accumulation. This result indicates that investment decisions rely more on fundamental and long term factors, than on short term aspects. Regression results also indicate a strong persistency in the investment decision. Lagged dependent variable displays a positive and highly significant coefficient in all specifications. The results also indicate a positive trend for capital accumulation.

We have also tested the zero autocorrelation in first-differenced errors. The results are depicted in Table 6.2 below. The nil hypothesis is no autocorrelation. In all the specification, we reject the nil hypothesis for the first moments, but not for the second ones. Arellano and Bond show that there is a first order serial correlation in the transformed error terms as expected, and that the second order serial correlation is rejected. Hence, using the second lag of the dependent variable as an instrument for the transformed lagged dependent variable is feasible.

CONVERGENCE IN BSEC GOVERNANCE INSTITUTIONS

In this section, we investigate whether regional integration among BSEC countries has led to convergence in governance within the region. We also

Table 6.2   Arellano-Bond test for zero autocorrelation in first-differenced errors

H0: no autocorrelation	AQ	PS	PA	GOV1	GOV2
Prob > z|					
Order 1	0	0	0	0	0
Order 2	0.1635	0.1952	0.2216	0.2798	0.2557

Source: Authors' calculations.

ask whether this convergence has helped to reduce the gap in governance with respect to the EU-12. To address the first question, we have examined the intra-BSEC coefficients of variation for seven individual governance indicators used in the regression estimation above. We find that BSEC countries have achieved visible intra-regional convergence in five out of seven governance indicators: bureaucratic quality, law and order, ethnic tensions, government stability and internal conflicts (Table 6.3). With respect to corruption control, intra-BSEC convergence is limited and there is evidence of intra-BSEC divergence with respect to democratic accountability.

Table 6.3 also indicates that the process of convergence has been subject to volatility. From 1984 to 1992 (the year in which BSEC was formed), variation between BSEC governance quality indicators either increased slightly or remained the same. However, in the period 1992–1998 that corresponded to the initial stage of transition to market economy, intra-BSEC variation between quality indicators increased significantly at the beginning of the sub-period, before some convergence could be observed in the second half of the period. Finally, in the period 1998–2005, the coefficients of variation for four governance indicators (bureaucratic quality, corruption control, ethnic tensions and internal conflict) have dropped, but they have increased for the remaining three indicators (law and order, government stability and democratic accountability). Despite this evident volatility in the process of convergence, the evidence enables us to conclude that the trend since 1992 (when BSEC was established) points in the direction of intra-BSEC convergence in five out of seven governance indicators.

To address the second question, we have calculated the difference between EU-12 and BSEC averages of the quality indicators in 1992, 1996, 2000 and 2005. Table 6.4 below indicates that BSEC countries, after 1992, have narrowed the governance quality gap with EU-12 countries in five out of seven indicators: law and order, government stability, internal conflicts, ethnic tensions and democratic accountability. Corruption and bureaucratic quality

Does economic governance matter?

Table 6.3   Coefficients or variation for BSEC governance indicators

Year	Bureaucratic quality	Corruption	Law and order	Ethnic tension	Government stability	Internal conflict	Democratic account.
1984	0.639	0.261	0.357	0.465	0.179	0.208	0.204
1985	0.639	0.254	0.335	0.515	0.120	0.194	0.178
1986	0.639	0.263	0.335	0.565	0.127	0.158	0.223
1987	0.639	0.266	0.335	0.543	0.187	0.157	0.325
1988	0.639	0.316	0.335	0.429	0.330	0.189	0.343
1989	0.639	0.400	0.348	0.442	0.410	0.230	0.319
1990	0.414	0.319	0.333	0.419	0.094	0.224	0.137
1991	0.465	0.267	0.335	0.300	0.247	0.198	0.173
1992	0.447	0.149	0.267	0.317	0.334	0.131	0.305
1993	0.447	0.167	0.209	0.341	0.227	0.147	0.278
1994	0.447	0.159	0.205	0.327	0.114	0.179	0.274
1995	0.447	0.165	0.202	0.440	0.051	0.192	0.187
1996	0.447	0.351	0.169	0.355	0.143	0.191	0.215
1997	0.443	0.404	0.202	0.365	0.087	0.213	0.197
1998	0.501	0.340	0.155	0.331	0.049	0.290	0.316
1999	0.471	0.417	0.207	0.290	0.057	0.223	0.337
2000	0.471	0.426	0.234	0.314	0.135	0.124	0.245
2001	0.471	0.416	0.234	0.292	0.149	0.111	0.364
2002	0.442	0.278	0.225	0.295	0.193	0.113	0.409
2003	0.437	0.272	0.224	0.295	0.146	0.101	0.380
2004	0.442	0.230	0.208	0.264	0.159	0.076	0.347
2005	0.471	0.217	0.205	0.288	0.146	0.089	0.328

Source: Authors' calculations.

are the two indicators where BSEC diverged away from the EU-12 average. The rate of convergence was the highest for internal conflict, ethnic tensions and government stability, while it was the least for democratic accountability.

In order to ascertain the impact of convergence in governance on capital accumulation in the BSEC region, we simulated how much investment would have gone up if governance had converged to the EU-12 levels. Calculations were done by using the proportion of each governance index affecting GOV2, the coefficient coming from the regression and the gap between BSEC and EU-12 averages. Results for the final year show that an improvement in bureaucratic quality and corruption would contribute the most, with an investment ratio increased by 0.29 per cent each year when BSEC average converges to that of EU-12. The law and order and democratic accountability are the second most effective governance indicator that has the potential to increase investment rate by 0.17 per cent

Table 6.4   *Difference of governance quality indicators: EU-12 average –*
BSEC average

	1992	1996	2000	2005	Trend
Law and order	1.7	1.2	1.7	1.4	Positive
Government stability	0.9	1	0.7	0.5	Positive
Internal conflicts	1.5	0.9	0.7	−0.4	Positive
Ethnic tensions	1.7	1.1	2.4	0.6	Positive
Democratic accountability	1.7	1.2	1.2	1.5	Positive
Corruption	1.7	1.7	2.2	2.0	Negative
Bureaucracy quality	1.2	1.8	1.8	2.1	Negative

Source: Authors' calculations.

Table 6.5   *Contributions of governance quality to investment: simulation*
results

	1992	1996	2000	2005
Corruption	0.25	0.25	0.32	0.29
Bureaucracy quality	0.16	0.25	0.24	0.29
Law and order	0.22	0.15	0.22	0.17
Government stability	0.12	0.13	0.09	0.07
Internal conflicts	0.19	0.11	0.08	−0.06
Ethnic tensions	0.24	0.15	0.33	0.08
Democratic accountability	0.20	0.15	0.14	0.18

Source: Authors' calculations.

and 0.18 per cent respectively (see Table 6.5). On the other hand, improvement in government stability and ethnic tension appears to have a slight contribution to capital accumulation.

CONCLUSION

Good governance and institutions are an assurance to guarantee property rights and minimize transaction costs, thus creating an environment conducive to investment and growth. Since its foundation in 1992, BSEC countries have gone through a transition process and, to a large extent, this has been about institutional transformation. In this chapter, we have examined this institutional transformation for several governance indicators and have reported that institutional convergence has taken place within the region during 1992–2005 in the control over corruption, quality of the bureaucracy, law and order, internal conflicts and ethnic tensions. This transformation has contributed to the region's institutional convergence towards the EU-12 average and has been associated with better economic performance indicators over the same period.

We have estimated the impact of governance institutions on investment using a panel of 43 countries from 1995–2005. Various dimensions of the quality of the administration (control over corruption, quality of bureaucracy, law and order), of political stability (government stability, internal conflict, ethnic tensions) and of democratic accountability (civil liberties, political rights, democratic accountability) show a positive and significant impact on investment. This result is all the more important for the BSCE countries, because of the potential for improvement in governance that still exists in the region. Filling the gap with the EU-12 would stimulate further investment and growth, facilitating in return a future integration in the EU. By using our econometric results we show, in particular, that investment could increase 0.58 per cent per year if bureaucracy quality and control over corruption caught up with the EU-12 average. This increase would be 0.17 and 0.18 per cent per year respectively for law and order and democratic accountability. Improvements in government stability and ethnic tension, however, display a lower contribution to capital accumulation. These results provide empirical support to the arguments that the quality of governance institutions has a positive impact on economic performance in general and on investment in particular. To our knowledge, the results are also the first estimates of how enhanced governance quality may enable BSEC countries to improve their investment potentials.

ACKNOWLEDGEMENT

Conference participants at Economic Research Forum (ERF), 17th Annual Conference, 20–22 March 2011, Antalya, Turkey, the Ninth International Conference of Middle East Economic Association, 24–26 June 2010, Istanbul Technical University, Istanbul, Economic Governance Institutions, Economic Outcomes and the Crisis: An International Conference, 4 June 2010, University of Greenwich, London UK and James Robinson, Mehmet Ugur, Philip Arestis provided useful comments on the previous version of the chapter. We are very grateful to all of them while retaining sole responsibility for any errors or misinterpretations. This work was sponsored by Economic Research Forum (ERF) and has benefited from financial and intellectual support. The contents and recommendations do not necessarily reflect ERF's views.

REFERENCES

Akai, N., Y. Horiuchi and M. Sakata (2005), 'Short-run and long-run effects of corruption on economic growth: evidence from state level cross-section data for the United States', *CIRJE (Center for International Research on the Japanese Economy)*, 1–30.

Alesina, A. and R. Perotti (1996), 'Income distribution, political instability, and investment', *European Economic Review*, **40**, 1203–1228.

Arellano, M. and S. Bond (1991), 'Some tests of specification for panel data: Monte Carlo evidence and an application to employment equations', *Review of Economic Studies*, **58**, 277–297.

Aysan, A.F., M. Nabli and M. Véganzonès-Varoudakis (2007), 'Governance institutions and private investment: an application to the Middle East and North Africa', *The Developing Economies,* **45** (3), 339–377.

Barro, R.J. (2001), 'Human capital and growth', *American Economic Review*, **91** (2), 12–17.

Blundell, R. and S. Bond (1997), 'Initial conditions and moment restrictions in dynamic panel data models', University College London Discussion Paper, July.

De Gregorio, J. (1992), 'Economic growth in Latin America', *Journal of Development Economics*, **39** (1), 59–84.

Doucouliagos, H. and M. Ulubaşoğlu (2008), 'Democracy and economic growth: a meta-analysis', *American Journal of Political Science*, **52** (1), 61–83.

Fischer, S. (1993), 'The role of macroeconomic factors in growth', *Journal of Monetary Economics*, **32**, 485–512.

Galor, O., O. Moav, and D. Vollrath (2005), 'Land inequality and the emergence of human capital promoting institutions', *Development and Comp Systems*, 0502018, Economic Working Paper Archive at WUSTL.

ICRG (1999), 'Brief Guide to the Rating System', New York: International Country Risk Guides, Political Link Service Group.

Kaufmann, D., A. Kraay and M. Mastruzzi (2003), *Governance Matters III, Governance Indicators for 1996–2002*, Washington, DC: World Bank.

Le, Q.V. (2004), 'Political and economic determinants of private investment', *Journal of International Development*, **16** (4), 589–604.

Lucas, R. (1988), 'On the mechanics of development', *Journal of Monetary Economics,* **22** (1), 1–175.

Mo, P.H. (2001), 'Corruption and economic growth', *Journal of Comparative Economics,* **29** (1), 66–79.

Pastor, M. and J.H. Sung (1995), 'Private investment and democracy in the developing world', *Journal of Economic Issues,* **29** (1), 223–221.

Pritchett, L. (1996), 'Where has all the education gone?', *World Bank, Policy Research Working Paper*, **1581**.

Rauch J.E. and P.B. Evans (2000), 'Bureaucratic structure and bureaucratic performance in less developed countries', *Journal of Public Economics*, **75** (1), 49–71.

Rodrik, D. (1991), 'Policy uncertainty and private investment in developing countries', *Journal of Development Economics,* **36** (2), 229–242.

Rodrik, D. (1999), 'Institutions for high-quality growth: what they are and how to acquire them', Paper presented at the IMF Conference on Second Generation Reforms, Washington, November, pp. 8–9.

Sachs, J. and A. Warner (1997), *Natural Resource Abundance and Economic Growth*, Cambridge, MA: Centre for International Development, Harvard University.

World Bank (2004), 'Better governance for development in the Middle East and North Africa: enhancing inclusiveness and accountability', Washington, DC: MENA Development Report, World Bank.
World Bank (2010), 'World Development Indicators', Washington, DC: World Bank.

APPENDIX

Table 6A.1   List of countries used in regression analysis

Albania	Dominican Republic	Malawi	South Africa
Armenia	Ecuador	Malaysia	Sri Lanka
Azerbaijan	Egypt	Moldova	Thailand
Bahrain	El Salvador	Nicaragua	Togo
Bangladesh	Ghana	Nigeria	Trinidad &Tobago
Bolivia	Greece	Panama	Turkey
Bulgaria	Guatemala	Papua New Guinea	Ukraine
Cameroon	Honduras	Paraguay	Uruguay
Chile	Hungary	Peru	Venezuela
China	India	Philippines	Zambia
Colombia	Indonesia	Romania	Zimbabwe
Costa Rica	Jordan	Russia	
Cote d'Ivoire	Kenya	Sierra Leone	

Table 6A.2   Principal Component Analysis (PCA) for the administrative quality (AQ) indicator

Component		Eigenvalue	Cumulative R^2
P1		1.87	0.62
P2		0.57	0.81
P3		0.55	1
Loadings	P1	P2	P3
Corruption	0.57	−0.43	0.69
Bureaucracy quality	0.57	−0.37	−0.72
Law and order	0.57	0.81	0.03

Note: AQ = P1*(0.62) + P2*(0.19) + P3*(0.19).

Source: Authors' calculations.

Table 6A.3 PCA for the political stability (PS) indicator

Component		Eigenvalue	Cumulative R²
P1		1.70	0.56
P2		0.80	0.83
P3		0.49	1.00
Loadings	P1	P2	P3
Government stability	0.52	0.74	0.41
Ethnic tensions	0.64	−0.03	−0.76
Internal tensions	0.55	−0.67	0.49

Note: PS = P1*(0.56) + P2*(0.27) + P3*(0.17).

Source: Authors' calculations.

Table 6A.4 PCA for the public accountability (PA) indicator

Component		Eigenvalue	Cumulative R²
P1		2.29	0.76
P2		0.56	0.95
P3		0.14	1.00
Loadings	P1	P2	P3
Democratic accountability	0.50	0.80	0.07
Political rights	0.61	−0.29	−0.72
Civil liberties	0.60	−0.41	0.68

Note: PA = P1*(0.76) + P2*(0.19) + P3*(0.05).

Source: Authors' calculations.

Table 6A.5   PCA for the Governance1 (GOV1) indicator

Component	Eigenvalue	Cumulative R²
P1	3.35	0.36
P2	1.82	0.56
P3	1.26	0.70
P4	0.75	0.80
P5	0.53	0.85
P6	0.46	0.90
P7	0.40	0.95
P8	0.25	0.98
P9	0.13	1.00

Loadings	P1	P2	P3	P4	P5	P6	P7	P8	P9
Corruption	0.30	0.17	0.47	0.43	0.41	0.48	0.18	0.22	0.02
Bureaucracy quality	0.30	0.26	0.49	0.23	0.14	0.72	0.04	0.12	0.01
Law and order	0.39	0.38	0.06	0.13	0.33	0.02	0.37	0.66	0.01
Government stability	0.24	0.23	0.32	0.69	0.48	0.27	0.05	0.03	0.01
Internal conflicts	0.39	0.28	0.31	0.02	0.49	0.06	0.03	0.65	0.06
Ethnic tensions	0.29	0.01	0.51	0.49	0.42	0.3	0.37	0.1	0.01
Democratic accountability	0.40	0.22	0.27	0.16	0.23	0.27	0.71	0.22	0.11
Political rights	0.33	0.55	0.01	0.06	0.01	0.06	0.23	0.02	0.73
Civil liberties	0.34	0.53	0.07	0.04	0.02	0.10	0.36	0.09	0.68

Note: Governance1 = P1*(0.37) + P2*(0.20) + P3*(0.14) + P4*(0.10) + P5*(0.05) + P6*(0.05) + P7*(0.05) + P8*(0.03) + P9*(0.02).

Source: Authors' calculations.

Table 6A.6   PCA for the Governance2 (GOV2) indicator

Component	Eigenvalue	Cumulative R²
P1	2.90	0.41
P2	1.22	0.59
P3	0.89	0.71
P4	0.71	0.82
P5	0.54	0.89
P6	0.45	0.96
P7	0.25	1.00

Loadings	P1	P2	P3	P4	P5	P6	P7
Corruption	0.35	0.46	0.37	0.22	0.41	0.51	0.22
Bureaucracy quality	0.37	0.47	0.3	0.21	0.13	0.7	0.12
Law and order	0.49	0.10	0.03	0.39	0.34	0.12	0.69
Government stability	0.30	0.34	0.69	0.12	0.48	0.27	0.03
Internal conflicts	0.46	0.33	0.00	0.05	0.49	0.06	0.66
Ethnic tensions	0.29	0.49	0.55	0.17	0.43	0.40	0.08
Democratic accountability	0.34	0.32	0.03	0.84	0.20	0.06	0.17

Note: Governance2 = P1*(0.41) + P2*(0.18) + P3*(0.12) + P4*(0.11) + P5*(0.07) + P6*(0.07) + P7*(0.04).

Source: Authors' calculations.

Table 6A.7   PCA for the structural reform (SR) indicator

Component	Eigenvalue	Cumulative R²
P1	1.29	0.58
P2	0.70	1.00

Loadings	P1	P2
Trade policy	0.71	–0.71
Domestic credit	71	0.71

Note: SR = P1*(0.58) + P2*(0.32).

Source: Authors' calculations.

Table 6A.8   PCA for the human capital (H) indicator

Component		Eigenvalue		Cumulative R²
P1		2.53		0.63
P2		0.87		0.85
P3		0.37		0.94
P4		0.21		1.00

Loadings	P1	P2	P3	P4
Life Expectancy	0.53	−0.18	0.81	−0.14
H1	0.28	0.94	0.05	0.13
H2	0.56	−0.04	−0.5	−0.65
H3	0.55	−0.25	−0.29	0.73

Note: H = P1*(0.63) + P2*(0.22) + P3*(0.09) +P4*(0.06).

Source: Authors' calculation.

Table 6A.9 PCA for the macroeconomic stability (MS) indicator

Component	Eigenvalue	Cumulative R²
P1	1.39	0.69
P2	0.60	1.00

Loadings	P1	P2
Inflation	0.7	0.7
External debt	70	−0.7

Note: SR = P1*(0.69) + P2*(0.21).

Source: Authors' calculations.

7. Taxes, foreign aid and quality of governance institutions

José Antonio Alonso, Carlos Garcimartín and Luis Rivas

INTRODUCTION

Economists have traditionally identified the causes of development in terms of the amount of inputs available and the aggregated level of efficiency. However, a new perspective, unlike this vision but not necessarily incompatible, has emerged in recent decades. This view calls for attention to be paid to the ways in which governance institutions condition development by defining incentives and penalties, shaping social behaviour and articulating collective action. (See for example, Hall and Jones, 1999; Acemoglu et al., 2002; Rodrik et al., 2002; Henisz, 2000; Tavares and Warcziarg, 2001; Varsakelis, 2006.) Once the role of institutions in development is acknowledged, it becomes important to investigate whether aid fosters (or hinders) institutional quality. In this sense, it has been argued that the former can be detrimental to the latter, giving rise to a sort of 'aid curse'.

Although empirical research is scarce in this area, some works have reported a negative impact of aid on institutional quality. Yet, in our opinion, most of these studies suffer from two main shortcomings. On the one hand, a prior investigation of the determinants of institutional quality is usually not implemented and, as a consequence, a serious problem of omitted variables can emerge, leading to biased results. On the other hand, as suggested in the literature on the aid–development nexus, aid may show decreasing returns, but this possibility is rarely taken into account. With the aim of overcoming these shortcomings, we have first analysed the determinants of institutional quality. According to our findings, four main factors determine the quality of institutions: development level, income distribution, tax revenue and education. Subsequently, we have incorporated aid into our regressions. Our main result suggests that aid impacts positively on institutional quality, but that it shows decreasing returns. In highly aid-dependent countries, the impact can be negative.

Since tax revenue is a crucial determinant of institutional quality, and because it has been argued that aid reduces the incentives to mobilize tax revenue, we have also investigated the relation between aid and taxes. Although the empirical evidence in this respect is ambiguous, in our opinion it shows three main shortcomings. First, some of the works do not implement a prior analysis of the determinants of tax revenue. Second, the possibility that the impact of aid on taxes might be conditional upon governance quality is rarely considered. Third, most (if not all) of the research using cross-country or panel databases considers only central government revenues. In samples including highly-decentralized countries and/or nations with high social contributions, as are usually the case, this can lead to significant mistakes. Our estimates suggest that, once these three aspects are taken into account, aid shows a positive impact on tax revenues, with this impact being dependent on the quality of institutions.

AID AND INSTITUTIONS

Traditionally, aid was assumed to exert a positive impact on governance quality in a recipient country. It was thought that the transfer of resources, expertise and technical capabilities should improve the institutional framework of recipient countries. In addition, an important share of aid has been devoted to strengthening governance institutions in poor countries, through capacity-building programmes.

Yet following Burnside and Dollar (2000) and the World Bank (1998), this view has changed. According to these studies, the impact of aid on development is conditioned by the quality of governance institutions, but aid does not have any influence on institutional quality. As a consequence of this approach, some donors tried to incorporate governance quality as a condition for aid distribution.

More recently, some authors have argued that aid can have an impact on the quality of institutions, but that impact is negative, giving rise to a sort of 'aid curse', which arises for the following reasons:

1. Rent-seeking activities and corruption can emerge as a consequence of discretionary fund allocations (Alesina and Weder, 2002; Djankov et al., 2008).
2. Budget planning can be more difficult if aid funds experience large variations.
3. Since aid softens budget constraints, it can promote unsustainable projects and policies (Bräutigam and Knack, 2004; Killick, 2004).

4. Since aid influences both the dimension and the composition of public expenditure, the former can increase more than proportionally (McGillivray and Morrissey, 2000; Remmer, 2004), while simultaneously favouring public consumption (Khan and Hoshino, 1992).
5. The recruitment of local technicians by foreign aid agencies can reduce the amount of qualified workers available for local administrations (Bräutigam, 2000).
6. In highly aid-dependent countries, government accountability can be directed towards donors rather than to citizens (Moore, 1998; Alonso and Garcimartín, forthcoming).
7. Aid can disincentive tax revenue efforts (Kimbrough, 1986; Bräutigam and Knack, 2004).

Although empirical research is scarce, some works have found a negative impact of aid on institutional quality. For example, Knack (2000) regresses the change in the ICRG quality-of-governance index on its initial value, aid, population growth and GDP per capita growth. Aid is considered endogenous, and it is instrumented by infant mortality in 1980 and initial GDP per capita (as indicators of recipient needs) and initial population and Franc Zone and Central America dummies (as measures of donors' interest). His estimates show that aid reduces institutional quality. Bräutigam (2000) builds a similar model, and she finds that aid is associated with deterioration in governance quality. A similar result is found in Bräutigam and Knack (2004), but according to their results and interpretation, the negative impact of aid vanished after 1990 because from that decade onward, donors engaged more actively in programmes to improve institutional quality, and they simultaneously targeted aid more selectively.

In our opinion, these three studies are very representative of the shortcomings that the empirical research on the impact of aid on institutional quality exhibits. The estimated models are Barro-type convergence regressions, in the sense that the variation of the dependent variable is regressed on its initial value plus the determinants of long-run institutional quality. According to the regressions implemented, these determinants are aid, population growth and GDP per capita growth. This implies that long-run institutional quality depends solely on these three variables; nothing else matters. Furthermore, a country's long-run institutional quality is not influenced by its income level, but by its rate of growth. It does not matter whether a country is rich or poor; what counts is whether it grows at a faster or slower rate. In our opinion, it is hard to see why this should be the case. However, since in their estimates aid is the only significant variable, long-run institutional quality depends exclusively on the amount of aid received. This conclusion is far from convincing.

Another interesting analysis is presented by Djankov et al. (2008). They use two proxies of institutional quality: the scales of democracy provided by the Polity IV project, and the Database of Political Institutions (DPI) constructed by Keefer et al. (2001). As explanatory variables, they consider oil resources, changes in the terms of trade, the initial value of political institutions quality, school enrolment and the origin of each country's legal system. They employ several estimation techniques: OLS, 2SLS and dynamic panel data analysis. The only significant variables are the initial value of institutional quality, ODA, and (to a lesser extent) oil rents. Again, these results imply that long-run institutional quality is almost exclusively determined by foreign aid; nothing else matters.

In our opinion, all these works suffer from two main shortcomings that make their conclusions less tenable. First, they lack a prior investigation on the determinants of institutional quality. They control for some variables, like income per capita growth or terms of trade shocks, but not for others that can determine institutional quality. As a consequence, a serious problem of omitted variables can emerge, leading to biased results. We believe that aid's emergence as the only determinant of long-run institutional quality is a reflection of this problem.

The second shortcoming of these empirical works is that decreasing returns to aid are not considered. Many works on the aid–development nexus have pointed out the existence of decreasing returns to aid, indicating that, although aid can foster development, there is a threshold in terms of aid volume. Once this threshold is crossed, aid has a negative impact on development. Hadjimichael et al. (1995), Durbarry et al. (1998), Hansen and Tarp (1999) and Rajan and Subramanian (2005), among others, have confirmed this result, although the threshold level varies across studies. Thus, according to Hadjimichael et al. (1995), the critical level of aid is about 25 per cent of GDP, a figure which rises to 40–45 per cent in Durbarry et al. (1998) and to 41–58 per cent in Lesink and White (1999).

ON THE DETERMINANTS OF INSTITUTIONAL QUALITY

Institutions respond to problems stemming from social interaction in an uncertain world, where agents take non-coordinated decisions within a framework of imperfect information. In this context, governance institutions constitute a mechanism to reduce discretional behaviours and to limit opportunism. In addition, since they shape social behaviour, institutions foster collective action, reducing coordination costs. Yet it cannot be taken for granted that institutions are always an efficient response to social transaction costs. They are also a mechanism through which social actors express their strategies and power. Hence, a society does not necessarily have all institutions it needs, nor are its existing institutions necessarily optimal.

Since institutions do not really work if they are not capable of shaping behaviours, it is important to analyse not only the rules that institutions define, but also the motivations by individuals to fulfil them. Therefore it is as relevant to study the incentives framework in which agents operate as why agents behave according to such a framework. It is necessary to discover why some rules are observed while others are not. Hence, the legitimacy of an institution becomes a basic feature conditioning its effectiveness.

According to this approach, governance institutions have two basic economic functions: (1) reducing transaction costs, thus granting certainty and predictability to social interaction; and (2) facilitating the coordination of economic agents. With these functions in mind, the quality of governance institutions might be defined by four basic properties (Alonso and Garcimartín, 2010):

1. Static efficiency: the institution's capacity to promote efficient equilibria.
2. Legitimacy: the institution's capacity to define credible intertemporary contracts. In other words, the institution's ability to generate a normative framework that truly modulates agents' behaviour in an effective way.
3. Predictability: an institution fulfils its function if it reduces the uncertainty associated with human interaction.
4. Adaptability (or dynamic efficiency): the institutional ability to be able to anticipate social changes, or at least to generate the incentives that facilitate agents' adjustment to these changes, as stressed by North (2005).

These properties must be taken into account when the determinants of institutional quality are analysed. In fact, in the empirical strategy followed by Alonso and Garcimartín (2010), the variables that match these criteria are identified prior to implementing any regression. One such variable is the level of development. The latter conditions the availability of resources for building good governance institutions and generates higher demand for good-quality institutions. As such, it is related to static efficiency of institutions, and the positive relationship between both variables has been confirmed by previous research (Chong and Zanforlin, 2000; Islam and Montenegro, 2002; Rigobon and Rodrik, 2004, among others).

Income distribution is the second variable considered by Alonso and Garcimartín (2010). This is expected to affect institutional predictability and legitimacy for three reasons. First, strong inequality causes divergent interests among different social groups and this, in turn, leads to conflicts, socio-political instability and insecurity. Secondly, inequality makes it easier for institutions to remain under the control of powerful groups, whose actions are orientated to their particular interests rather than to the common good. Thirdly, inequality diminishes social agents' disposition toward cooperative action; instead it fosters corruption and rent-seeking activities. This relationship was also supported by previous studies (Alesina and Rodrik, 1993; Alesina and Perotti ,1996; Easterly, 2001); though in some cases the results depend on the inclusion of regional dummies (Islam and Montenegro, 2002). In addition, Engerman and Sokoloff (1997, 2002, 2005, 2006) argue that highly unequal income distribution encourages institutions that, in turn, tend to perpetuate inequality, thus generating a vicious circle between inequality and low institutional quality.

International openness is the third factor that, according to Alonso and Garcimartín (2010), can encourage institutional quality. It is related to the dynamic efficiency of institutions. Firstly, international openness creates a dynamic, sophisticated and demanding environment, which fuels a larger demand for good institutions. Secondly, it encourages a more competitive environment and can therefore hinder rent-seeking activities, corruption and nepotism. Finally, openness can facilitate learning processes and the imitation of good practices from other countries. For example, Rodrik et al. (2002) confirm that openness has a positive impact on institutional quality, but their estimates do not control for development level. Rigobon and Rodrik (2004) find a positive, though weak, relationship between trade openness and the rule of law, but that relationship becomes negative in the case of democracy. Also, Islam and Montenegro (2002) state that, when controlling for development level, openness affects some institutional quality variables but not others. Finally, the work of Knack and Azfar (2003), in reference to corruption, shows that the results are very sensitive to the country sample used.

Education is the fourth factor considered by Alonso and Garcimartín (2010) as a determinant of institutional quality. It is a variable related to an institution's dynamic efficiency. A more educated population demands more transparent and dynamic institutions and permits them to be built. This is a variable seldom considered in empirical research. As an exception, the work of Alesina and Perotti (1996), which confirms the positive impact of education on institutional quality, must be pointed out. Also, in the literature on corruption, the education effect has been detected in works such as those of Glaeser and Sacks (2006) or Evans and Rauch (2000).

Finally, the fifth determinant of institutional quality is taxes. To our knowledge, only Alonso and Garcimartín (2010) have argued that taxes are a crucial variable that affects both the static efficiency and legitimacy of institutions. A sound tax system not only provides the resources necessary to build high-quality governance institutions, but also underpins a social contract that gives rise to a more demanding relationship between the state and citizens. Thus the resulting higher transparency and accountability leads to better institutional quality (Tilly, 1992; Moore, 1998). This may not be the case with public revenues collected from other sources, such as state-owned companies or natural resources.

The model estimated by Alonso and Garcimartín (2010) directly responds to determinants related to the previously defined institutional quality criteria. In particular, the estimated equation was:

$$IQ = \alpha + \beta_1 Y + \beta_2 G + \beta_3 T + \beta_4 Ed + \beta_5 OR + Di \qquad (1)$$

where IQ stands for institutional quality; Y is per capita GDP; G is income distribution, measured by the Gini index; T represents tax revenues as a percentage of GDP; Ed is education; OR is openness rate; and Di are regional dummies. The data for these variables used in this study is the same as that used by Alonso and Garcimartín (2010) – with the exception of overseas development aid (ODA), which we incorporate as a new determinant of institutional quality here. Variable definitions and data sources can be seen in the appendix to this chapter.

Our previous study showed that per capita GDP, income distribution, openness rate and tax revenue should be considered endogenous, while the results were not robust in the case of education. Therefore this variable was considered as both exogenous and endogenous. The equation was estimated by instrumental variables, using the following instruments: for GDP per capita, its 15-year lagged value; for the Gini index, the 15-year lagged GDP per capita, its square value, and ethnic fragmentation index and regional dummies; for the tax ratio, the percentage of fuel exports on total exports and regional dummies; and for openness rate, total population.

All variables showed the expected sign and were significant, except the openness rate. Therefore, the results suggested that a higher development level, a more equitable income distribution, a better educated population and a sounder tax system lead to higher institutional quality. These findings were robust to the use of alternative institutional quality indicators. As such, the findings of Alonso and Garcimartín (2010) suggest that institutional quality is determined by those variables directly related to the aforementioned institutional properties – that is efficiency, legitimacy, predictability and adaptability.

AID AND INSTITUTIONAL QUALITY: EMPIRICAL EVIDENCE

Having identified the determinants of institutional quality, we can now incorporate aid into the model, with the confidence that omitted variables will not seriously bias the results. Thus, using the same database employed by Alonso and Garcimartín (2010), we have included aid (ODA) into the regressions by measuring it as a percentage of GDP. It has been considered endogenous, employing as instrument its 5-year average lagged value.

In Table 7.1, we regress institutional quality only on its lagged value and aid (ODA). Both variables are significant and aid shows a negative sign, thus confirming the results obtained by the studies mentioned in section one. Yet, when we incorporate ODA into our fully-specified institutional quality model, ODA does not significantly differ from zero (Table 7.2, column 2).

As stated above, institutional quality may show decreasing returns to aid. In order to test this possibility, we have included the squared value of aid into the model (ODA^2). In that case, the aid parameter becomes positive and significant (at 95 per cent probability), while (ODA^2)is negative and significant (at 90 per cent probability), thus confirming that aid has a positive impact on the quality of institutions, but the impact can be mitigated or even reversed if the amount of aid is larger than 3.8 per cent of GDP (Table 7.2, column 2).

On the other hand, it may be inappropriate to compute aid as a

Table 7.1   Impact of aid on institutional quality

Variable	Value (t-ratio)
Initial institutional quality	0.93 (28.29)
ODA	−0.02 (−3.90)
Adjusted R^2	0.84
Number of observations	166
Infra-identification test: Kleibergen-Paap statistic (probability)	0.03

Note: Endogenous: ODA 2005; Instrument: ODA 2000; Instrumental variables; robust estimates.

Table 7.2   Aid-inclusive determinants of institutional quality (I)

Variable	ODA		ODA and ODA^2		ODA (PPP)		ODA and ODA^2 (PPP)	
	Value	t-ratio	Value	t-ratio	Value	t-ratio	Value	t-ratio
Per capita GDP	0.36	2.58	0.48	3.08	0.40	2.48	0.49	2.97
Gini Index	−0.58	−1.98	−0.59	−2.07	−0.60	−2.09	−0.64	−2.26
Taxes	0.67	2.79	0.58	2.50	0.61	2.36	0.55	2.38
Education	0.31	1.50	0.27	1.36	0.28	1.38	0.27	1.43
ODA	0.055	1.20	0.283	2.16	0.13	0.34	0.554	2.05
ODA^2			−0.037	−1.79			−0.14	−1.96
ECA	−0.42	−2.68	−0.35	−2.20	−0.40	−2.48	−0.36	−2.22
MENA	−0.55	−2.58	−0.60	−3.47	−0.56	−2.78	−0.57	−3.26
N	79		79		79		79	
Centred R^2	0.79		0.81		0.80		0.81	
Underidentification test (Kleibergen-Paap rk LM statistic (P-value)	0.0332		0.0390		0.0553		0.0617	
Hansen J statistic (overidentification) (P-value)	0.1255		0.1675		0.1240		0.1756	

Notes:
Endogenous: Per capita GDP , Gini Index, taxes, ODA2005 and (ODA2005)^2
Instruments: Per capita GDP 1990, (Per capita GDP 1990)^2, fuel exports, ethnic fragmentation, ODA2000 and regional dummies
ECA: Europe and Central Asia; MENA: Middle East and North Africa.

percentage of GDP using current exchange rates. Aid is measured in US$, but national GDPs are given in national currencies, and therefore the latter must be converted (into US$). However conversion by means of current exchange rates can generate large and artificial fluctuations in the aid/GDP ratio. To avoid this problem, we have also calculated these ratios by converting national GDPs into PPP US$.[1] The results obtained are quite similar to those shown above, although it must be noted that the squared aid parameter increases its significance (Table 7.2, columns 3 and 4).

Another possible source of bias stems from the use of the World Bank Governance Indicators. These indicators measure each country's institutional quality in relative rather than absolute terms, normalizing each value with respect to the sample average, which by construction is zero. Since the rest of variables are measured in absolute terms, we have re-estimated the model with all variables transformed to relative terms

Table 7.3   Aid-inclusive determinants of institutional quality (II)

Variable	ODA		ODA and ODA^2		ODA (PPP)		ODA and ODA^2 (PPP)	
	Value	t-ratio	Value	t-ratio	Value	t-ratio	Value	t-ratio
Per capita GDP	0.36	2.60	0.48	3.10	0.41	2.51	0.49	3.01
Gini Index	−0.58	−1.97	−0.6	−2.08	−0.6	−2.08	−0.64	−2.25
Taxes	0.66	2.79	0.58	2.49	0.61	2.36	0.55	2.37
Education	0.31	1.50	0.27	1.40	0.28	1.38	0.28	1.47
ODA	0.17	1.22	0.862	2.16	0.19	1.37	0.774	2.08
ODA^2			−0.277	−1.79			−1.409	−1.99
ECA	−0.42	−2.68	−0.35	−2.2	−0.4	−2.48	−0.36	−2.21
MENA	−0.55	−2.58	−0.61	−3.5	−0.56	−2.78	−0.57	−3.27
N	79		79		79		79	
Centred R^2	0.79		0.81		0.80		0.81	
Underidentification test (Kleibergen-Paap rk LM statistic (P-value)	0.0331		0.0388		0.0548		0.0623	
Hansen J statistic (overidentification) (P-value)	0.1261		0.1662		0.1243		0.1768	

Notes:
Endogenous: Per capita GDP, Gini Index, taxes, ODA2005 and (ODA2005)^2
Instruments: Per capita GDP 1990, (Per capita GDP 1990)^2, fuel exports, ethnic
fragmentation, ODA2000, (ODA2000)^2 and regional dummies
ECA: Europe and Central Asia; MENA: Middle East and North Africa.

(dividing each country's value by the sample average). As shown in Table 7.3, the main conclusions remain unchanged.

Note that regional dummies in Tables 7.2 and 7.3 are all negative and statistically significant – indicating that country characteristics of transition and Middle East and North African countries have a negative effect on institutional quality.

THE IMPACT OF AID ON TAXES

As stated above, taxes are an important factor determining institutional quality. A sound tax system provides the resources necessary for building high quality institutions, also enabling the consolidation of a social contract that gives rise to a more demanding relationship between state and citizens. As pointed by the OECD (2008): 'Tax is not the sole determinant of rapid development but it is one pillar of an effective state, and may also provide the basis for accountable and responsive democratic systems.'

Some scholars have argued that aid can damage the capacity of states to create a sound tax system. Since taxes can be unpopular and more subject to social scrutiny, governments may be induced to use aid as a substitute for taxes or as a means for delaying tax reforms. In such cases, aid can depress tax revenues. However, empirical research is inconclusive on this subject. Pioneering studies found a negative impact of aid on tax revenues (Heller, 1975; Cashel-Cordo and Craig, 1990; Khan and Hoshino, 1992), but more recent works are more ambiguous.[2] For example, Bräutigam and Knack (2004) report that aid reduces tax revenue in the recipient country, while Gupta (2007) and Brun et al. (2007) find a positive relationship between aid and revenue performance. Finally, Morrissey et al. (2007), Teera and Hudson (2004) and Ouattara (2006) do not find any robust effect of aid on tax revenues.

In our opinion, three main shortcomings can be identified in the literature on the aid–tax revenue nexus. Firstly, while some works do explicitly investigate the impact of variables other than aid on tax revenue, key variables are missing in others. Empirical research has identified income per capita, the share of agriculture and fuel/mining sectors in GDP, international openness and inflation as key determinants of tax revenue (although the effect of some of these variables is ambiguous). However, some studies on the aid–tax revenue nexus do not include these variables in their regressions. Secondly, the literature on the impact of aid on development has stressed that this impact depends on the quality of institutions, and therefore a multiplicative variable should be included. Some works, like Brun et al. (2007), have incorporated this multiplicative variable into their regressions, but many others have not. Finally, there is a serious problem in most studies using cross-country data sets: they employ central government data provided by the IMF Government Finance Statistics, or by the World Bank Development Indicators. For countries that are highly decentralized and/or where social contributions amount to a significant percentage of GDP, the use of central government data may lead to very inaccurate estimates and conclusions. As an example of this last shortcoming, let us quote the work by Gupta (2007), who states that: '. . . countries like Argentina, Brazil, Peru, Panama, United Arab Emirates, etc. have revenue performance indices well below 0.75, which suggests that they have yet to achieve their full revenue potential'.

This is a clear-cut example of misleading conclusions stemming from the use of central government data. On average for the period 1996–2006, central government tax revenue in Brazil reached 14.2 per cent of GDP; a figure that seems to support Gupta's findings. Yet Brazil is a very decentralized country where social contributions amount to a large percentage of GDP. Indeed, general government tax revenue (including social contributions) is 30.4 per cent of GDP, more than twice as large as central government revenue and very close to the tax revenue of some rich countries. So in other words, Brazil is not far from reaching its revenue potential, as stated by Gupta; in fact the opposite is true. The same error occurs with respect to some other countries that, according to Gupta, have failed to achieve their revenue potential: Argentina, Colombia, Costa Rica, Panama, Slovak Republic or Lithuania.

To our knowledge, only Gupta et al. (2003) point out this problem but they consider it appropriate to use central government data, on the grounds that: 'Since most foreign assistance is routed through the central government Budget, the nonavailability of data on revenue collected at the subnational level should not be a major handicap.'[3]

Still, the argument is extremely weak. It holds true only for single-country studies, where central government revenues are independent of regional government revenues, and only for a sample period when the territorial financing system has not been reformed. Finally, it should be noted that, to our knowledge, Brun et al. (2007) is the only non-regional cross-country analysis in the tax-aid literature not using the IMF Government Finance Statistics or the World Bank Development Indicators. They build up their own database, but unfortunately they do not specify whether general or central government tax revenues are employed.

TAX REVENUE DETERMINANTS AND THE IMPACT OF AID ON TAXES: NEW ESTIMATES

In order to investigate the impact of aid on taxes, we shall first analyse how well the traditional tax determinants identified in the literature explain revenues in our dataset. With this aim, we have considered as explanatory variables income per capita, metal and fuel exports, agriculture, urban population, openness rate and inflation rate. In addition, we have included another variable that, in our opinion, may have a significant impact on tax revenues: income distribution. A very unequal income distribution can encourage the informal economy, increase fiscal evasion and favour the resistance of the elites to pay taxes and implement tax reforms. Income distribution has been rarely considered as a factor conditioning tax revenue in the aid–taxes empirical research. In this sense, one must consider the work by Gupta (2007), who finds that the tax structure influences tax revenue: as the weight of direct taxes increases, so does total revenue. According to his interpretation, since indirect taxes tend to be regressive, they exacerbate inequality and reduce the tax base.[4] However, the tax structure is a poor proxy for income distribution, so we prefer to use the Gini index as a measure of income distribution. Unfortunately, since no single database covers enough countries and years, income distribution has been considered to be constant over time for each country.[5]

Our panel covers developed and developing countries, the number of which varies across estimates, since it is an unbalanced panel. The sample period ranges from 1996 to 2007, and each variable has been computed as a three-year average. Therefore, there are four time observations for each variable and country, which means that the time dimension of our panel is small. Unfortunately accurate data are lacking not only for Gini indices, but for tax revenues as well. On the other hand, this time period allows us to employ the World Bank Governance Indicators as institutional quality proxies, which, in our opinion, are more accurate than other indicators, having a longer time dimension. In addition, since we have only one observation per country for the Gini index, we have also estimated the different models using the database employed in the institutional quality regressions. Finally, it must be noted that aid, income distribution, and income per capita are considered endogenous. The former two need no further explanation, and with respect to the latter, taxes can indirectly impact on income through institutional quality, as shown above.

With regard to cross-country estimates, only three variables are significant in the OLS regression (Table 7.4): income per capita, income distribution, and inflation (with a positive sign). Due to collinearity problems between agriculture and urban population, we have re-estimated the model dropping the last variable, but the results change only slightly. When we estimate using instrumental variables (IVs), the main conclusions still hold.

Regarding the panel database, income per capita and income distribution are significant and show the expected sign both in OLS and in IV regressions. Inflation is only significant when we use instrumental variables and openness when we employ OLS (Table 7.5). In the fixed effects regression no variable is significant (Table 7.6) since this estimation technique does not take into account information across countries, but only over time. Hence fixed effects estimation may be misleading if the time dimension of the panel is short. Therefore, when we use random effects, income per capita, openness and the Gini index become significant (the latter at 90 per cent probability) and show the expected sign. In addition, the Hausman test indicates that random effects should be used.

Table 7.4   Determinants of tax revenue: cross-section

Variable	OLS				IV			
	Value	t-ratio	Value	t-ratio	Value	t-ratio	Value	t-ratio
Per capita GDP	0.25	3.10	0.24	−3.28	0.27	2.20	0.23	2.49
Gini Index	−0.32	−2.19	−0.32	−2.25	−0.90	−3.02	−1.01	−3.82
Fuel and metals	−0.05	−1.56	−0.05	−1.73	0.01	0.61	0.01	0.21
Agriculture	−0.08	−1.10	−0.08	−1.09	−0.02	−0.29	−0.02	−0.29
Urban population	−0.02	−0.22			−0.09	−0.63		
Openness rate	0.02	0.21	0.02	0.15	0.12	1.61	0.11	1.40
Inflation	0.01	2.54	0.01	2.54	0.01	2.94	0.01	2.82
N	91		91		88		88	
Adjusted R^2 (centred in IV)	0.52		0.53		0.51		0.49	
Underidentification test (Kleibergen-Paap rk LM statistic (P-value)					0.0		0.0	
Hansen J statistic (overidentification) (P-value)					0.41		0.30	

Notes:
Endogenous: GDP per capita, Gini index
Instruments: Per capita GDP 1990, (Per capita GDP 1990)^2, ethnic fragmentation, regional dummy for Eastern Europe
Robust estimates.

Finally, if we use dynamic panel techniques, only agriculture becomes significant in the dif-GMM regression, while no variable is significant in the sys-GMM regression (Table 7.7). In our opinion, this result cannot be interpreted as evidence of the irrelevance of the variables considered in our estimation, but rather as a consequence of the short time dimension of our panel and the fact that one of the most powerful explanatory variables (the Gini index) has been held constant, due to the lack of data.

In view of these results, it seems reasonable to drop urban population from the estimates, since it is never significant and it correlates with agriculture and GDP per capita. On the other hand, fixed effects estimates do not seem to be appropriate, since this technique reduces the panel information to a large extent (exploiting time information but not cross-country information), the Gini index parameter cannot be estimated and the Hausman test suggests that the use of random effects is more efficient. OLS regressions do not seem adequate either, since they raise problems

Table 7.5 Determinants of tax revenue: pooled panel

Variable	OLS				IV			
	Value	t-ratio	Value	t-ratio	Value	t-ratio	Value	t-ratio
Per capita GDP	0.22	6.54	0.24	7.89	0.37	2.58	0.37	2.90
Gini Index	−0.54	−6.75	−0.53	−6.67	−0.78	−3.22	−0.78	−3.21
Fuel and metals	−0.004	−0.35	−0.001	−0.1	0.004	0.26	0.001	0.09
Agriculture	−0.01	−0.43	−0.02	−0.52	0.12	1.10	0.13	1.03
Urban population	0.05	1.07			−0.06	−0.46		
Openness rate	0.10	2.97	0.10	2.98	0.09	1.91	0.02	1.10
Inflation	0.02	1.28	0.02	1.42	0.02	1.46	0.03	2.90
N	427		427		425		423	
Adjusted R^2 (centred in IV)	0.59		0.59		0.56		0.56	
Underidentification test (Kleibergen-Paap rk LM statistic (P-value)					0.0		0.0	
Hansen J statistic (overidentification) (P-value)					Equation exactly identified		Equation exactly identified	

Notes:
Endogenous: GDP per capita, Gini index
Instruments: ethnic fragmentation, regional dummy for Eastern Europe (due to over-identification problems, per capita GDP 1990 and its squared value were eliminated as instruments)
Robust estimates.

of endogeneity. Finally, dynamic panel techniques must also be excluded, since all explanatory variables (even GDP per capita) are non-significant, the time period is short (10 years and four observations per country) and the panel is very unbalanced.

In fact, only two variables seem robust: income per capita and income distribution (and to a lesser extent inflation, but its sign is contrary to expected, according to the Tanzi-Olivera effect).[6] If income per capita is considered the only independent variable, the R^2 reaches 0.23–0.30 (Table 7.8). If we add the Gini index to the regression, it increases to 0.49–0.57, while the inclusion of the rest of the variables only accounts for a marginal increase of the R^2. In short, income per capita and income distribution are the most powerful explanatory variables of the tax revenue differences across countries.

Having analysed the tax revenue determinants, we can now incorporate aid into the model. With this aim, we have considered ODA as

Table 7.6   Determinants of tax revenue: fixed and random effects

	Fixed effects				Random effects			
	Value	t-ratio	Value	t-ratio	Value	t-ratio	Value	t-ratio
Per capita GDP	1.09	0.50	1.60	1.74	0.33	1.81	0.31	2.51
Gini Index					−0.76	−1.42	−0.87	−1.70
Fuel and metals	−0.01	−0.36	−0.01	−0.58	0.01	1.19	0.01	1.22
Agriculture	0.30	0.43	0.45	1.48	0.08	0.95	0.07	0.76
Urban population	0.30	0.32			0.03	0.16		
Openness rate	−0.12	−0.24	−0.23	−0.96	0.08	2.09	0.07	1.98
Inflation	0.02	0.49	0.02	1.25	0.01	0.83	0.01	0.95
N	425		425		425		425	
Groups (average per group)	118 (3.6)		118 (3.6)		118 (3.6)		118 (3.6)	
R^2 (overall)	0.51		0.50		0.58		0.58	
Hausman Test	0.89		0.79		0.89		0.79	

Notes:
Endogenous: GDP per capita, Gini index
Instruments: ethnic fragmentation, regional dummy for Eastern Europe and birth rate
(birth rate is included as instrument because otherwise the GDP per capita coefficient
could not be estimated in the fixed effects regression, since the rest of instruments are
constant)
Robust estimates.

endogenous, using as instruments birth rate (as indicator of recipient
needs) and population (as proxy for donors' interest).[7] The main findings
are reported in Table 7.9. First, the impact of aid is positive in all estimations, but it is only significant (at 90 per cent probability) in the cross-
section and pooled regressions. However, cross-section estimates are not
very robust, since the aid coefficient is much higher than those computed
using the panel sample, and the R^2 is much lower than that found in the
previous equation. Second, income per capita and income distribution are
significant in all cases. Finally, regarding the remaining variables, openness is significant in all regressions (at 90 per cent probability in panel
regressions), while inflation is significant in the cross-section and pooled
regressions, but not when random effects are used.

In sum, although its sign is positive, aid does not seem to have a robust
impact on tax revenue, once we have controlled for other potential determinants of tax revenue and all government levels have been taken into
account.[8] Still, some researchers have pointed out that, as with regard
to growth, the impact of aid on taxes can be conditioned by institutional quality. For example, Azam et al. (1999) build a theoretical model

Table 7.7   Determinants of tax revenue: dynamic panel

Variable	Dif-GMM, two-step (robust)				Sys-GMM, two-step (robust)			
	Value	t-ratio	Value	t-ratio	Value	t-ratio	Value	t-ratio
Lagged tax revenue	0.302	0.48	0.692	3.44	0.846	3.08	0.766	4.25
Per capita GDP	0.127	1.10	0.108	1.29	0.123	1.34	0.041	0.46
Gini Index	−0.083	−0.23	−0.060	−0.27	0.327	0.96	0.214	0.64
Fuel and metals	0.005	0.34	0.010	0.74	0.020	1.53	0.019	1.33
Agriculture	−0.063	−2.87	−0.066	−2.78	−0.058	−1.38	−0.053	−1.04
Urban population	0.339	0.49			−0.479	−1.56		
Openness rate	0.024	0.30	0.078	1.27	0.089	1.45	0.089	1.03
Inflation	0.029	1.71	0.020	1.00	0.025	1.21	0.021	0.95
Groups (average per group)	108	(1.82)	108	(1.82)	115	(2.71)	115	(2.71)
N instruments	15		14		19		18	

Note: Additional instruments: ethnic fragmentation, regional dummy for Eastern Europe and birth rate.

Table 7.8   A comparison of the R^2

Independent variable	Cross-section		Pooled		Random effects
	OLS	IV	OLS	IV	IV
Only GDP per capita	0.31	0.32	0.29	0.23	0.30
GDP per capita and Gini index	0.53	0.49	0.57	0.54	0.57
All variables	0.53	0.49	0.59	0.56	0.58

including the interaction between aid and institutional quality. Empirical research that includes an interaction variable is scarce. Gupta et al. (2003) investigate the impact of aid on tax revenue by constructing sub-samples according to corruption levels. They find that the positive impact of loans on tax revenue decreases as corruption rises. Brun et al. (2007) include in their regressions as an independent variable the cross-product of aid by institutional quality. This variable turns out to be positive in the case of bureaucracy quality.

We have followed the approach suggested by Brun et al. (2007), incorporating into our previous regressions the cross-product of aid by institutional

Table 7.9   Aid-inclusive determinants of tax revenue

Variable	IV cross-section		IV pooled panel		IV RE panel	
	Value	t-ratio	Value	t-ratio	Value	t-ratio
Per capita GDP	0.46	2.16	0.37	5.77	0.37	4.56
Gini Index	−0.83	−3.22	−0.88	−10.03	−0.86	−5.14
Fuel and metals	0.01	1.15	−0.003	−0.18	0.01	1.12
Agriculture	−0.05	−0.32	0.07	1.21	0.09	1.73
Openness rate	0.24	2.66	0.07	1.71	0.07	1.93
Inflation	0.009	2.48	0.04	2.06	0.009	0.85
ODA	0.22	1.72	0.04	1.9	0.02	0.92
N	87		423		423*	
Centred R^2	0.35		0.54		0.57 (overall)	
Underidentification test (Kleibergen-Paap rk LM statistic (P-value)	0.0		0.0			
Hansen J statistic (overidentification) (P-value)	0.73		0.59			

Notes:
*117 groups; avg. per group 3.6
Endogenous: GDP per capita, Gini index, ODA
Instruments: per capita GDP 1990, (Per capita GDP 1990)^2, ethnic fragmentation, regional dummies, birth rate and population
Robust estimates.

quality, using for the latter the World Bank Governance Indicators average. Although this product is composed of endogenous variables, it has been considered exogenous for the following reasons. First, aid and institutional quality move in opposite directions. Second, the correlation coefficient between the cross-product of aid by institutional quality and aid is −0.16, and 0.32 between that product and institutional quality. In other words, it is acceptably low. Third, the correlation coefficients between the residuals and the cross-product of aid by institutional quality are also small, especially in the random effects regression, suggesting that there are no endogeneity problems. Finally, according to the Wu-Hausman Test, the cross-product of aid by institutional quality can be considered exogenous.

According to our estimates, aid and the cross-product of aid by institutional quality are positive in all regressions (with at least 95 per cent probability) (Table 7.10). This means that aid contributes to increase tax revenues, but its effect can be amplified, reduced or even reversed by the quality of

Table 7.10   Aid- and institutions-inclusive determinants of tax revenue: instrumental values estimation with current US$

Variable	IV cross-section		IV pooled panel		IV RE panel	
	Value	t-ratio	Value	t-ratio	Value	t-ratio
Per capita GDP	0.64	3.54	0.36	5.38	0.36	5.29
Gini Index	−0.69	−2.59	−0.92	−10.22	−0.92	−7.53
Fuel and metals	−0.003	−0.19	−0.004	−0.28	−0.004	−0.36
Agriculture	0.15	1.19	0.07	1.16	0.07	1.22
Openness rate	0.20	1.89	0.04	1.11	0.04	1.11
Inflation	0.007	1.49	0.04	2.48	0.04	2.25
ODA	0.37	2.26	0.07	2.20	0.07	2.78
ODA * Inst. Qual.	0.32	1.77	0.06	2.06	0.06	3.29
N	87		423		423*	
Centred R^2	0.34		0.55		0.56 (overall)	
Underidentification test (Kleibergen-Paap rk LM statistic (P-value)	0.08		0.00			
Hansen J statistic (overidentification) (P-value)	0.63		0.36			
Wu-Hausman Test (P-value)	0.45		0.22			
Correlation Aid * Inst. Qual. / residuals (absolute value)	0.14		0.24		0.03	

Notes:
*117 groups; avg. per group 3.6
Endogenous: GDP per capita, Gini, ODA
Instruments: Per capita GDP 1990, (Per capita GDP 1990)^2, ethnic fragmentation, regional dummies, birth rate and population
Robust estimates.

governance institutions. Since governance indicators range between –2.5 and 2.5, the net effect can be negative for those countries with an institutional quality below –1.1. Regarding the rest of the variables, income per capita and income distribution are significant and show the expected sign in all regressions, while inflation is significant in panel estimates and openness in the cross-section regression (at 90 per cent probability).

As we stated above, measuring national GDPs in current US$ can generate artificial variations in the aid/GDP ratios across countries and over time. In addition, since institutional quality is measured in relative terms, the rest of variables should be relative as well. To check out whether these

Table 7.11   Aid- and institutions-inclusive determinants of tax revenue: instrumental values estimation with PPP$

Variable	IV cross-section		IV pooled panel		IV RE panel	
	Value	t-ratio	Value	t-ratio	Value	t-ratio
Per capita GDP	0.54	3.13	0.33	4.73	0.33	5.34
Gini Index	−0.62	−2.96	−0.90	−9.71	−0.87	−6.29
Fuel and metals	−0.04	−1.14	−0.02	−0.95	0.002	0.18
Agriculture	0.07	0.67	0.04	0.58	0.05	1.02
Openness rate	0.13	1.75	0.04	1.05	0.07	1.58
Inflation	0.006	1.68	0.04	2.01	0.02	1.32
ODA	0.75	2.49	0.24	2.22	0.19	2.20
ODA * Inst. Qual.	0.56	1.90	0.24	2.40	0.18	2.72
N	87		348		348*	
Centred R^2	0.46		0.57		0.63 (overall)	
Underidentification test (Kleibergen-Paap rk LM statistic (P-value)	0.04		0.00			
Hansen J statistic (overidentification) (P-value)	0.78		0.60			
Wu-Hausman Test (P-value)	0.25		0.37			
Correlation Aid * Inst. Qual. / residuals (absolute value)	0.15		0.24		0.04	

Notes:
*87 groups, 4 obs. per group
Endogenous: GDP per capita, Gini, ODA
Instruments: Per capita GDP 1990, (Per capita GDP 1990)^2, ethnic fragmentation, regional dummies, birth rate and population
Robust estimates.

measurement errors could bias the results obtained in previous estimates, we have re-estimated the former equation by dividing all observations by the sample average and using PPP US$ GDPs. Unfortunately, this implies that the panel must be balanced (otherwise relative variables can change simply due to changes in the sample), which in turn means a significant loss of observations. According to the new estimates, the conclusions obtained above still hold (Table 7.11). Aid and the cross-product of aid by institutional quality are positive and significant in all regressions. With regard to the rest of variables, income and income distribution are significant and show the expected sign, while openness rate and inflation lose robustness.

Table 7.12   Aid- and institutions-inclusive determinants of tax revenue: random effects

Variable	Whole sample		ODA recipient countries	
	Value	t-ratio	Value	t-ratio
Per capita GDP	0.48	10.90	0.37	5.37
Gini Index	−0.91	−13.07	−0.76	−5.53
Fuel and metals	0.03	3.39	0.02	2.28
Agriculture	0.22	1.23	0.09	1.38
Openness rate	0.02	0.77	0.09	2.15
Inflation	0.02	1.94	0.01	0.55
ODA	0.05	2.92	0.04	1.95
ODA * Inst. Qual.	0.03	2.73	0.03	2.00
N	423*		289*	
Overall R^2	0.87		0.80	

Notes:
*117 groups, 3.6 obs. per group
**85 groups, 3.4 obs. per group
Endogenous: GDP per capita, Gini, ODA
Instruments: ethnic fragmentation, regional dummies, birth rate and population
Countries with a positive dummy (95 per cent): Brazil, Burundi, Comoros, Djibouti, Kenya, Lesotho, Moldova, Morocco, South Africa, Swaziland, Uzbekistan, Vietnam, Zambia
Countries with a negative dummy (95 per cent): Albania, Bangladesh, Bhutan, Cambodia, Egypt, Guinea-Bissau, Iran, N. Korea, Kyrgyz Republic, Lao, Mexico, Tanzania, Venezuela
Robust estimates.

Finally, let us remark that the coefficients of determination of the previous estimations are relatively low, reaching a maximum value of about 0.6. This means that something important is missing. One possible reason is that, although tax revenues have common determinants, they can also have country-specific factors. In other words, tax/GDP ratios are also influenced by political, social and historical issues particular to some countries, which are not captured either by regional dummies or by random effects. In fact, we have detected some important outliers in the sample employed. As shown in Tables 7.12 and 7.13, the inclusion of some country dummies significantly increases the coefficient of determination. Regarding the coefficients of aid and the cross-product of aid by institutional quality, they are positive and significant.

Table 7.13   Aid- and institutions-inclusive determinants of tax revenue: random effects (using PPP ODA, all variables are in relative terms)

Variable	Whole sample		ODA recipient countries	
	Value	t-ratio	Value	t-ratio
Per capita GDP	0.46	8.77	0.42	3.18
Gini Index	−0.90	−10.87	−0.75	−2.43
Fuel and metals	0.02	1.95	0.02	1.59
Agriculture	0.14	3.56	0.04	0.61
Openess rate	0.01	0.39	0.02	0.26
Inflation	0.03	2.30	0.02	1.35
ODA	0.28	3.41	0.36	2.15
ODA * Inst. Qual.	0.21	3.29	0.27	2.28
N	348*		234**	
Overall R^2	0.87		0.80	

Notes:
*87 groups, 4 obs. per group
**62 groups, 4 obs. per group
Endogenous: GDP per capita, Gini, ODA
Instruments: ethnic fragmentation, regional dummies, birth rate and population
Countries with a positive dummy (95 per cent): Brazil, Comoros, Kenya, Lesotho, Moldova, Morocco, South Africa, Vietnam, Zambia
Countries with a negative dummy (95 per cent): Bangladesh, Bhutan, Egypt, Guinea-Bissau, Iran, Korea, Mexico, Venezuela
Robust estimates.

CONCLUDING REMARKS

In the first part of this chapter we pointed out the shortcomings that, in our opinion, affect most of the empirical research studying the impact of aid on institutional quality. On the one hand, a prior analysis on the determinants of institutional quality is usually omitted and, as a consequence, a serious problem of omitted variable bias can emerge. On the other, the literature on the growth–aid nexus has shown that the impact of aid on income is subject to decreasing returns, and therefore this could also be the case for institutional quality. In sum, prior to analysing the impact of aid on institutional quality, the determinants of the latter must be investigated. Otherwise, empirical findings may mask the true relation between aid and the quality of governance institutions.

To this end, we have first singled out the four properties that, according to Alonso and Garcimartín (2010), define institutional quality: static efficiency, dynamic efficiency, legitimacy and predictability. On the basis of these properties, four main determinants of institutional quality can be identified: development level, income distribution, tax revenue and education. Development fosters good institutions. In addition, high-quality institutions are expected to develop in equitable societies with a sound tax system and educated population. Once these factors were identified, we incorporated aid into the Alonso and Garcimartín model (2010). According to our findings, aid impacts positively on institutional quality but with decreasing returns. In highly aid-dependent countries, the impact can be negative.

The second part of the chapter was devoted to the analysis of the effect of aid on tax revenue – taking issue with the argument that aid reduces the incentives to mobilize tax revenues. Although the empirical evidence in this respect is ambiguous, in our opinion it shows three main shortcomings in existing literature. First, some of the works do not control for all relevant variables. Second, only in a few cases is the possibility considered that the effect of aid on taxes is conditional upon the quality of governance institutions. Third, most if not all of the research that uses cross-country or panel data considers only central government revenue. In samples including highly-decentralized countries and/or nations where social contributions amount to a high percentage of GDP, as is usually the case, this can lead to important estimation errors. In fact, our estimates suggest that, once these factors are taken into account, aid has a positive impact on tax revenues, and this impact is dependent on the quality of governance institutions. However, given the limitations of our database, this result must be taken cautiously.

Finally, let us remark that, according to our research, a sound tax system improves institutional quality, which in turn favours the impact of aid on the former. In addition, aid contributes to raising the quality of institutions, thus further generating an indirect impact on taxes. In other words, our estimates reveal a complex set of relations between aid, taxes and institutional quality, which can generate either vicious or virtuous circles – with the vicious circle more likely to be the case in low-income low-governance-quality countries.

NOTES

1. Djankov et al. (2009) also measure the aid/GDP ratio in PPP terms.
2. See Brun et al. (2007) for a survey on the aid-tax revenue nexus.
3. Bird et al. (2004) also point out that the use of central government data can lead to an underestimation of tax revenues in those countries where subnational governments are important. However, they use central government data in their analysis.

4. Bird et al. (2004) also find that inequality decreases tax revenue, but their result is not very robust.
5. Since our sample period is not very long (ranging from 1996 to 2007) and income distribution changes occur very slowly, we do not believe that holding the Gini index constant can create serious problems.
6. According to the Tanzi-Olivera effect, in an inflationary environment, tax revenues can decrease in real terms due to the lag between tax payments and tax obligations.
7. As indicators of recipient needs, also employed were infant mortality, fertility rate and life expectancy. Since the results obtained did not change much, we decided to use birth rate, given that more data were available for this variable.
8. We also implemented the same regressions using as control variables only income per capita and income distribution. Concerning ODA, the estimates were similar to those in Table 7.9.

REFERENCES

Acemoglu, D., S. Johnson and J.A. Robinson (2001), 'The colonial origins of comparative development: an empirical investigation', *American Economic Review*, **91** (5), 1369–1401.
Acemoglu, D., S. Johnson and J.A. Robinson (2002), 'Reversal of fortunes: geography and institutions in the making of the modern world income distribution', *Quarterly Journal of Economics*, **117** (4), 1231–1294.
Alesina, A. and R. Perotti (1996), 'Income distribution, political instability and investment', *European Economic Review*, **40** (6), 1203–1228.
Alesina, Alberto and Dani Rodrik (1993), 'Income distribution and economic growth: a simple theory and some empirical evidence', in Alex Cukierman, Zvi Hercovitz and Leonardo Leiderman (eds), *The Political Economy of Business Cycles and Growth*, Cambridge, MA: MIT Press.
Alesina, A. and B. Weder (2002), 'Do corrupt governments receive less foreign aid?', *American Economic Review*, **92**, 1126–1137.
Alesina, A., A. Devleeschauwer, W. Easterly and S. Kurlat (2003), 'Fractionalization', *Journal of Economic Growth*, **8** (2), 155–194.
Alonso, J.A. (2007), 'Inequality, institutions and progress: a debate between history and the present', *CEPAL Review*, **93**, 61–80.
Alonso, J.A. and C. Garcimartín (forthcoming), 'The determinants of institutional quality. More on the debate', *Journal of International Development*.
Azam, J.P., S. Devarajan and S.A. O'Connell (1999), 'Aid dependence reconsidered', *Policy Research Working Paper*, **2144**, The World Bank.
Barro, R.J. and J-W. Lee (2000), 'International data on educational attainment: updates and implications', NBER Working Paper 7911, National Bureau of Economic Research, Cambridge, MA.
Bird, R.M., J. Martinez-Vazquez and B. Torgler (2004), 'Societal institutions and tax effort in developing countries', International Studies Program Working Paper, 04-06.
Bräutigam, Deborah (2000), *Aid Dependence and Governance*, Stockholm, Sweden: Almqvist and Wiksell.
Bräutigam, D. and S. Knack (2004), 'Foreign aid, institutions, and governance in sub-Saharan Africa', *Economic Development and Cultural Change*, **52** (2), 255–286.

Brun, J.F., G. Chambasand and S. Guerineau (2007), 'Aide et mobilisation fiscale', *Jumbo*, **21**, Agence française de développement (AFD), Paris.

Burnside, C. and D. Dollar (2000), 'Aid, policies and growth', *American Economic Review*, **90**, 847–868.

Cashel-Cordo, P. and S. Craig (1990), 'The public sector impact of international resource transfers', *Journal of Development Economics*, **32**, 17–42.

Chong A. and L. Zanforlin (2000), 'Law tradition and institutional quality: some empirical evidence', *Journal of International Development*, **12** (8), 1057–1068.

Djankov, S., J. Montalvo and M. Reynal-Querol (2008), 'The curse of aid', *Journal of Economic Growth*, **13** (3), 169–194.

Durbarry, D.C., R.N. Gemmell and D. Greenaway (1998), 'New evidence on the impact of foreign aid on economic growth', *CREDIT Research Paper*, **8**.

Easterly, W. (2001), 'The middle class consensus and economic development', *Journal of Economic Growth*, **6** (4), 317–335.

Easterly, W. and R. Levine (2003), 'Tropics, germs, and crops: how endowment influences economic development', *Journal of Monetary Economics*, **50** (1), 3–39.

Engerman, Stanley and Kenneth Sokoloff (1997), 'Factor endowments: institutions and differential paths of growth among new world economies. A view from economic historians of the United States', in Stephen Haber (ed.), *How Latin America Fell Behind: Essays on the Economic Histories of Brazil and Mexico, 1800–1914*, Stanford, CA: Stanford University Press.

Engerman, S.L. and K.L. Sokoloff (2002), 'Factor endowments, inequality, and paths of development among the new world economies', NBER Working Paper, **9259.**

Engerman, S.L. and K.L. Sokoloff (2005), 'Colonialism, inequality, and long-run paths of development', NBER Working Paper, **11057.**

Engerman, Stanley L. and Kenneth Sokoloff (2006), 'Colonialism, inequality, and long-run paths of development', in Abhijit Banerjee, Ronald Bénabou and Dilip Mookherjee (eds), *Understanding Poverty*, Oxford: Oxford University Press.

Evans, P. and P. Rauch (2000), 'Bureaucratic structure and bureaucratic performance in less developed countries', *Journal of Public Economics*, **75**, 49–71.

Gallup, J.L., J. Sachs and A. Mellinger (1998), 'Geography and economic development', NBER Working Paper, **6849.**

Glaeser, E.L. and R. Sacks (2006), 'Corruption in America', *Journal of Public Economics*, **90** (6–7), 1053–1072.

Glaeser, E. and A. Shleifer (2003), 'The rise of the regulatory state', *Journal of Economic Literature*, **41**, 401–425.

Gómez Sabaini, J.C. (2005), 'Evolución y situación tributaria actual en AL: una serie de temas para la discusión', CEPAL Discussion Paper, available at http://www.eclac.org/publicaciones/xml/1/27951/lcg2324e_CapI.pdf (accessed 1 May 2010).

Gupta, A.S. (2007), 'Determinants of tax revenue efforts in developing countries', IMF Working Paper, **07/184**.

Gupta, S., B. Clements, A. Pivovarsky and E.R. Tiongson (2003), 'Foreign aid and revenue response: does the composition of aid matter?', IMF Working Paper, **WP/03/176.**

Hadjimichael, M.T., D. Ghura, M. Mühleisen, R. Nord and E.M. Uçer (1995),

'Sub-Saharan Africa: growth, savings, and investment, 1986–1993', IMF Occasional Paper, **118.**

Hall, R.E. and C.I. Jones (1999), 'Why do some countries produce so much more output per worker than others?', *Quarterly Journal of Economics*, **114**, 83–116.

Hansen, H. and F. Tarp (1999), *The Effectiveness of Foreign Aid*, Copenhagen, Sweden: Development Economics Research Group, Institute of Economics, University of Copenhagen.

Heller, P.S. (1975), 'A model of public fiscal behaviour in developing countries: aid, investment and taxation', *American Economic Review*, **65** (3), 429–445.

Henisz, W.J. (2000), 'The institutional environment for economic growth', *Economics and Politics*, **12** (1), 1–31.

Islam, Roumeen and Claudio E. Montenegro (2002), 'What determines the quality of institutions?', in *World Development Report: Building Institutions for Markets*, Washington, DC: World Bank.

Ivanova, A., M. Keen and A. Klemm (2005), 'The Russian flat tax reform', IMF Working Paper, **WP/05/16**.

Keefer, P., T. Beck, G. Clarke, A. Groff and P. Walsh (2001), *New Tools and New Tests in Comparative Political Economy: The Database of Political Institutions*, Washington, DC: World Bank.

Khan, H.A. and E. Hoshino (1992), 'Impact of foreign aid on the fiscal behaviour of LDC governments', *World Development*, **20** (10), 1481–1488.

Killick, T. (2004), 'Politics, evidence and the new aid agenda', *Development Policy Review*, **22** (1), 29–53.

Kimbrough, K.P. (1986), 'Foreign aid and optimal fiscal policy', *Canadian Journal of Economics*, **19** (February), 35–61.

Knack, S. (2000), 'Aid dependence and the quality of governance: a cross-country empirical analysis', World Bank Policy Research, Working Paper, **2396**, Washington, DC: World Bank.

Knack, S. and O. Azfar (2003), 'Trade intensity, country size and corruption', *Economic Governance,* **4** (1), 1–18.

La Porta, R., F. López de Silanes, A. Shleifer and R.W. Vishny (1999), 'The quality of government', *Journal of Law, Economics and Organization*, **15** (March), 222–279.

Lesink, R. and H. White (2001), 'Are there negative returns to aid?', *Journal of Development Studies*, **37** (August), 42–65.

McGillivray, M. and O. Morrissey (2000), 'Aid fungibility in assessing aid: red herring or true concern?', *Journal of International Development*, **12** (3), 413–428.

Moore, Mick (1998), 'Death without taxes: democracy, state capacity, and aid dependence in the fourth world', in Gordon White and Mark Robinson (eds), *Towards a Democratic Developmental State*, Oxford: Oxford University Press, pp. 67–88.

Morrissey, O., O. Islei and D. M'Amanja (2007), 'Aid loans versus aid grants: are the effects different?', *CREDIT Research Paper*, **06/07.**

North, Douglass (2005), *Understanding the Process of Economic Change*, Princeton, NJ: Princeton University Press.

OECD (2008), *Governance, Taxation and Accountability Issues and Practices*, Paris: OECD.

Ouattara, B. (2006), 'Foreign aid and government fiscal behaviour in developing countries: panel data evidence', *Economic Modelling*, **23** (3), 506–514.

Rajan, R.G. and A. Subramanian (2005), 'Aid and growth: what does the cross-country evidence really show?', IMF Working Paper, **05/127.**

Remmer, K.L. (2004), 'Does foreign aid promote the expansion of government?', *The American Journal of Political Science*, **48** (1), 77–92.

Rigobon, R. and D. Rodrik (2004), 'Rule of law, democracy, openness, and income: estimating the interrelationships', NBER Working Paper, **10750.**

Rodrik, D., A. Subramanian and F. Trebbi (2002), 'Institutions rule: the primacy of institutions over geography and integration in economic development', IMF Working Paper, **02/189**.

Sachs, J. and A. Warner (1997), 'Sources of slow growth in African economies', *Journal of African Economies*, **6**, 335–376.

Tavares, J. and R. Wacziarg (2001), 'How democracy affects growth', *European Economic Review,* **45** (8), 1341–1378.

Teera, J. and J. Hudson (2004), 'Tax performance: a comparative study', *Journal of International Development,* **16** (6), 785–802.

Tilly, Charles (1992), *Coercion, Capital and European States, AD 990–1992*, Cambridge, MA: Basil Blackwell.

Treisman, D. (2000), 'The causes of corruption: a cross-national study', *Journal of Public Economics,* **76** (3), 399–457.

Varsakelis, N.C. (2006), 'Education, political institutions and innovative activity: a cross-country empirical investigation', *Research Policy*, **35**, 1083–1090.

World Bank (1988), *Assessing Aid. What Works, What Doesn't and Why?*, Washington, DC and Oxford: The World Bank/Oxford University Press.

APPENDIX: DATA SOURCES AND DESCRIPTION OF VARIABLES

Determinants of Institutional Quality

All variables are in logs, except ODA and the World Bank Governance Indicators (since they can be zero or negative)

Data used are the same employed in Alonso and Garcimartín (2010), with the exception of fuel (a larger sample has been employed) and ODA:

- Institutional Quality: 2006 World Bank Governance Indicators average.
- Per capita Income: constant PPP per capita GDP. 2004. Source: World Bank.
- Gini Index: latest year available. Source: World Bank.
- Education: average years of school for the population aged over 25 years. Source: Barro and Lee (2000).
- Taxes: for Latin America, Gómez Sabaini (2005) has been employed, except for Venezuela, whose data corresponds to the World Bank. For the OECD countries, OECD. For other countries, two sources have

been used. Firstly, the World Bank in countries for which data is available and reliable. The WB provides data from income tax excluding social security, also providing data for the latter separately. Therefore, these two figures have been added. The University of Michigan World Tax Database is the second source used, in countries for which the WB has no data, http://www.bus.umich.edu/OTPR/otpr/ or where data is not reliable. Data year is 2000. In some cases, where data was not available for a given year, we selected the closest year available, with a maximum difference of three years. When possible, data cover General Government and include social security contributions.

- Ethnic Fragmentation. Source: Alesina et al. (2003).
- Fuel: percentage of fuels, ores, metals, precious stones, and non-monetary gold on total exports. 2004. Source: UNCTAD.
- ODA: 5-year average net ODA less Humanitarian Aid, Food Aid, and Debt Relief. Source: OECD.

Determinants of Tax Revenue

All variables are in logs, except ODA and the World Bank Governance Indicators (since they can be zero or negative) and computed as a 3-year average (except the Gini index and institutional quality).

- Institutional quality: World Bank Governance Indicators average. Before 2002, they are available only for the years 1996, 1998 and 2000. Therefore, for the period 1996–1998 we have computed the 2-year average between 1996 and 1998, while for the period 1999–2001, we have used the value for 2000.
- Taxes:

    a) OECD countries: OECD.
    b) Latin American countries: ECLAC.
    c) African countries: African Development Bank (African Statistical Yearbook), except where otherwise indicated.
    d) Asian countries: Asian Development Bank, except where otherwise indicated.
    e) Bulgaria, Cyprus, Estonia, Latvia, Lithuania, Malta, Romania, and Slovenia: Eurostat.
    f) Croatia: Central Bureau of Statistics.
    g) Russia: Ivanova et al. (2005).
    h) Ukraine: Institute for Economic Research and Policy Consulting.
    i) South Africa: South African Revenue Service.

j)   Tanzania: Tanzania Revenue Authority.
k)   Ethiopia: Ministry of Revenue.
l)   India: Ministry of Finance.
m)   China: National Bureau of Statistics of China.
n)   Nigeria, Senegal, Comoros, Sierra Leone, Armenia, Kazakhstan, Moldova, Syria, Yemen, Brunei, Cambodia, Laos, and Mongolia: IMF Country Reports.
o)   Rest of countries: World Bank WDI.

- Taxes refer to General Government, except for those countries whose data source is AFDB, the World Bank, or ADB (except Bangladesh, Georgia, Kiribati, Kyrgyz Republic, Pakistan, Philippines, Sri Lanka, and Tajikistan, whose data refer to General Government).
- Taxes include social contributions except for Algeria, Angola, Benin, Bhutan, Botswana, Burundi, Cameroon, Central African Republic, Congo D. R., Congo R., Djibouti, Egypt, Equatorial Guinea, Fiji, Gambia, Guinea Bissau, Jamaica, Kenya, Kuwait, Kiribati, Kyrgyz Republic, Laos, Lebanon, Liberia, Madagascar, Malawi, Malaysia, Maldives, Mali, Micronesia, Myanmar, Niger, Papua New Guinea, Philippines, Rwanda, Singapore, Solomon, Sudan, Swaziland, Thailand, Togo, Tonga, Turkmenistan, Tuvalu, Uganda, Uzbekistan, Vanuatu, Vietnam and Zimbabwe. No social contributions data are available for these countries.
- Per capita Income: constant PPP per capita GDP. Source: World Bank
- Gini Index: latest year available. Source: World Bank.
- Fuel: percentage of fuels, ores, metals, precious stones, and non-monetary gold on total exports. 2004. Source: UNCTAD.
- Agriculture: agriculture value added (percentage of GDP). Source: World Bank.
- Urban: Urban population (percentage of total). Source: World Bank.
- Openness rate: exports plus imports as a percentage of GDP. Source: World Bank.
- Inflation: GDP deflator (annual percentage). Source: World Bank.
- Ethnic Fragmentation. Source: Alesina et al. (2003).
- ODA: (percentage of GDP). Net ODA less Humanitarian Aid, Food Aid, and Debt Relief. Source: OECD.
- Population: source: World Bank.
- Birth rate: source: World Bank.

8. Economic governance and full employment

Constantine E. Passaris

INTRODUCTION

The mission and mandate of public policy and its accompanying institutional architecture requires realignment so that governments can respond to challenges posed by two recent economic events: the emergence of the new global economy and the financial crisis of 2008. Whilst the emergence of the new global economy has eroded national borders and increased the degree of policy arbitrage, the financial crisis of 2008 had a devastating effect on growth and employment, challenged the belief in market efficiency and revealed the structural fault lines within contemporary economic governance institutions.

Therefore, we argue in this chapter that the institutional architecture of economic governance requires change with a view to provide an anchor for economic policy options concerning full employment. We propose a new set of guiding principles for economic governance and articulate a road map for achieving full employment which is congruent with the structural parameters of the new global economy.

ECONOMIC GLOBALIZATION AND THE FINANCIAL CRISIS: THE CHALLENGE FOR ECONOMIC GOVERNANCE INSTITUTIONS

The new economy is shaped by three interactive forces, which include financial integration, trade liberalization and the diffusion of the Information and Communications Technology (ICT) revolution. The role of innovation as a catalyst that drives the engine of economic growth has become a fundamental postulate of the new global economy (Passaris, 2006). Furthermore, the pivotal role of a country's human resources and the unique economic value of its human capital endowment (which is reflected in educational attainment, technical competencies and special skills of the population) have become essential prerequisites for empowering the new economy and facilitating the integration of labour in the knowledge-based industries (Passaris, 2001, 2003 and 2006).

With the advent of economic globalization, governance principles, the institutional architecture and a country's economic policies should be adapted to conform to the realities of the global economy. Global economic integration results in diminished national and domestic policy autonomy. This is further accentuated by the existence of multinational and transnational corporations in the private sector that have embraced the benefits of economic globalization for a very long time. Given this context, the modern rules of economic engagement require the adoption of governance principles that provide for achieving often conflicting policy objectives – including fiscal propriety, competitiveness, renewed economic infrastructure, full employment, embracing the ICT revolution, reformatting tax policies, revising the regulatory mechanism and promoting a stable economic environment for domestic and foreign investment.

All of the above suggest that the contemporary economic landscape, in some cases, has increased the responsibilities of national governments; and in other cases, it has modified or renewed them. Therefore, the existing economic governance institutions and architectures require a refit and renewal in some cases and in others a modern economic governance institutional architecture needs to be built from the ground up. The management of these new or renewed governance institutions should also reflect the forces of global economic integration and interdependence.

On the other hand, globalization has also created limitations and reduced the degrees of freedom for governments with respect to economic governance domestically as well as the operational features of the domestic market mechanisms. These constraints can create tensions for domestic and global governance systems, which must be more inclusive, resilient, focused, rule-based and serve as anchors for national and international economic policies.

Given this background, the financial crisis of 2008 took everybody by surprise. In addition, the recovery in the aftermath of the financial crisis has not produced a sustained and significant level of employment creation. Unlike previous regional financial crises there does not appear to be a rebound in employment opportunities. The combination of fiscal deficits, declining tax revenues and the burden of a huge public debt is limiting the ability of governments to engage in expansionary fiscal policies. In addition, the private sector does not look likely to make up for job losses in the public sector. Instead, it tends to increase its profit margins by minimizing its payroll costs during economic recovery (Passaris, 2008).

These post-crisis trends notwithstanding, shortcomings in job-creation functions of both the private and public sector had been visible in the 1990s and 2000s too. The public sector had been cognitive of its role in stimulating the economy, but tended to be guided by a short-term horizon in its job creation strategy. The private sector, on the other hand, responded to globalization by downsizing the labour component of the production process. This may have been necessary to maintain competitiveness in the face of global competition, but it has also had the perverse outcome of giving up on a comprehensive strategy towards full employment.

The adverse consequences of losing sight of the job-creation function are likely to be exacerbated by the looming demographic storm for most advanced industrialized countries. The financial crisis and the subsequent economic crisis have distracted us from the longer term consequences of a forthcoming demographic and labour market crisis that is bound to have serious consequences. Most advanced industrialized countries have an aging population, which implies an increase in the dependency ratio and the contraction of the economically active portion of the labour force. In some countries the process of addressing this issue has already begun (EFMD, 2007). However, the demographic challenges remain – at least in the form of increased budgeting allocations for pensions, healthcare, social programmes and old age assistance. These challenges are likely to be exacerbated by the advent of the knowledge economy, which requires an elevated threshold of education and training at post-secondary level, including university degrees, community college certificates or diplomas, apprenticeship, industry credentials or professional qualifications. This trend is predicted to continue into the future (Gordon, 2009).

THE ECONOMIC GOVERNANCE LESSONS OF THE KEYNESIAN ERA

The advent of Keynesian economics during the second half of the twentieth century was aimed at preventing the repeat of the Great Depression of the 1930s. It would do so by establishing an institutional norm whereby government would play a supportive role in economic decision making and management. More precisely, government along with the private sector would collectively and collaboratively fulfill the fundamental macroeconomic objectives of price stability, employment creation and a high rate of economic growth. This new formula would create the fundamentals for the pursuit of full employment (Passaris, 2008).

The most significant inconsistency in this new context was the potential conflict between political expediency and economic rationale. Governments are elected with a political mandate and consequently develop an opportunistic time frame, usually around four years, in order to confirm their political and economic success that would result in their re-election. On the other hand, achieving the desired macroeconomic objectives requires a longer time frame, certainly in excess of the four year electoral cycle. In consequence, the economic governance institutions that emerged along with and supported the Keynesian economic policy framework were not effective in preventing the short-term political cycle from prevailing at the expense of a longer-term economic time frame (Passaris, 2008).

The conflict between the economic rationale and political consideration that characterized most of the Keynesian era has prompted debate on good governance, which consists of interactive and complementary dimensions such as accountability, transparency, inclusiveness, participation, equality, consensus building and efficiency. Accountability is both a mindset and a goal. The spirit and practice of accountability involves a commitment to announce and defend the actions, policies and legislation of the government so that they can be held up to public scrutiny. Transparency in governance means that the process of decision-making is clear, widely known and has earned the public trust. Furthermore, transparency requires that the decisions taken and their implementation are done in a manner that is consistent, predictable and follows established rules, regulations and guidelines.

The inclusiveness characteristic of good governance dates back to the eminent Greek philosopher Aristotle, who pointed out in the fourth century BC that liberty and equality – the main premises of a democracy – will be best attained 'when all persons alike share in the government to the utmost' (Barnes, 1984, IV.1291b34). Good governance also requires consensus building – a norm that encourages different ideas and varied perspectives to formulate future objectives.

AN ECONOMIC GOVERNANCE APPROACH TO THE CONFLICT BETWEEN ECONOMIC RATIONALE AND POLITICAL EXPEDIENCY

Economic governance is an area of study that analyses how economic governance institutions affect the decisions of economic agents, the design and implementation of public policies and the interaction between the public and private economic spheres. One strand examines the ways in which institutions (understood as formal and informal rules, norms and values), affect economic outcomes through their effects on market structures, collective action outcomes, principal–agent problems, credibility and accountability of public policy and quality of regulation. The other tends to examine bottom-up processes leading to emergence of norms, rules and social networks that function as privately-ordered economic governance institutions (Dixit, 2008).

The economic governance literature may provide some pointers as to how the economic institutions of the twenty-first century could respond to the emergence of the new global economy and the consequences of the financial crisis of 2008. The economic governance framework suggests that the institutional architecture can shape expectations and inform decisions so that economic agents can develop new ways of addressing the structural implications of globalization and post-crisis growth/employment trajectories indicated above. It is now more evident that contemporary issues are multifaceted in their genetic composition and they intertwine economic, social and environmental issues simultaneously. Therefore, they call for novel ways of developing public policy and implementing solutions in a manner that are holistic and comprehensive. The economic governance framework can enable policy-makers and business people to develop such holistic and comprehensive approaches to practical/structural problems because it focuses on methods and rules through which the game that governs the transactions between economic agents is framed. Put differently, it points out the ways in which transaction costs are minimized, conflicts are mitigated and mutual gains are maximized (Williamson, 2005).

It should be underlined that economic governance also shapes the organizational structure that promotes compliance with the legal, statutory and regulatory frameworks. Governance institutions include the machinery of government, the economic and financial markets as well as government agencies, boards and commissions, all of whom formulate and implement principles, norms, rules and decision-making protocols that impact upon the economic behaviour of individuals and groups. It goes without saying that the critical analysis of economic governance as well as the design of new organizational structures must include both the governance organisations and the institutional environment.

As the Keynesian economic policy framework had become dented by the conflict between economic rationale and political expediency, economic governance rules and norms have developed a marked tendency to favour market mechanisms. This translated into privatization, deregulation and an emphasis on quasi-markets as solutions to public-sector inefficiencies. There was a discernable trend towards new forms of contractual arrangements between the government and the private sector and an extension of market instruments into the public sector. Indeed, the public sector became more entrepreneurial in its mission and mandate. This retrenchment has resulted in a sharp decline in government intervention in Canada and the USA as well as a more restricted, limited and targeted reliance of government interventions. It most assuredly has meant a retraction from an influential presence in the organizing and the controlling of production activities to a more peripheral role in the form of a facilitator and catalyst for private sector activities and initiatives. Against this background of downsizing of government economic initiatives and of increased reliance on market mechanisms, the public sector's institutional architecture has been neglected and allowed to atrophy to the point that it has reached a minimalistic state of existence (Passaris, 2008).

Therefore, it can be argued that the economic governance norms and institutions that purportedly emerged to address the major conflict of the Keynesian era have in fact circumvented the conflict and boiled down to pulling the rug from underneath the process of designing and implementing public policy. The occurrence of the financial crisis in 2008 and the lacklustre performance in job creation under globalization are clearly related to this institutional bias. This bias has led to redirection of influence and leadership on the economic landscape to favour the market mechanism and the private sector. All of this has generated an adverse effect on macroeconomic stabilization and employment efforts and the role of the public sector in the economy.

There is no denying that an increase in government failures has shifted the pendulum towards a greater reliance on market mechanisms. One of the most frequently cited reasons for government failure is the inadequacy of the information it can have prior to economic decisions being taken. A second reason for government failure is the lack of direct competition for cost-effectiveness and maintaining a competitive edge that exists in the profit-seeking private sector. Nevertheless, an effective economic governance model in the contemporary context requires a re-examination of the scope and substance of public policy for the purpose of modernizing its thrust and effectiveness – not the demise of government or public policy. Otherwise, we face the risk of losing sight of the synergies between government and the private sector or between economic policy and social policy. What are needed, therefore, are economic governance institutions that promote complementarity and inter-independence between economic policy, social policy and environmental policy in the twenty-first century.

Such institutions are needed for becoming more proactive and incorporating a longer term horizon in the decision-making processes of both governmental and non-governmental economic actors. This is in contrast to the previous mode of governance that was propelled by the electoral cycle which was more suited to a short term and reactive mode. This may take the form of restructuring existing institutions through renewal or institutional innovation or building new ones from the ground up. In addition, technological advances in information and communications have provided a degree of public scrutiny that is unprecedented. They have raised the bar on the interchange between civil society and public institutions. There is no denying that public expectations of government performance are now higher than at any time in the past. Modern technology has resulted in public demand for government disclosure regarding their vision, policies, strategies, performance and actions (Passaris, 2008).

Good economic governance is not a static concept. It should evolve in order to accommodate the structural changes on the economic landscape. Clearly it is a concept that is not only time sensitive but also responsive to societal permeations. In this regard Dixit points out that 'different governance institutions are optimal for different societies, for different kinds of economic activity, and at different times. Changes in underlying technologies of production, exchange and communication change the relative merits of different methods of governance' (Dixit, 2008: 673).

All of this requires redefining the role, functions and modern economic mission of government. Clearly, business as usual is not an option. There is evident need for institutional change, which should support the formulation of enlightened public policy and its strategic implementation. This is necessary to address the shortcomings of the private sector in matching demand for and supply of human resources. The clearing mechanism for human endeavour is different from the trade of physical assets inasmuch as it embraces the risks and benefits of investing in human capital. In this context, the externalities and collective benefits associated with the public sector's purpose in investing in skills and education is manifested in the government's contribution towards promoting and subsidizing the accumulation of individual human capital. This often takes the form of free or subsidized tuition for attendance at schools, community colleges and universities as well as subsidized student loans, government supported worker retraining and skill upgrading and worker mobility programmes. In addition, collateral investments and benefits may take the form of public health programmes, workplace health and safety institutions and subsidized or government provided health care. North American governments have adopted as part of their economic mission a commitment to invest public funds in the creation and dissemination of knowledge.

ECONOMIC GOVERNANCE AND EMPLOYMENT: GETTING THE NORM RIGHT

Unemployed human resources lead to significant economic and social costs for any country. The economic costs include loss of income as well as loss of goods and services to the economy as a whole. The social costs consist of loss of self-esteem and self-worth for the unemployed, and a wide range of associated social consequences such as family break-ups, ill-health and life style choices that have negative effects both on the unemployed themselves and society at large.

At the current juncture, the employment horizon is dotted with what appear to be insurmountable problems. The private sector is downsizing and contributing to massive layoffs. Governments are restructuring and shedding jobs in order to cope with the consequences of the financial crisis for public finances. The demographic trends that combine the retirement of the baby boomers and the decline in the birth rate are causing the labour pool to shrink. Furthermore, the economic recovery that is slowly unfolding is showing signs of remaining a jobless recovery.

These developments are taking place in the context of significant and pervasive structural change, which happens at rare intervals. In fact the last time it happened was more than 200 years ago and it was called the Industrial Revolution. The contemporary transformational change is called the IT revolution, which is impacting not only the economy but every aspect of our daily lives including how we bank, travel, access health care, entertain ourselves and educate ourselves.

On the economic front, there is one significant difference between the IT revolution and the Industrial Revolution. The introduction of machinery into the production process took a 'leisurely' 100 years to complete. The required adjustments and corrections were less hurried and more protracted. In addition, workers who were laid off due to the introduction of new machines found alternative employment in the factories making the machines. The process was without a significant loss to the strategic utilization of the full labour force.

Fast forward to the introduction of information and communications technologies and we notice that structural change is taking place at a faster pace and more abruptly. The IT revolution is not showing any signs of repeating the smooth labour absorption that was experienced during the industrial revolution. That is primarily due to the entry level requirements for the new jobs that are being created in the wake of the introduction of the information and communications technologies into the workplace. The new jobs require higher levels of academic qualifications, specialized skills and new competencies. All of this is creating new barriers for the absorption of workers who are laid off because of the introduction of the new and highly sophisticated technology (Miner, 2010).

Unless we are prepared to live with a lengthy and protracted period of unduly high unemployment, we need to come to grips with the fact that the old model of matching the unemployed with the existing job opportunities is not going to work in the new economy. We need a new employment model that is informed by appropriate institutional norms and responsive to the structural parameters of the new economy at the same time. In what follows, we will highlight the structural parameters of the skills requirements in the new economy, and introduce the institutional norm that could function as an anchor for labour market policy, and propose an employment commission that embodies the institutional norm and is responsive to the skills requirements of the new economy.

The modern economy requires a combination of educational attainment and specialized skills that, in turn, require a more integrated system between universities, community colleges, polytechnics and technical schools. All too often the contemporary labour market demands a university degree as well as a college diploma or certificate. In other words, the modern workforce should be equipped with academic education and employable skills. Governments has been the traditional provider of the infrastructure and programmes for education and skills. In Canada, the private sector is also a source of apprenticeships, in-house training, skills upgrading and other types of company schemes.

While the government has been providing this service, the contribution of the private sector has been minimal and the latter may be criticized for maintaining a benign neglect at best or for engaging in free-riding at worst. It is indeed regrettable that employer-sponsored training has not become a high priority for the industrial sector. The range of reasons provided for this systematic neglect have included lack of government assistance, difficulty in calculating and/or internalizing the benefits from investment in training, a risk of poaching by competitor firms and the high cost of customized training (Hughes and Grant, 2007).

Yet, it is now recognized that skill enhancement and life-long learning are necessary ingredients for competitiveness and growth. For example, the European Foundation for Management Development (EFMD) states that: 'The economy and competitiveness of the companies will much depend on the skills of the workforce. It is mainly in the mind of high skilled workers that we can find innovative solutions and competitive advantage' (EFMD, 2007, p. 10). Furthermore, an article by the Canadian Policy Research Network put it this way: 'The social and economic importance of encouraging adults to engage in continuous learning throughout their working lives is undisputed' (Myers and de Boucher, 2006, p. 1).

On the other hand, and as indicated above, high levels of unemployment, coupled with the shrinkage of the active labour force, pose serious and immediate challenges to developed economies and are destined to do so for emerging market economies in the future. Therefore, the raison d'être of John Maynard Keynes' pre-occupation with unemployment is still a relevant concern. Keynes was not an advocate of 'pump priming' policies that resort to raising aggregate demand through lowering taxes, increasing government spending or reducing interest rates but rather he was in favour of 'targeted' spending programs (Wray, 2009). Keynes' approach to targeted spending concentrated on government spending aimed at enhancing social policy goals as well as government spending in sectors that are operating below capacity – all of this with the overarching objective of reducing unemployment and enhancing aggregate effective demand.

The institutional norm that would inform and anchor the full-employment policy can be developed on the basis of a job guarantee principle. The latter has been discussed by some economists, who argue that the government should act as the employer of last resort by providing employment for every citizen who is able and willing to work. Their work proposes a conceptual model for harnessing the productive capacity of a country's human resources and achieving full employment through a job guarantee at a basic fixed wage (Wray, 2009).

This model incorporates a counter-cyclical and built-in stabilizer feature. More specifically, when the demand for workers declines during an economic downturn it is anticipated that the private sector will contribute to higher unemployment rates which in turn will be absorbed into this government-operated employment programme. Conversely, during an economic upturn the private sector will start hiring workers away from the employment programme. It goes without saying that the budgetary appropriation for this type of employment programme would also follow a counter-cyclical rhythm enhancing the government's stabilizing efforts by ensuring a sustainable level of consumer demand during a robust economy as well as a weak economy (Wray, 2009).

The job guarantee rule should not be considered as only a pragmatic (and hence time-limited) response to perceived problems – it should in fact be considered as a natural component of the third-generation human rights obligations. In effect a job guarantee embraces the economic objective of optimizing a country's economic potential as well as the social dimension of an economic right within the umbrella of modern human rights. Wray and Forstater (2004) argue that the right to work is essential for achieving social justice in as much as income from employment guarantees access to resources for one's livelihood. Some economists also contend that a job is a right in the context of fundamental human rights or natural rights (Wray, 2009). Indeed, these assertions gain validity within the context of international legal statutes such as the United Nations Universal Declaration of Human Rights – especially with the extension of civil and political rights to include social and economic rights.

Advocates of a job guarantee maintain that the free market does not provide efficient mechanisms for full employment and that those who are the most vulnerable in society are penalized disproportionately in terms of access to employment opportunities. They point out that the individual and collective costs of unemployment afflict those members of society who have been marginalized and disadvantaged such as women, aboriginals, persons with disabilities, immigrants, racial and ethnic minorities, younger and older citizens and those with lower educational achievement. In the allocation of human resources within the market system there is also a conflict of a micro and a macro dimension in the sense that the micro-level self-interest of the firm does not necessarily promote the macro-level efficiency for aggregate human resource absorption (Wray, 2009).

The literature points to a lively debate regarding worker remuneration within the proposed job guarantee programme. Some economists recommend a tiered remuneration scale for a public sector job for citizens who are unable to find employment with remuneration approximating a 'market wage' (different from the minimum wage) which allows for a differentiated wage structure based on education and skill level, that is, more highly educated and skilled workers would receive higher pay. Others economists propose a different model for remuneration whereby the government provides the financial support for a job creation programme that offers a standard hourly wage (similar to a minimum wage) and a package of benefits. The advantage of this latter programme is that it does not create any competition or tension between the private sector and the public sector (Wray, 2009). The consensus of opinion suggests that a government employment guarantee programme should be set at the minimum wage with the proviso that the latter provides an acceptable standard of living for those at that income bracket. The full employment programme should also include, in addition to the minimum wage, all the associated workers benefits such as health care and ancillary benefits that are considered an entitlement for residents of that country.

A government-funded employment programme is not without its critics. Sawyer (2003) argues that a job guarantee is inflationary. He resorts to a version of the Phillips curve argument whereby at the lower unemployment rates the process induces higher levels of inflation. Others suggest that such a plan would adversely affect the work ethic and create higher private sector costs by encouraging workers to adopt lax attitudes since they could always move to employment in the government plan in the event they lost their jobs. They also argue that such a programme would be so massive an undertaking that it would become virtually impossible to manage (Wray, 2009). Still others expressed fears of corruption, suggesting that there will not be enough worthwhile jobs for those in the programme and that it would be difficult to discipline workers in this programme. Finally, opponents of this programme suggest that a job guarantee is too expensive and will cause budgetary deficits to reach unprecedented heights (Aspromourgos, 2000; King, 2001).

On the other hand, proponents for a job guarantee (Mitchell and Wray, 2005) respond to some of the criticisms by arguing that critics overlook the difference between aggregate-demand pumping which results in inflationary pressures and targeted spending which will only provide jobs for those unemployed that the private sector is not prepared to employ. They emphasize that the remuneration that is set at the minimum wage will prevent the wage from falling below that level, but this does not automatically lead to wage increases in the private sector. Finally, there is the counter-cyclical premise for a government employment programme which automatically stabilizes the economy as government spending increases during a recession and falls during an economic expansion.

ECONOMIC GOVERNANCE AND EMPLOYMENT: A PROPOSAL

The pursuit of good economic governance will require the creation of a new organization that is informed by the economic governance norm described above to promote full employment. The conceptual framework for this new organization can draw on the template of a central bank. This new organization will be mandated to achieve a full-employment target that would be specified on the basis of existing research and would embrace a long-term decision-making horizon that would minimize the conflict between political expediency and rational policy objectives. It can be named as the National Employment Commission. The structure of this new commission should be non-political, at arm's length of government and devoid of any government interference. An independent agency will ensure that politics and policy are kept apart in the pursuit of full employment. The commission should report to the national parliament and be governed by a board of directors that will include representatives of government, the private sector, professional experts as well as representatives from the social economy and the not-for-profit sector. The National Employment Commission should be capable of making long-term economic and human resources decisions rather than focusing on the short-term electoral cycle.

There is no denying that the mission and mandate of a National Employment Commission is a daunting task. Nevertheless, it is an imperative machinery of institutional engineering that we need to put in place in order to come to grips with a new model that is congruent with the challenges and opportunities of the new global economy.

The broad purpose of this institution is to serve as an economic intelligence gathering, labour force forecasting unit and a catalyst for full employment. There is no doubt that forecasting labour market requirements is no easy task; however doing nothing to predict the changing economic landscape at a time of a rapidly-changing environment is not an option. The global economy is going through a process of renewal and transformational change. Old economy jobs are becoming obsolete and disappearing. New economy jobs are emerging but they require new skills, talents and educational competencies. The Employment Commission will also be tasked with co-ordinating the efficient and effective deployment of a country's human resources. This means taking into account the quantitative and qualitative demands of the private, public and social sectors.

More specifically, the mission and mandate of this Commission will involve monitoring the evolution of the employment landscape and serving as a catalyst for new economic and employment policy initiatives; assessing the educational and training priorities of the new economy and recommending remedial action in terms of absorbing the unemployed; undertaking labour forecasting, human resource planning and management; correcting for labour supply shortages and production bottlenecks; facilitating the economic integration of immigrants; co-ordinating an ongoing labour market dialogue with the public, private and social sectors; enhancing curriculum planning with post secondary institutions, universities, polytechnics and community colleges; promoting the acquisition of human capital through enhanced levels of education, skills and competencies and anticipating structural changes to the economic landscape. In the final analysis, the umbrella mandate of such a body would be to ensure the strategic, efficient and effective deployment of a country's human resources in order to achieve the maximum economic and social benefits.

This new institution must earn the respect and confidence of its stakeholders as well as the general public. It should do so by being accountable, transparent and embrace the highest standards of operational efficiency and effectiveness. The undeniable benefit of an Employment Commission is to serve as a catalyst for optimizing the contribution of a country's human capital assets in the most effective and efficient manner in order to maximize a country's productive capacity and standard of living. The creation of a new commission with a mandate to promote full employment will undoubtedly involve an additional operational cost. Those costs will be offset by the direct and indirect benefits that will accrue to the economy and society by pursuing and achieving full employment. It should be emphasized that inaction with regard to unemployment also incurs significant costs. Indeed, the most persuasive argument for full employment is the importance of human capital in the engineering and structure of the new global economy. No country can achieve its full economic potential in the absence of the total utilization and optimization of its human resources. In short, it is not a matter that society cannot afford the allocation of resources in the pursuit of full employment but that we cannot afford the economic and social costs of unemployment. Furthermore, a full employment programme will decrease the economic costs of unemployment and enhance the aggregate economic benefits of the effective utilization of a country's human resources. The realities of the new global economy and the pursuit of full employment require the re-engineering of our inherited economic and social institutional architecture and the introduction of a new economic architecture that is more conducive to meeting the challenges and taking advantage of the opportunities of the twenty-first century.

CONCLUSION

The mission and mandate of economic governance and its accompanying institutional architecture requires realignment to conform to the realities of the new global economy. Two recent economic events, the emergence of the new global economy and the financial crisis of 2008, have precipitated the need for a renewal of our governance principles, our inherited institutional architecture and a country's economic policies in order to conform to the realities of the contemporary landscape. The modern rules of economic engagement require the adoption of governance principles of fiscal propriety, enhancing competitive advantage, renewing the economic infrastructure, achieving full employment, embracing the tools of the ICT revolution, reformatting tax policies, revising the regulatory mechanism and promoting a stable economic environment for domestic and foreign investment.

The modern institutional architecture of economic governance should reflect the complementarity and inter-independence between economic policy, social policy and environmental policy. Indeed, there is room for new economic institutions that are targeted towards specific economic challenges, embrace a proactive approach and incorporate a longer term horizon in their decision making mandate. To that effect, the principle of job guarantee can be drawn upon as a norm that will shape expectations and inform new policy and organizational choices with respect to labour market policy. Under this norm, the government is the employer of last resort who should provide employment for every citizen who is able and willing to work. This norm is not a pragmatic reaction, but ties in with international human rights standards that now include not only civil and political rights but also social and economic rights.

This norm can inform and anchor the establishment of a National Employment Commission whose mandate is to promote and achieve full employment – that is, the efficient absorption of a country's human resources and their effective integration in the new economy. This organization should be at arm's length from government influence and direction and serves as a catalyst for achieving full employment.

REFERENCES

Aspromourgos, T. (2000), 'Is an employer-of-last-resort policy sustainable? A review article', *Review of Political Economy*, **12**(2), 141–155.

Barnes, J. (ed.) (1984), *The Complete Works of Aristotle: The Revised Oxford Translation*, Princeton, NJ: Princeton University Press.

Darity, W. (1999), 'Who loses from unemployment?', *Journal of Economic Issues*, **33**(2), 491–496.

Dixit, A. (2008), 'Economic governance', in Steven N. Durlauf and Lawrence E. Blume (eds), *The New Palgrave Dictionary of Economics*, 2nd edition, Basingstoke and New York: Palgrave Macmillan.

EFMD (European Foundation for Management Development) (2007), 'Aging workforce: what future for the knowledge worker?', Brussels: EFMD, available at http://www.efmd.org/attachments/tmpl_1_art_070219sqku_att_070219xvqb. pdf (accessed 12 May 2010).

Gordon, A. (2009), 'Jobs of the future, science and technology enabled employment for 2020–2030', available at http://futuresavvy.net/2009/08/jobs-of-the-future-technology-enabled-employment-for-2020-2030/ (accessed 18 March 2010).

Hughes, D.P. and M. Grant (2007), 'Learning and development outlook 2007', available at http://www.conferenceboard.ca/documents.aspx?did=1995 (accessed 21 May 2010).

King, J.E. (2001), 'The last resort? Some critical reflections on ELR', *Journal of Economic and Social Policy*, **5**(2), 72–76.

Miner, R. (2010), 'People without jobs, jobs without people', available at http://www.collegesontario.org/research/other/people-without-jobs-jobs-without-people-final.pdf (accessed 26 April 2010).

Mitchell, W.F. and J. Muysken (2008), *Full Employment Abandoned: Shifting Sands and Policy Failure*, Cheltenham, UK and Northampton, MA, USA: Edward Elgar.

Mitchell, W.F. and L.R. Wray (2005), 'In defence of employer of last resort: a response to Malcolm Sawyer', *Journal of Economic Issues*, **39**(1), 235–245.

Myers, K. and P. de Boucher (2006), 'Too many left behind: Canada's adult education and training system', Canadian Policy Research Network Inc. Research Report, **w/34**, available at http://www.cprn.org/doc.cfm?doc=1479 (accessed 29 March 2010).

Passaris, C. (2001), 'Schumpeter's legacy of technological innovation in the context of the twenty-first century', in V. Orati and S.B. Dahiya (eds), *Economic Theory in the Light of Schumpeter's Scientific Heritage*, Rohtak, India: Spellbound Publications, pp. 1985–2009.

Passaris, C. (2003), 'Schumpeter and globalization: innovation and entrepreneurship in the new economy', *Fifth Annual International Schumpeter Lecture, Viterbo (Italy)*, International Institute of Advanced Economic and Social Studies, pp. 9–95.

Passaris, C. (2006), 'The business of globalization and the globalization of business', *Journal of Comparative International Management*, **9**(1), 3–18.

Passaris, C. (2008), 'Macroeconomic policy in the new global economy of the twenty first century', Proceedings of the Society of Heterodox Economists Conference on Contemporary Issues for Heterodox Economics, Sydney, Australia, 8–9 December , pp. 109–137.

Sawyer, M. (2003), 'Employer of last resort: could it deliver full employment and price stability?', *Journal of Economic Issues*, **37**(4), 881–908.

Williamson, Oliver E. (2005), 'The economics of governance', *American Economic Review*, **95**(2), 1–18.

Wray, L.R. (2009), 'The social and economic importance of full employment', available at http://www.levyinstitute.org/pubs/wp_560.pdf (accessed 26 April 2010).

Wray, L.R. and M. Forstater (2004), 'Full employment and economic justice', in D. Champlin and J. Knoedler (eds), *The Institutionalist Tradition in Labor Economics*, Armonk, NY: M.E. Sharp, pp. 253–272.

PART III

The governance and regulation interface

9. The political economy of deregulation in the US gas distribution market

Vladimir Hlasny

Since the late 1800s, regulation of public utilities in the United States has undergone many changes in structure and conceptual approach. The most recent upheaval took place in the early 1990s, when state-level public service commissions abandoned traditional cost-plus ratemaking regime for performance-based regulation. Some states fixed prices that utilities could charge, some introduced financial incentives for utilities to exceed certain performance standards, and others allowed utilities to compete among themselves for customers. Utilities went along with, if not welcomed, the changes. The first large incentive programs in the gas distribution industry were introduced 15 years ago, and many states have adopted them since then. As of 2007, half of US states and two-thirds of utilities still operated under rate-of-return regulation. To this day, motives behind regulatory reform across individual states remain unclear. Understanding them can help us determine the relative importance of legitimate economic factors, and of political capture motives, in bringing about policy reform. This understanding can also help us predict future patterns of deregulation.

This chapter extends empirical evidence on factors behind regulatory reform in utility industries, using panel data on all natural-gas utilities in the continental United States. Among state-level political factors, frequency and timing of commissioner re-elections, system of selection of commissioners and party composition of the commissions and state legislatures are significant in explaining the pattern of deregulation. Demonstration effects from regulatory regimes in surrounding states and particularly from other utility industries in a state appear to play a role. A negative significant association between the prevalence of restructuring, and of price cap deregulation across states is identified. This may result from the adoption of price cap regulation to block restructuring. It may also result from the preference for price cap regulation in less competitive regions, and restructuring in regions with a sufficient potential for competition. Finally, utilities' prices and capacity, and market concentration, are shown to help explain the outcome and timing of regulatory reform.

BACKGROUND OF REGULATION

Prior to the 1860s, federal government oversaw utility industries from wellheads to city gates. Individual municipalities oversaw distribution companies. Because of simple structure and balkanization of utility industries, there appeared little need for state-level regulation. Between the 1860s and 1920s, utility industries became more integrated, as companies increased the scope of their services and regional reach, and their operations spanned out across multiple commodities. Trusts and monopolies arose in railroad and other public utility industries. State commissions emerged, as a Populist (1880s) and Progressive (1890s–1910s) response to these trusts. In fact, most state commissions called themselves railroad commissions for many decades even though their function included telecommunications, energy, gas, water and other utilities. The primary objective of the commissions was initially to protect core (that is, residential and small commercial) customers from being abused to the benefit of larger consumers or utilities themselves (Stigler and Friedland, 1962; Priest, 1993). Over time, state commissions took on more responsibilities, with regard to infrastructure provision and enforcement of efficiency at companies. Today they are the most influential body responsible for supervision of transportation and distribution companies in utility industries.

State commissions have adopted different regulatory approaches across different utility industries, depending on the complexity of service to consumers, ownership and cost of key assets and the prospect of technological innovation. The gas distribution market was traditionally kept under rate-of-return regulation, because of its status as classical natural monopoly. State commissions used tight regulation in order to hold utilities' returns and consumer prices within narrow ranges. In the 1960s, rate-of-return regulation regime came under attack for giving utilities insufficient incentives to manage costs and revenues, and encouraging them to strategically overcapitalize and pass up risky long-term cost-reducing investments (Averch and Johnson, 1962). In protecting core customers' bottom line, regulators had discouraged utilities from marketing to off-grid industrial consumers and procuring gas in innovative ways.

In 1978, the National Energy Act unified the intrastate and interstate transmission markets, and Orders 380 and 436 gave gas providers open access to transmission companies' pipelines. Through the 1978 Natural Gas

Policy Act and the 1989 Wellhead Decontrol Act, wellhead prices became competitive. Utilities' options for using their resources and procuring commodity widened. As the national gas market became more integrated, state officials, consumer advocates and utilities themselves started calling for lighter-handed, more flexible and more efficient regulatory regimes. The 1992 FERC Order 636 facilitated regulatory reform by extending utilities' access to transmission, and simplifying price structure in transmission.

Price cap regulation became debated as the means of promoting efficiency. Price caps gave utilities the full reward for efficiency in capital investment and in risk-taking in gas procurement and infrastructure management. The difference between price caps and rate-of-return regulation was, in reality, dampened by regulatory imperfections and constraints. Regulatory lags, rate case moratoria and prudence reviews reduced the efficiency disadvantages of rate-of-return regulation. Accounting for Z factors in the calculation of rates, and the possibility of ex-post renegotiation of allowed rates reduced the utilities' incentives under price caps. Even though price cap regulation required less regulatory oversight than rate-of-return regulation, it did not represent true regime change because – theoretically and empirically – it did not depart sufficiently from the rate-of-return regulation paradigm. Companies' costs and their allowed rates remained tied, and companies' sunk investments remained protected by a safety net. Price-cap regulation also required regulators to correctly predict future costs and technology improvements, otherwise utilities could earn excessive returns or default on their responsibilities. Perhaps because of these reservations, price cap regulation was adopted in a 'gradual and sometimes haphazard manner' in the United States (Crew and Kleindorfer, 1996: 212).

In the mid-1990s, several state commissions started advancing incentive or performance-based regulation to give utilities incentives in particular areas of operation. Rewards for outstanding performance were reflected in their allowed consumer rates. The first stab at such deregulation, named capacity-release and off-system sale plans, allowed utilities to share benefits from exceptional performance in utilization of marginal resources. The first was adopted in North Carolina in 1993. Some states, starting with Mississippi in 1994, introduced monetary rewards for superb customer service. When these programs were deemed successful, more aggressive incentive programs were authorized to give utilities a wider space for decision-making, such as attracting off-system industrial customers (earnings-sharing mechanisms) and purchasing the commodity from various sources (gas cost incentive mechanisms). Utilities were allowed to influence their rate of return on capital by retaining a portion of the difference between actual and benchmark costs or revenues (Comnes et al., 1995).

Table 9.1   Cumulative number of policies in the dataset (by year)

	1996	1997	1998	1999	2000	2001	2002	2003	2004
Sliding scale plans (Utilities)*	28	39	48	56	60	63	70	70	71
Price caps (Utilities)	13	15	16	18	19	20	21	21	21
Consumer choice (States)	0	1	8	14	19	19	20	20	20

Note: * This count does not include Wyoming utilities (44), who all receive 10 per cent of gas cost savings under state legislation.

Sliding scale programs currently used by US state commissions have several major variations. Margin-sharing plans promote efficient management and divestiture of resources on the margin: off-system sales and pipeline capacity release plans reward utilities for using excess gas or capacity in their pipelines. Gas cost incentive mechanisms offer utilities an incentive for efficient gas procurement, in commodities, futures and derivatives markets. Earnings-sharing mechanisms encourage negotiation of special contracts with new industrial customers to make gas competitive with other fuels. Once again, adoption of sliding scale programs did not represent a true regulatory reform, merely partial, controlled deregulation. Similarly to price cap regulation, sliding scale plans retained much of the link between companies' costs and prices, and continued to restrict companies' returns to be within certain ranges.

In 2000, state commissions started departing from the regulatory paradigm based on viewing utilities as natural monopolies. They restructured the gas distribution market by unbundling gas distribution service into several service areas, and approving several utilities and independent marketers to compete in individual segments (Table 9.1). Introduction of consumer choice programs arguably represented true regulatory reform, as it brought about a new view and treatment of individual utilities, industrywide structural changes and changes in state commission' role. Moreover, entry of unregulated interstate marketers gave states access to new sources of gas, undercut existing vertical regional supply chains, and helped to further unify the gas market.

REGULATORY LITERATURE

Most research on public utilities has focused on the electric and telecommunications industries, and has evaluated performance of regulatory regimes, rather than reasons for their adoption. Hlasny (2006, 2008a, 2008b) reviews these studies. Economic studies of the causes of regulatory reform have identified various governance-related factors behind deregulation in utility industries. These include political factors (Bailey and Pack, 1995); presence of infrastructure necessary for restructuring (Comnes et al., 1995); political party in power and composition of public service commissions; commissioner re-elections (Dalbo, 2006; Hagerman and Ratchford, 1978); pressure from various interest groups (Hilton, 1972; Stigler, 1971; Posner, 1974; Peltzman, 1976; Becker, 1983); and satisfaction with restructuring in surrounding states or industries (Flippen and Mitchell, 2003). Other economic factors include monopolistic behaviour and high prices of incumbent firms (McCraw, 1975; Ando and Palmer, 1998; Hlasny, 2011); recouping of stranded costs of utilities' long-term investments (Flood, 1992; Gilbert and Newbery, 1994; Salant, 1995; White et al., 1996); and other economic trends (Joskow et al., 1989; Dal Bo and Di Tella, 2003).

Empirical evidence on the consequences of regulatory reform has been mixed. In the electricity industry, the process of regulator-selection has had little impact on the stringency of regulation in terms of the consumer prices (Costello, 1984; Primeaux et al., 1984; Primeaux and Mann, 1986; Boyes and McDowell, 1989; Campbell, 1996; Kwoka, 2002; Besley and Coate, 2003), and in terms of allowed rates of return (Joskow, 1972; Hagerman and Ratchford, 1978; Harris and Navarro, 1983). However, regulator selection has had some impact on the length of regulatory lag (Atkinson and Nowell, 1994). Similarly, the creation of consumer advocate groups seems to have affected the stringency of the regulator's price setting and cost review (Holburn and Spiller, 2002; Holburn and Vanden Bergh, 2006). In telecommunications, the price-effects of the regulator-setting process (Smart, 1994) and of campaign contributions (Edwards and Waverman, 2004; DeFigueiredo and Edwards, 2005) have been noted.

ESTIMABLE MODEL OF REGULATORY CHOICE

The empirical analysis herein is loosely based on a theoretical model of rational regulatory choice, following Peltzman's (1976) capture model. At the centre of the regulatory process is a regulator who chooses among regulatory regimes P_{ij} with the objective to maximize a measure of his political returns $W_i(P_{ij})$. The regulator's return may be in the state-wide consumer or producer surplus, state revenue, chances of re-election, financial contributions, popularity, prestige, sense of righteousness or a combination of these. The regulator selects the regime that yields the greatest returns.

$$W_i(P_{ij}) = \sum_{g=1}^{G} [n_g \cdot f_g(P_{ij})] \tag{1}$$

In this expression, subscript i is for the regulator, and j is for the utility under consideration. P_{ij} is a categorical policy variable whose Π possible realizations include the decision to retain the status quo regime. Regulator i's political returns are a sum of the returns obtained from G groups of stakeholders. G includes non-overlapping groups such as other governmental bodies, taxpayers, voters, different classes of consumers, shareholders, utility workers, other utilities and others. The returns from each group g depend on the size of the group, n_g, and the measure of support from a typical member of g for the policy reform in question, $f_g(P_{ij})$. The form of $f_g(\cdot)$ depends on the marginal support that a typical member of g tenders for P_{ij} when the present value of his wealth increases by one dollar as a result of introduction of P_{ij}. Thus, $f_g(\cdot)$ may depend on an individual's existing wealth, time preference and risk aversion.

f_g can be a probability that an individual grant his support for P_{ij}, or the money or utility transfer to the regulator, conditional on P_{ij}, or a vector of variables of interest. $f_g(\cdot)$ may be increasing and weakly concave, because of positive non-increasing marginal contribution of individuals' net benefits of regulation to their support for P_{ij}. Different groups may have different functional forms of f_g. Without information on the exact variable whose value state commission strives to maximize, no other restriction should be placed on f_g. Specifically, $f_g(P_{ij})$ may depend on the present value of direct benefits from particular policy reform, costs to implement and enforce the new regime, and mitigate or appease opposition, and costs of organizing within the group g.

Direct benefits from policy reform may depend on the change in individuals' earnings (for example, from off-system sales) or savings (from lower prices) anticipated if the new regime is adopted, including direct costs of adoption. Costs to enforce a policy may depend on the necessary spending (for example, information gathering and dissemination or concealment) and transfers to other groups to ensure adoption of a policy. Costs of organizing a group may depend on the difficulty of tallying individual members' valuation and organizing them (overcoming free riding and mobilizing members), and may therefore be a function of the size of a group. Direct benefits from policy reform, T_g, may be positive or negative. We may have $\Sigma_{g=1}^{G}(T_g) \neq 0$ for a particular P_{ij}, or $\Sigma_{P_{ij}=1}^{\Pi}(T_g) \neq 0$ for a particular g. Costs to enforce a policy, K_g, may be $K_g(P_{ij}) < 0$ if g receives a transfer from another group h ($h \in G$, $h \neq g$) to enforce a policy (particularly if groups differed in their voting rights or weights in the regulator's objective). Both $T_g(\cdot)$ and $K_g(\cdot)$ may depend on the sizes of other interest groups n_h.

In reality, regulatory decisions are not made by the state commission alone. Various stakeholders, including the utility in question, have input in the process. Back and forth negotiation weakens the power that the regulator or utility may exercise in implementing policy reform (Mathios and Rogers, 1989; Greenstein et al., 1995). Equation (1) allows for these considerations. The regulator faces a tradeoff in the support he receives from different interest groups, and selects policy reform P_{ij}^* that maximizes their sum. Knowledge of the individual parts of equation (1) would shed light on why particular regulatory regime is adopted at a utility-regulator pair at a particular point in time, and which forms of regulation are likely to be used in the future.

For simplicity of presentation, equation (1) omits time subscripts. The regulator's problem is of course dynamic. The size of individual interest groups, the net benefits expected by them and the rules of admissibility of their support change over time. Flows of net benefits, costs of lobbying and of organizing groups occur at different points in time, with different certainty. Furthermore, the regulator's identity and the form of his political returns may change over time.

Empirical Approach

Decisions about alternative policies should be studied jointly, since the regulator has a number of deregulatory options from which to choose, and the decision to adopt a particular policy depends on the set of available policy options. The likelihood and timing of implementation of a particular mechanism are thought to depend on expectations of all stakeholders regarding the net benefits from a particular form of deregulation, as compared to other policy alternatives.

One can study the revealed choice at each regulator-utility pair to identify factors affecting the decisions as well as the individual parts of $W_i(P_{ij})$. Ideally, one would infer the support function $f_g(\cdot)$ of a typical stakeholder in each interest group g for each considered deregulatory regime P_{ij}. Unfortunately, information on utility functions of individual public service commissions and all stakeholders is missing. The exact functional form and arguments of $f_g(\cdot)$ are unknown, and are difficult to estimate for policy regimes that have not been enacted. The identity and size of all interest groups is also unknown. Most data are available only at the state or utility level. As a result, the following empirical model studies factors behind deregulation at the levels of the public commission and the utility.

Given the available data, several conjectures suggested by previous literature can be tested. One conjecture related to the capture theory is that the process of selecting public service commissioners may influence the form of deregulation. Whether the selection is through appointment by state legislature or through public election, number of (re)appointments in the current year and the length of election cycles may matter. Unfortunately, the direction of these effects is a priori unclear, as it depends on commissioners' campaign programs and voters' sentiments, unobservable in this analysis.

Another conjecture testable using the available data is that previous experience with similar forms of deregulation in other industries in the state, or in the gas market in surrounding states, yields demonstration effects that impact the expected benefits of deregulation. Provided that the previous experience is positive, one could expect positive demonstration effects.

Among economic factors, one conjecture is that higher consumer prices of a utility encourage deregulation. They may increase the expected price reductions under deregulation relative to the status quo. A benevolent regulator may be sympathetic to the consumers' cause particularly of high prices.[1]

Another interesting economic conjecture is that the measure of effective industry concentration encourages the adoption of price caps. Even though most utilities are monopolies in their local markets, they compete to attract off-grid customers and to win regulator's support in cost review cases and performance evaluations (for example service quality awards). For these reasons utilities strive to compare favourably to other utilities in the state. The higher the concentration of utilities, the less effective competition of this sort may exist, and the more of monopolistic and exploitative behaviour one may observe. The regulator may then prefer price caps to rate-of-return regulation. Price caps treat a utility in isolation, fixing the service quality and other operating standards, and inducing the utility to increase its efficiency, regardless of how low competitive pressures from outside are. Sliding scale and consumer choice programs, on the other hand, may be expected to operate best in industries with lower concentration. Sliding scale plans are based on a comparison of a utility's performance against the performance of other utilities. Among sliding scale plans, earnings-sharing plans reward utilities explicitly for acquiring new customers and margin-sharing plans reward a utility for sharing its resources with other utilities profitably. Consumer choice programs require the presence or the potential for entry of competing providers of unbundled services.

A related conjecture is that utility size affects the expected benefits from deregulation. Larger utilities have larger interest groups (n_g) that may be better organized; have generally been in existence longer and may have earned more trust from the regulator; and may be perceived as less competitive by general public (because of their sheer size). For these reasons, utility size may affect the benefits from deregulation expected by the utility and consumers. A priori, it is unclear whether utilities' size should be related positively or negatively to the likelihood of deregulation relative to the status quo. Among the possible forms of deregulation, we may believe that larger utility size is conducive of utility-level incentive programs. Utility size is unimportant or may be harmful when regulatory reform relies on effective competition among utilities.

One may formulate other hypotheses of interest beside those above. Unfortunately, many hypotheses cannot be tested using currently available data. In particular, direct pressure by various interest groups, or utilities' rates of return, stranded costs and reserve margins are missing. Some conjectures are difficult to test because of interplay of competing effects in the real world. For example, incomes affect consumers' marginal utility of money, but also voting behaviour, preferences and attitude toward risk; prices of alternative fuels affect each stakeholder differently, and may be correlated with unobserved features of state-wide gas industry.

Cox Model of Time to Deregulation

The Cox proportional-hazard model is estimated to predict the time to deregulation of utilities that have not deregulated yet, using information on the timing of deregulation at presently deregulated utilities. The standard model is advanced to allow for competing risks of adoption of one or more of the alternative deregulatory plans. In a discrete-time model, the hazard (likelihood) of an event is the probability that the event occurs in a time period, conditional on the fact that it has not occurred until then. The hazard rate of adoption of a program π at each regulator–utility pair ij in year t, $\lambda_{ij\pi t}$, is frequently modelled as an exponential function of determining factors, multiplied by an estimated baseline hazard rate of adoption:

$$\lambda_{ij\pi t} = \exp(\gamma_\pi \cdot Y_{ijt}) \cdot \lambda_{00\pi t} \qquad (2)$$

In this expression, Y_{ijt} is a vector of time-varying explanatory variables specific to each regulator–utility pair ij, γ_π is the associated vector of coefficients specific to policy π, and $\lambda_{00\pi t}$ is a duration-dependence baseline hazard rate of policy π as of time t.

Y_{ijt} includes time-varying factors suggested by hypotheses in the previous section: political and electoral factors pertaining to the state commission, experience with deregulation in surrounding industries, utilities' capacity and prices, concentration of the natural gas market and fiscal climate in states. In particular, political and electoral factors include the number of commissioners appointed in a year, whether the appointment is by state legislature or by public election, length of election cycles for commissioners, size of the state commission and party composition of the commission and of state legislature. Average state personal income and marginal business income tax rate help to control for fiscal climate in states.

Explanatory variables are thus at the levels of utility, state commission and gas market. To the extent that each regulator–utility pair has a particular expectation of conditions resulting under each policy alternative, the model should include policy-specific controls. However, such expectations could differ between the regulator and the utility, and information on such expectations is missing. Detailed provisions of each utility-specific mechanism are also unknown.

$\lambda_{00\pi t}$ is the hazard rate of adopting π conditional on all control variables being set to zero, and therefore does not depend on the regulator's or the utility's characteristics. Typically, one needs to estimate $\lambda_{00\pi t}$ along with all model coefficients. This need can be eliminated using a partial-likelihood maximization method, by focusing only on the contribution of ij's time to deregulation to the ordering of times across all regulator–utility pairs, conditional on the set of regulator–utility pairs that have not deregulated as of t.

Equation (2) is fitted using maximum likelihood methods. To allow for competing risks of alternative regulatory regimes, the likelihood of adoption of a policy must be independent of the choice set of available deregulatory programs.[2] Empirically, only some combinations of policies or progressions between policies are feasible. However, modelling of the allowed relationships among available policies would be difficult. It is implicitly assumed that any policy can be implemented alongside any other policy, and arbitrary progression between any two policies over time is allowed.

Data

Data for this analysis come from several public sources, most importantly the Department of Energy, National Association of Regulatory Utility Commissioners and webpages of state public service commissions. The data covers all large-capacity utilities in the continental USA reporting to the Department of Energy's EIA-176 from 1996–2004. To limit the heterogeneity of utilities in the sample, three-quarters of utilities with the smallest capacity are dropped, reducing the sample size from 2,222 utilities (12,941 observations) to 659 utilities (3,646 observations). Small utilities appear to be regulated differently from medium-size and large utilities,

Table 9.2   Inventory of policies in the sample

Program	States	Utilities	Observations
Consumer choice – pilot or implemented[a]	22	216	721
Price cap[b]	4	7	20
Sliding scale plan[ab]	21	37	134
Sample size	47	659	3,646

Note: The reported number of states, utilities and observations have information on years prior to deregulation, needed for the analysis. Programs implemented before 1996 are dropped.
[a] Of these numbers, 10 states, 16 utilities and 29 observations have both consumer choice programs and sliding scale plans.
[b] Of these numbers, 2 states, 4 utilities and 8 observations have both price caps and sliding scale plans.

and have other systematic differences. Information on why each of these utilities is different is missing, and dropping them appears to be the best option. However, the analysis was repeated using all utilities, and all qualitative results remained valid.

Hawaii and Alaska are outliers in the dataset, both conceptually and empirically, and suffer from missing data. These states are excluded. Californian utility industries have undergone extensive structural and political changes in recent years. During the period under analysis, the state experienced energy industry price-fixing scandals, financial crises and the resulting policy changes. After evaluating the effects of the uncompetitive activities on regulation in the region, California was not dropped from the analysis, because its presence does not alter the results greatly.

Information on the form of regulation comes from a custom survey of state public service commissions, conducted for accuracy three times between 2001 and 2007 (Hlasny, 2006, 2008a). Table 9.2 describes the presence of deregulatory programs in the sample, including their joint distribution. Information on the composition of state public service commissions, system of selection of commissioners and times of (re)appointments comes from NARUC (2010), Beecher (2007, 2010) and commissions' websites. Other data on state and national elections are taken from the US Census. Hlasny (2011) reports the source and description of economic control variables.

The number of commissioner positions open for (re)appointment, process of selecting new commissioners and length of election cycles control for time-variation in regulatory motives at the state level. The size and composition of the commission and the political party prevalent in the state legislature control for party objectives. Controlling for the state commissions' experience with deregulation is the number of deregulatory programs in the gas market in surrounding states, and the number of deregulatory programs in other utility industries within the state, as of year *t-1*.

The Herfindahl-Hirschman Index (HHI) for the concentration of utilities in the state gas distribution market measures inversely the amount of interaction among utilities and strength of competitive forces in the industry. It is defined as the sum of squared market shares of all distribution companies in a state, where market shares are computed using the sum of volumes of gas sold to all consumer classes. The state is chosen as the definition of utilities' market on the assumption that this measure of market concentration is closely related to the effective amount of competition that a utility faces, and for a lack of better information. State boundaries provide some effective restrictions on utilities' operations (for example, requirements to be licensed in a state to compete there, and to deal with transmission companies in a state), and so the HHI in the state market is expected to be a better measure of the effective interaction among utilities regardless of state size than, say, a uniform-size market definition.

State per capita incomes, unemployment rates, bankruptcy rates, personal and business income tax rates proxy for the fiscal environment in the state, including consumers' ability to pay. Residential prices, capacity, operation type and ownership are used to control for utilities' observable and unobservable time-varying characteristics and performance.

With the exception of categorical variables and the HHI, all variables are normalized by the nationwide average of the variables for a year. This normalization picks up relative differences across utilities (or states) rather than variation over time, and is insensitive to nationwide year-specific shocks. Units of the normalized variables are the percentage deviations from the national mean. Another set of controls is obtained by normalizing variables by their average for the utility (or state) in all prior years. This normalization picks up year-to-year shocks rather than differences across utilities, thus measuring time-varying factors at a utility. Both sets of variables – those normalized by a nationwide average, and those normalized by a utility's prior average – were evaluated simultaneously. This allowed the model to distinguish variation in a regressor across utilities, and over time, as distinct factors affecting the time to deregulation. Furthermore, the mean of these normalized variables is zero. This implies that the computed baseline hazards can be interpreted as the likelihoods of adopting policies by a typical utility in a typical state.

Some of the needed variables are unobservable or measured imprecisely in the data. Policies are measured by binary indicators for the adoption of the policies at a utility, regardless of the detailed provisions of the policies. This is a limitation to the extent that the same policies may vary across utilities by their incentive power, number of affected customer classes, number of customers, agreed upon time span and other factors. Utilities with the same policy are thus implicitly assumed to be regulated subject to similar gas procurement, pricing, cost recovery and rate-of-return rules. In reality, policy with a greater incentive power, extent and time span may be more difficult to implement. Inclusion of these factors would render the above model difficult to solve. The degrees of freedom would also fall with the number of categories of regulatory outcomes. Finally, information on the detailed provisions is often missing or unclear.

Earnings-sharing, margin-sharing and gas cost incentive plans are studied jointly as sliding scale programs. Some of these programs are adopted very rarely. In the analysis, even fewer occurrences may appear if some of the independent variables are missing for a utility with the program. With a small portion of the sample under policy treatment, the estimated coefficients would be imprecise. The second reason is that the degrees of freedom in the analysis falls with the number of competing policies, because each policy requires estimation of another set of coefficients and another baseline likelihood. Making different sliding scale plans interchangeable with each other is acceptable, provided they are similar in their adoption processes.

RESULTS

This section reports the results of Cox regressions, estimating the time-dependent likelihood of adoption of each policy. Table 9.3 reports on the Cox hazard models where all deregulatory programs are evaluated jointly, thus controlling for the risk of adoption of other programs at the utility. Hazards presented in Table 9.3 account for the fact that several alternative policies compete for adoption simultaneously.[3] Baseline hazard in this model is assumed the same across the three policies, but most regressors are allowed to contribute differentially to the respective hazards. Each policy thus has a different hazard (likelihood) of adoption.

The first three columns in Table 9.3 make the likelihood of regulatory reform a simple function of political factors at the state level. Selection process of state commissioners, size of the state commission and political party in power account for the political climate in the commission and in the public sphere. In particular, the number of seats up for reassignment on the state commission, the party responsible for the selection and the composition and tenure of state commission control for commissioners

Table 9.3   Cox proportional-hazards model estimation results

	Sliding scale	Price cap	Choice	Sliding scale	Price cap	Choice
Commissioners – chosen in t	0.005	1.111	−0.711***	−1.781*	1.562	−1.110***
	(0.715)	(0.873)	(0.168)	(1.052)	(1.105)	(0.214)
Appointed – v. elected	0.799	0.27	1.154***	0.022	−3.048**	0.455*
	(0.550)	(0.618)	(0.268)	(1.047)	(1.441)	(0.244)
Election cycle – length	0.042	−0.308	−0.201***	0.1	−1.234***	−0.197**
	(0.215)	(0.298)	(0.068)	(0.480)	(0.269)	(0.084)
Democrats – on commission	0.207**	0.184	−0.102***	0.154	0.889**	−0.158***
	(0.085)	(0.157)	(0.033)	(0.174)	(0.362)	(0.049)
Democrats – in Upper House	−1.668	−0.164	−0.547	0.328	6.410*	−2.183***
	(1.051)	(1.613)	(0.672)	(1.679)	(3.888)	(0.717)
Commission – Members	−0.497**	−0.788	0.323***	−0.888*	−2.616***	0.388***
	(0.251)	(0.507)	(0.065)	(0.517)	(0.769)	(0.105)
Sliding scale plans – in electricity industry				−1.037		1.084***
				(0.699)		(0.264)
Price caps – in telecom industry					6.134***	−1.498***
					(1.960)	(0.297)
Price caps – in electricity industry					0.236	−0.443*
					(1.163)	(0.227)
Sliding scale plans in – gas industry in region				−0.138		0.590***
				(0.314)		(0.081)
Price caps in – gas industry in region					−0.194	−0.430***
					(0.575)	(0.145)
Choice programs in – gas industry in region						−1.658***
						(0.360)
Price of gas – v. other utilities				0.290***	0.077***	−0.117***
				(0.063)	(0.020)	(0.034)
Price of gas – v. previous years				−0.797***		0.079
				(0.198)		(0.051)

Table 9.3   (continued)

	Sliding scale	Price cap	Choice	Sliding scale	Price cap	Choice
Utility volume				0.006***	0.023***	0.001
– v. other utilities				(0.002)	(0.005)	(0.001)
Herfindahl-Hirschmann Index				0.224	0.786**	–0.051
				(0.252)	(0.326)	(0.062)
Personal income				1.234***	1.417**	0.418***
– v. other states				(0.335)	(0.608)	(0.102)
Personal income				–3.652**	–6.629***	–3.566***
– v. previous years				(1.619)	(1.711)	(0.361)
Business income tax				0.147**		0.147**
– v. other states				(0.061)		(0.061)
Utilities (States)	659 (47)			657 (47)		
Log pseudo-likelihood	–2,134.51			–1,635.75		
Chi-square	400.03			1,275.78		

Note: * statistically significant at 10%; ** 5%; *** 1%, two-sided tests.

objectives and the climate in which they make decisions. Political leaning in the Upper House of state legislature controls for state-level political climate. The three columns on the right control for regulatory experience from other industries and economic factors, to identify better the partial effects of political factors on regulatory reform. Deregulation status in the telecommunications and the electricity industries in the state, and deregulation status of natural gas utilities in other states in the region, control for demonstration effects. Economic control variables at the utility level include residential price of gas, utility's capacity, type and ownership. At the state level, other economic controls include concentration of the gas industry, state per capita income, business income tax rate and prices of related fuels. They help proxy for fiscal and regulatory climate in the state.

The first six rows in Table 9.3 report on the effects of political factors on the likelihood of adoption of the three competing regulatory regimes: sliding scale, price cap and restructuring with consumer choice. The number of commissioner seats up for election or re-election in a year is positively related to the likelihood of deregulation via price caps, and negatively related to the likelihood of other forms of deregulation. It appears that deregulation via sliding scale and consumer choice programs is politically more difficult (statistically significant) than adoption of price caps or retention of status quo in years when many commissioners seek to be appointed. The process of commissioner selection also appears to affect regulatory reform, with appointments by state legislature favouring sliding scale regulation or restructuring, and public elections favouring price caps. Thus, when public sentiment is needed in commissioner appointments, state commissions tend to push through price caps, even against the status quo rate-of-return regulation. They appear to shy away from other forms of deregulation. This is further confirmed in the third row: the more often the commissioner selection is conducted – because of shorter election cycles – the higher the likelihood of price caps compared to consumer choice and particularly compared to sliding scale plans. In sum, the extent of commissioner elections in a year, the involvement of general public in them, and frequency of elections, tend to favour price caps, over other possible deregulatory regimes or the status quo.

The fourth and fifth rows of the table report on the effects of political-party composition of state commissions and state legislatures. Democratic leaning of the commission and of state legislature tends to favour deregulation via price caps (weakly even sliding scale plans) against restructuring. This may agree with our beliefs regarding Democratic and Republic legislators' attitudes toward competitive forces in the marketplace and toward economic governance. One interesting finding worth studying further is that commissions that have fewer members tend to favour price cap and sliding scale deregulation, and avoid restructuring. This may be an artifact of complexity inherent in full-blown restructuring, and of other facets of the decision-making process behind regulatory reform.

The following six rows in Table 9.3 show that policies adopted in other utility industries in the state, and in the gas industry in other states have a strong effect on the likelihood of adoption of the same policy at a gas utility. Prevalence of price caps in the telecommunications and electricity industries in the state affects the likelihood of price cap deregulation positively, and that of restructuring negatively. Prevalence of sliding scale plans in the electricity industry in the state surprisingly has a negative effect on the likelihood of this form of deregulation in the gas industry (insignificant), and a positive effect on the likelihood of restructuring.[4] Deregulation in the gas industry in surrounding states appears to have the unexpected effect on deregulation in a state: experience with restructuring (sliding scale plans or price caps, respectively) in surrounding states lowers the likelihood of restructuring (sliding scale or price cap adoption, respectively) in a state. This is significant for the likelihood of restructuring. The one expected result is that the prevalence of sliding scale plans (price caps, respectively) in surrounding states raises (lowers, respectively) the likelihood of restructuring in a state. Once again we find a strong negative relationship between the usage of price caps, and of consumer choice programs across utility industries in a state, and across US regions. On the other hand, there appears to be a positive relationship between the adoption of sliding scale plans and consumer choice programs.

The next three rows show coefficients on utility-level economic variables. First, an attempt is made to differentiate the effect of premiums in utilities' residential prices relative to other utilities, and jumps in prices relative to previous years. The first variable is normalized by its mean across all utilities for the year. These coefficients are interpreted as contributions of a percentage premium in the variable, compared to values in other utilities, to the likelihood of adoption. The second variable is normalized by its up-to-date mean at the utility level. These coefficients are interpreted as contributions of a percentage change in the variable, compared to its previous levels, to the likelihood of adoption. The residential price of gas affects the likelihood of sliding scale plans and price caps positively, and consumer choice negatively. Compared to the levels in previous years, higher prices of gas tend to decrease the likelihood of sliding scale plans. These price effects may together imply that utilities that are less efficient than their peers – in the sense of charging higher regulated prices – tend to be assigned incentive regulation tailored to the particular utilities: price caps or specific forms of sliding scale plans. Regulators may hope to change utilities' performance under new utility-level payoff regimes. Furthermore, sliding scale plans may be granted only when the utilities show some improvement in prices over previous years.[5]

Utility's capacity increases the likelihood of regulation via sliding scale plans and price caps, and has no effect on the prospect of restructuring. Although the effect of utility size on deregulation (holding market concentration fixed) is theoretically unclear, the estimated effect is not surprising, implying that the amount of resources and experience – and perhaps even the effective or perceived market power, ability to lobby regulators or absolute level of benefits to ratepayers – at the utility can raise the expected success of utility-level deregulation. These same factors are unimportant or counterproductive to facilitating competition under restructuring.

The last four rows show the estimated effects of state-level economic controls, as varying across states or years. HHI for the state gas market has a positive effect on the likelihood of sliding scale plans and price caps, and no effect on restructuring. Thus, concentration of utilities in the market has similar influence on regulatory efforts as utilities' size, a nice expected result.

The next two rows attempt to differentiate the effect of premiums in income levels compared to other states, and jumps in income levels

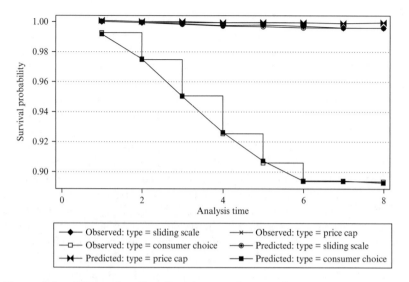

*Figure 9.1   Observed and predicted survival curves for competing
regulatory regimes*

compared to previous years. Higher per capita incomes (relative to other
states) are associated with higher likelihood of adoption of each deregulatory program. Jumps in per capita earnings (relative to previous years) are
associated with a large fall in the likelihood of adoption of all programs.
Variation in corporate income tax rates across states is related positively
to the likelihood of sliding scale plans and consumer choice. (To preserve
degrees of freedom, the coefficients were restricted to be identical in the
two equations, and the variable was omitted from the price cap equation.)
    There is one potential limitation of the models presented in Table 9.3 that
should be mentioned. The likelihood model relies on the assumption of proportional hazards (likelihoods) – that is, for any two utilities, the ratio of
the estimated likelihoods should remain constant regardless of what other
plans are available. Kaplan-Meier observed and predicted survival curves
(Figure 9.1) can help us evaluate this assumption (Kaplan and Meier, 1958).
The closer the observed values are to the predicted values, the less likely the
proportional hazards assumption has been violated. The predicted curves
are very close to the observed values, thus alleviating fears that the important assumption was violated. This is confirmed in Figure 9.2, showing the
Kaplan-Meier log-log survival curves of individual policies against log-
time. The proportional-hazards assumption appears to be valid for these
survival curves, because the curves are nearly perfectly parallel.
    Figure 9.3 shows the baseline hazard (likelihood) estimates (smoothed

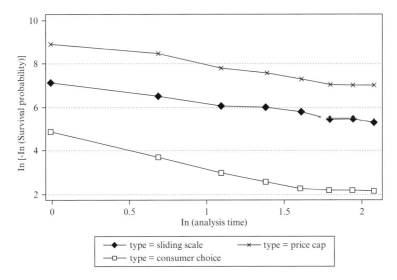

Figure 9.2   Log-log survival curves for competing regulatory regimes

using kernel density estimation) for each deregulatory regime at the means of all covariates. The likelihood of adoption of sliding scale and price cap forms of regulation falls over time, whereas the likelihood of restructuring rises. This corresponds to the fact that the vast bulk of the sliding scale plans and price caps were adopted in the late 1990s, while consumer choice programs started to spread only after the year 2000. The three graphs indicate that the assumption of equal baseline likelihoods across policies would not be valid. Clearly, no two policy alternatives can be combined into one, and each policy should be modelled with own baseline hazard.

CONCLUSIONS

This chapter has evaluated selected political and economic factors affecting the likelihood and timing of regulatory reform in the gas distribution market. Three deregulatory regimes were studied jointly: sliding scale incentive regulation, price cap regulation and restructuring with consumer choice. Results indicate that the process of selecting state public service commissioners is an important determinant of regulatory choice for gas utilities. The extent of commissioner elections in a year, the involvement of general public in them and frequency of elections, tend to favour price caps, over other possible deregulatory regimes or the status quo. Political-party composition of state commissions and state legislatures contributes.

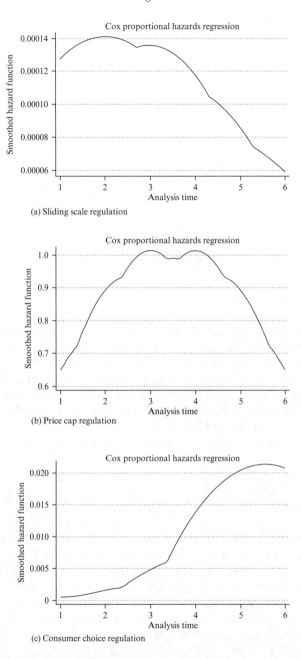

Figure 9.3   Smoothed estimates of baseline hazards of competing regulatory regimes

Democratic leaning of the commission and of state legislature tends to favour price caps against restructuring.

Adoption of price caps and consumer choice programs in other utility industries in the state has a positive and significant demonstration effect on the adoption of these norms in the gas industry. Demonstration effects from the gas industry in surrounding states are weak and unclear. This may correspond with the fact that policy reforms have not been success-ful in all states where they were undertaken from 1996–2004. Whether demonstration effects will become clearer and positive in the coming years presumably depends on actual performance of existing programs.

After controlling for a number of political and economic factors, there remains a clear negative association between the prevalence of consumer choice – together with sliding scale – regimes on the one hand, and price cap deregulation on the other hand, across utility industries in a state, and across the continental United States. The systematic negative association between restructuring and price cap regulation may be caused by the usage of price cap regulation to block restructuring, and the adoption of sliding scale plans as a preparatory step for successful restructuring. This associa-tion may also result from the correlatedness of political climates, electoral systems, composition of gas industry and availability of resources (such as gas wells, underground storages or pipeline capacity) across US states. Sliding scale regulation appears to have similar criteria for adoption as restructuring, while the criteria for price cap regulation are contrary.

At the utility level, residential prices and utilities' size affect the likeli-hood that the utility will be subject to regulatory reform, and the effect is positive for price caps and sliding scale plans, and negative or insignificant for consumer choice. The estimated effect of utilities' size may imply that the amount of resources and experience at the utility – and perhaps even the effective or perceived market power, ability to lobby regulators or absolute level of benefits to ratepayers – can increase the expected success of utility-level regulatory reform. These same factors are unimportant or counterproductive to facilitating competition under restructuring. Concentration of utilities in the market has similar influence on regulatory reform.

NOTES

1. High prices may signify improprieties by the utility. Also, while utilities may be thought to have constant marginal utility of money, consumers' marginal utility increases with prices. Regulators may be particularly sympathetic to residential consumers, who face diminishing marginal utility of money, for whom utility bills represent a large portion of incomes and whose support in $W_i(P_{ij})$ can be substantial.

2. To evaluate reasonableness of this assumption, the results of a joint competing-risks model are compared against a model stratified by policy alternatives or by distinct time periods (Harrell and Lee, 1986). The results are available on request. Since restructuring became a viable policy option only in year 1999 (after the initial pilot programs proved feasible, and upon support from federal legislation), periods 1996–1998 and 1999–2004 are distinct in the effective menu of available policies, and can be used for stratification. (The experience with restructuring in California and Georgia became known only in the second time period. Delaware and Wisconsin also discontinued their pilot programs in the second time period.)

3. First, competing deregulatory programs were evaluated individually. In the study of implementation of policy *A*, utilities adopting policy *B* were treated as non-deregulated, and their observations as right-censored. Because competing policies were treated as equivalent to the benchmark rate-of-return regulation, coefficients in this model are interpreted as contributions of a variable to the hazard of adoption of a given policy, against the hazard of adopting another policy (including retention of the benchmark policy). An important limitation of the policy-specific model is that it evaluates the hazard of adoption of only one policy at a time, treating all other alternatives as equivalent to the benchmark. It is likely that the decision between rate-of-return regulation and restructuring, for example, depends on whether the utility currently operates under rate-of-return, price cap or sliding scale regulation. In addition, one of several types of deregulation can result, and a low estimated hazard of restructuring should not necessarily be interpreted as a high hazard of retention of rate-of-return regulation. One must remember what policy outcomes are contained and most prevalent in the benchmark when interpreting the coefficients. For these reasons, policy-specific analysis does not appear justified, and joint estimation is more appropriate.

4. This variable, as well as sliding scale and consumer choice regulation used in other states, price of gas compared to previous years and business income taxes are omitted from the price cap regression to preserve degrees of freedom. Table 9.2 has already reported that there are only seven subjects (20 observations) adopting price caps in our sample. If some explanatory variables are missing for those utilities, we would have even fewer adoptions in the regression. It also turns out that information on utilities' prices is sometimes missing. Business taxes are also less significant and less a priori relevant in the model.

5. Another explanation of this system of coefficients is that the two variables – demeaned across all utilities, or normalized by the average for all previous years – are collinear, and their coefficients may be spurious. However, the coefficients are statistically highly significant, and the two variables have low correlation. This indicates that multicollinearity is not a problem here.

REFERENCES

Ando, A. and K. Palmer (1998), 'Getting on the map: the political economy of State-level electricity restructuring', *Resources for the Future, Discussion Paper*, **98-19-REV**.

Atkinson, S. and C. Nowell (1994), 'Explaining regulatory commission behaviour in the electric utility industry', *Southern Economic Journal*, **60** (3), 634–643.

Averch, H. and L.L. Johnson (1962), 'Behavior of the firm under regulatory constraint', *American Economic Review*, **52** (5), 1052–1069.

Bailey, E. and J. Pack (1995), *The Political Economy of Privatization and Deregulation*, Aldershot, UK and Brookfield, VT, USA: Edward Elgar.

Becker, G. (1983), 'A theory of competition among pressure groups for political influence', *Quarterly Journal of Economics*, **98** (3), 371–400.

Beecher, J. (2007), 'The all commissioners list', *Institute of Public Utilities Research Note*, May.

Beecher, J. (2010), 'Commissioner demographics 2010', *Institute of Public Utilities Research Note*, March.

Besley, T. and S. Coate (2003), 'Elected versus appointed regulators: theory and evidence', *Journal of the European Economic Association*, **1** (5), 1176–1206.

Boyes, W. and J. McDowell (1989), 'The selection of public utility commissioners: a re-examination of the importance of institutional setting', *Public Choice*, **61** (1), 1–13.

Campbell, H. (1996), 'The politics of requesting: strategic behaviour and public utility regulation', *Journal of Policy Analysis and Management*, **15** (3), 395–423.

Comnes, G., S. Stoft, N. Greene and L.J. Hill (1995), 'Performance-based rate-making for electric utilities: review of plans and analysis of economic and resource-planning issues', Lawrence Berkeley National Laboratory, University of California Working Paper, lbl-37577 uc-1320.

Costello, K. (1984), 'Electing regulators: the case of public utility commissioners', *Yale Journal on Regulation*, **1**, 83–105.

Crew, M. and P. Kleindorfer (1996), 'Incentive regulation in the United Kingdom and the United Sates: some lessons', *Journal of Regulatory Economics*, **9** (3), 211–225.

Dal Bo, E. (2006), 'Regulatory capture: a review', *Oxford Review of Economic Policy*, **22** (2), 203–225.

Dal Bo, E. and R. Di Tella (2003), 'Capture by threat', *Journal of Political Economy*, **111** (5), 1123–1154.

DeFigueiredo, R. and G. Edwards (2005), 'Does private money buy public policy? Campaign contributions and regulatory outcomes in telecommunications', Working Paper, University of California, Berkeley.

Edwards, G. and L. Waverman (2004), 'The effects of public ownership and regulatory independence on regulatory outcomes: a study of interconnect rates in EU telecommunications', Working Paper, University of California, Berkeley.

Flippen, E. and A. Mitchell (2003), 'Electricity utility restructuring after California', *Journal of Energy and Natural Resources Law*, **21** (1), 1–18.

Flood, R. (1992), 'What is policy switching?', *Finance and Development*, **29** (3), 33–35.

Gilbert, R. and D. Newbery (1994), 'The dynamic efficiency of regulatory constitutions', *RAND Journal of Economics*, **25** (4), 538–554.

Greenstein, S., S. McMaster and P. Spiller (1995), 'The effect of incentive regulation on local exchange companies. Deployment of digital infrastructure', *Journal of Economics and Management Strategy*, **4** (2), 187–236.

Hagerman, R. and B. Ratchford (1978), 'Some determinants of allowed rates of return on equity to utilities', *Bell Journal of Regulation*, **9**, 46–55.

Harrell, F. and K. Lee (1986), 'Verifying assumptions of the proportional hazards model', *Proceedings of the SAS Users' Group International*, **11**, 823–828.

Harris, M. and P. Navarro (1983), 'Does electing public utility commissioners bring lower electric rates?', *Public Utilities Fortnightly*, **112**, 23–88.

Hilton, G. (1972), 'The basic behaviour of regulatory commissions', *American Economic Review*, **62**, 47–54.

Hlasny, V. (2006), 'Do gas cost incentive mechanisms work? A nation-wide study', *American Economist*, **50** (1), 51–68.

Hlasny, V. (2008a), 'The impact of restructuring and deregulation on gas rates', *Journal of Regulatory Economics*, **34** (1), 27–52.

Hlasny, V. (2008b), *Regulation of Utility Industries in the United States*, Saarbrucken, Germany: VDM.

Hlasny, V. (2011), 'Economic determinants of deregulation in the gas distribution market', *Journal of Economic Policy Reform*, **14** (2).

Holburn, G. and P. Spiller (2002), 'Interest group representation in administrative institutions. The impact of consumer advocates and elected commissioners on regulatory policy in the United States', *Proceedings of International Society for New Institutional Economics Conference*, Cambridge, Massachusetts, 27–29 September.

Holburn, G. and R. Vanden Bergh (2006), 'Consumer capture of regulatory institutions. The creation of public utility consumer advocates in the United States', *Public Choice*, **126** (1–2), 45–73.

Joskow, P. (1972), 'The determination of the allowed rate of return in a formal regulatory hearing', *Bell Journal of Economics*, **11**, 632–644.

Joskow, P., D. Bohi and F. Gollop (1989), 'Regulatory failure, regulatory reform and structural change in the electrical power industry', *Brookings Papers on Economic Activity*, 1989, 125–208.

Kaplan, E.L. and P. Meier (1958), 'Nonparametric estimation from incomplete observations', *Journal of the American Statistical Association*, **53**, 457–481.

Kwoka, J. (2002),'Governance alternatives and pricing in the US electric power industry', *Journal of Law, Economics and Organization*, **18** (1), 278–294.

Mathios, A. and R. Rogers (1989), 'The impact of alternative forms of State regulation of AT & T on direct-dial, long-distance telephone rates', *RAND Journal of Economics*, **20** (3), 437–453.

McCraw, T. (1975), 'Regulation in America', *Business History Review*, **49** (2), 159–183.

NARUC (2010), 'NARUC membership directory', *NARUC* Report (National Association of Regulatory Commissioners), February, 1–376.

Peltzman, S. (1976), 'Toward a more general theory of regulation', *Journal of Law and Economics*, **19** (2), 211–240.

Posner, R. (1974), 'Theories of economic regulation', *Bell Journal of Economics and Management Science*, **5** (2), 335–358.

Priest, G. (1993), 'The origins of utility regulation and the theories of regulation debate', *Journal of Law and Economics*, **36**, 289–323.

Primeaux, W. and P. Mann (1986), 'Regulator selection methods and electricity prices', *Land Economics*, **62** (1), 1–13.

Primeaux, W., J. Filer, R. Herren and D. Hollas (1984), 'Determinants of regulatory policies toward competition in the electric utility industry', *Public Choice*, **43** (2), 173–186.

Salant, D. (1995), 'Behind the revolving door. A new view of public utility regulation', *RAND Journal of Economics*, **26** (3), 362–377.

Smart, S. (1994), 'The consequences of appointment methods and party control for telecommunications pricing', *Journal of Economics and Management Strategy*, **3** (2), 301–323.

Stigler, G. (1971), 'The theory of economic regulation', *Bell Journal of Economics and Management Science*, **2** (1), 3–21.

Stigler, G. and C. Friedland (1962), 'What can regulators regulate? The case of electricity', *Journal of Law and Economics*, **5**.

White, M.W., P.L. Joskow and J. Hausman (1996), 'Power struggles. Explaining deregulatory reforms in electricity markets', *Brookings Papers on Economic Activity*, 1996, 201–267.

10. Electricity sector reforms and the tariff review process in Brazil

Cláudio de Araújo Wanderley, John Cullen and Mathew Tsamenyi

INTRODUCTION

Many countries have deregulated so-called public services utilities, causing changes in the institutional environment of this sector. The main justification for such reforms has been the policy makers' claim that privatised organisations would be more efficient and effective in their operations and services within a competitive environment (Boubakri and Cosset, 1998; Jaruga and Ho, 2002; Johnson et al., 2000; Ogden, 1995 1997; Jacobs, 2009; Tsamenyi et al., 2010). This chapter examines such reforms in the context of the Brazilian electricity sector by focusing on the development of the tariff review process and the effects of the latter on electricity sector outcomes such as investment and prices.

Electricity sector reforms in Brazil started with the privatisation programme between 1995 and 2002, which created about US$100 billion of revenue for the government (BNDES, 2002). Privatisation was a consequence of political decisions made by the Brazilian government, but these decision were taken under internal pressure for privatisation as well as external pressure from the World Bank and the IMF (International Monetary Fund), who played a significant role in the process of the utility sector's deregulation in Brazil (Amann and Baer, 2005). In the electricity sector, 23 distribution companies were privatised for roughly US$22 billion (Araujo, 2006). This represents about 70 per cent of the Brazilian energy distribution market.

The impact of privatisation on public services utilities has attracted the attention of a number of scholars (for instance, Thomas, 2006; Cole and Cooper, 2006; Amann and Baer, 2005; Branston, 2000). However, the literature on regulatory reform is still under-developed and most of the research in this area has been conducted in developed countries. Zhang and Thomas (2009: 33) point out that: 'So far, most literature has been concerned with regulatory reform in OECD countries, but not as much has been known about the experience in the other part of the world.' This chapter aims to address this limitation by providing evidence on the impacts of privatisation and structural reforms in emerging economies using Brazil's electricity sector as a case.

Ugur (2009: 348) points out that regulation of the electricity industry is a public policy problem, 'the resolution of which is complicated by information asymmetries, transaction costs, agency problems, and strategic inter-action between multiple actors such as consumers, suppliers, regulators, and governments'. Kirkpatrick and Parker (2004: 334) also comment that 'regulation is now recognised as an important instrument in the development policy toolkit, which can support market-led, pro-poor growth and development'. As a result, the role of the regulator is crucial as the entity responsible for coordinating the agents involved in the electricity industry.

Cubbin and Stern (2006: 117) suggest two main output measures for assessing regulatory governance quality in utility regulation: 'the level and rate of growth of technical efficiency and productivity (and the quality of service); and the level of capacity'. The authors point out that the rationale for designing a regulatory framework is the inability of governments to make credible and binding commitments about utility pricing to sustain private investment while retaining decision-making powers. Taking this underlying rationale into account, this chapter focuses on the important issue of setting the electricity tariff (the tariff review process) by describing and analysing the development of the tariff review process in Brazil. It is argued that a well-designed and well-implemented tariff review framework leads to good results in terms of the two main output measures for utility regulation stated above. Therefore, this chapter views the tariff review process as a governance regime with rules and contract types for shaping incentives and constraints faced by the agents, including the government, the regulator, companies and consumers.

The remainder of the chapter is organised into three main sections. First, an overview of the Brazilian tariff review process is provided. Then, the chapter moves on to explain the relationship between the electricity sector reforms and the tariff review process issues and the final section provides concluding comments.

TARIFF REVIEW PROCESS

Distribution companies' tariffs historically were established by the Brazilian government through a set of laws. This legal framework was a very complex system of subsidies and compensations which was applied to the distribution utilities to equalise the tariffs at national level (Alvarez, 2007). This system was implemented in 1974, when the electricity tariffs were equalised over the country. In 1993, distribution companies were authorised by law number 8,631 to set their own tariffs, subject to approval by the licensing authorities, in particular DNAEE (Department of Waters and Electric Energy). As a result, this law ended the guaranteed return on investment, as well as tariff equalisation among the distribution utilities, and annulled intra-sector debts (Alvarez, 2007; Araujo, 2006). This law adjusted tariffs according to the actual costs of service rendered by each utility (cost-plus methodology) in accordance with the future privatisation programme enacted in 1990.

Law number 8,987 (enacted in 1995) established the overall concession regime, introducing price cap regulation and competitive bidding for all public concessions. Price cap regulation occurs when the government and utility set caps on service tariffs that the utility is allowed to charge. The price is adjusted periodically to account for inflation, technological progress and exogenous changes (Lima, 2002). According to Kang et al. (2000: 113), price cap regulation 'is commonly referred to as RPI-X regulation, where RPI is the retail price index and X is a factor that reflects anticipated productivity gains, and specifies the rate at which the regulated firm's prices must fall in real terms on an annual basis'. Varela and Redolfi (2007) point out that in the price cap regulation, once the tariff is set for the settlement period (in the Brazilian case from four to five years), the utility is free to manage its costs and there is an incentive to convert the benefits resulting from the efficiencies obtained, which can be passed through to the customers in the subsequent tariff period, as at the end of the settlement period, X factor is reset by the government, and the process is repeated.

According to the Brazilian tariff rules, the electricity tariff to captive consumers can be adjusted through three processes (ANEEL, 2009):

- the periodic tariff review process (between four and five years);
- the annual tariff adjustment (IRT, in Portuguese) – this process will not be explained in this chapter due to space limitation; and
- the extraordinary tariff review, which can occur whenever the financial and economic equilibrium of the concession contract is broken. This process will not be dealt in this chapter, because this occurs only in exceptional cases.

THE PERIODIC TARIFF REVIEW PROCESS

The tariff revision process occurs every four or five years, depending on the concession contract. The first periodic tariff review process (2003–2006) was in accordance to ANEEL's resolution number 493/02, while the second periodic review (2007–2010) was regulated by ANEEL's resolution number 234/2006. The periodic tariff review process encompasses two stages: (1) tariff repositioning (RT, in Portuguese), which establishes the level of efficient operating costs and fair return on the capital invested; and (2) determination of the X factor (Rocha et al., 2007).

The tariff repositioning (RT) is represented by the following formula:

$$RT(\%) = \frac{Allowed\ Revenue - Other\ Revenues}{Verified\ Revenue}$$

The RT compares the allowed revenue for the test year (12-month period after the revision date) with the utility's verified revenue. The allowed revenue comprises the revenue necessary to cover efficient operating costs and to provide an adequate return on prudent capital invested. The verified revenue consists of the revenue that would be obtained with the tariffs in effect before the revision, applied to market sales in the test year. Other revenues are revenues that do not refer exclusively to the tariff, but they have an indirect relation with distribution service or with the operational distribution company's asset, in the Brazilian case other revenues are sharing network revenues. The allowed revenue is then reduced by the other revenues (90 per cent of the other revenues) to try to keep tariffs at moderate levels.

To determine the 'Allowed Revenue' of the distribution companies, the Brazilian regulator (ANEEL) adopts the traditional accounting based method of achieving financial-economic balance. In order to calculate the regulated revenue, ANEEL divides utility costs in two parts: Part A (uncontrollable costs) and Part B (controllable costs). The calculation is based on the forecast market for the first year of the new period (test year) (Alvarez, 2007). Uncontrollable costs (Part A) account for approximately 70 per cent of a distribution company's tariff, while controllable costs (Part B) account for 30 per cent (see Figure 10.1) (InstitutoAscendeBrazil, 2007).

The uncontrollable costs (Part A) are, a priori, beyond the utility's control and they are passed on in their entirety to the captive consumers. Uncontrollable costs (Part A) comprise:

- energy purchase costs (including commercial and technical losses);
- costs for the transmission system (energy transport); and
- taxes and sector charges.

Losses constitute a special case of uncontrollable costs. Distribution companies have two types of losses: (1) technical losses, which are

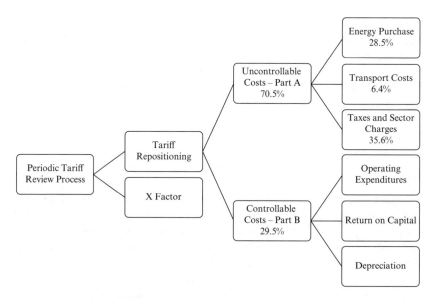

Figure 10.1   The periodic review process

associated with energy transport (joule effect, losses at the transformers, and so on); and (2) non-technical losses resulting from power thefts, measurement errors, and so on. In Brazil, the non-technical losses are a huge problem, as the percentage of non-technical losses is extremely high, in some cases more than 20 per cent of the energy purchase (Alvarez, 2007). Therefore, ANEEL establishes the efficient loss level in the regulated revenue. In the first review process, ANEEL required the distribution companies to submit a characterisation of their losses in their concession areas and a plan to combat their level of losses. In general, ANEEL recognised the average loss over the past three years as the regulatory value of losses. In the second review process (2007–2010), ANEEL used a mathematical network model based on the methodology adopted in the national electricity distribution procedure (PRODIST, in Portuguese) to determine the regulatory technical losses. The regulatory non-technical losses are determined on a case-by-case basis considering the information submitted by the utilities and based on the general criteria established in the ANEEL resolution number 234/2006, in particular, the complexity index, which takes into consideration the wide range of factors that influence the non-technical losses (for further detail about the complexity index see ANEEL Technical Note number 290/2008 SRE/ANEEL).

The controllable costs (Part B) are those under the distribution company's control and encompass:

- operating expenditures (OPEX), which involve the management, commercial, operating and maintenance expenditures which an efficient distributor should incur to supply the market;
- return on capital, which results from multiplying: (1) the net regulatory asset base (NBRA) by; (2) the opportunity cost to develop the distribution activity in Brazil; and
- depreciation: the regulatory depreciation is the value to be annually recovered to replace the assets at the end of their operational life, and it is obtained by multiplying: (1) gross regulatory asset base by; (2) the annual depreciation rate.

Operating expenditures (Opex) is calculated by applying the Reference Utility methodology, also known as Model Utility (Varela and Redolfi, 2007). This methodology is based on the concept that the operating costs can be determined by specifying the main tasks of distribution companies' activities, allocating the necessary resources (labour and materials) and evaluating them at the market price in concessionaire's area. Therefore, ANEEL aims to establish a market reference adjusted to the actual geographical and macroeconomic conditions in the utility's concession area to calculate the corresponding efficient Opex.

One of the most significant aspects of the regulatory system is the relationship between the regulator and regulated utilities, characterised by the so-called 'information asymmetry'. This refers to the reliance of the regulator on data supplied by the regulated company, when the firm has a great and better knowledge of its own operations (Tozzini, 2008). In order to overcome such a problem, ANEEL decided to adopt, among other measures, the Reference Utility methodology to determine the utilities' operational expenditures. The Reference Utility is a hypothetical distribution company tailored to economic conditions of the geographic area of the actual utility under analysis. ANEEL designs the Reference Utility based on its projection of what it considers to be efficient operation. As a result, the Reference Utility methodology seeks to design a model company against which the actual utility can compare its performance, as a result, this can create an incentive to operate at a lower cost than the standards set by the regulator.

Tozzini (2008) points out that there are at least two different methodologies which can be used to design the Reference Utility. First, the model utility is based on engineering principles taking into consideration the best practices and technologies. Second, the design of standard performance is made by comparing existing companies, both in relation to an efficient frontier and to average performance standards or indexes. ANEEL adopts the engineering principles to determine the model utility.

According to ANEEL Technical Note number 290/2008 SRE/ANEEL, the methodology adopted in Brazil to establish the operating expenditures is the Reference Utility approach based on a normative model. The main characteristic of a normative model is that it does not use actual data from distribution companies to determine the production function. Therefore, the Brazilian model is based on technical standards, instead of actual costs from utilities firms. In addition, the Brazil system uses the price market in accordance to the concession area, instead of price used by the companies, to evaluate the operating costs.

Burns and Estache (1998) point out that regulatory asset valuation has been proved to be an extremely controversial area in the tariff review process. This was also true in the Brazilian context; as Alvarez (2007) states, the determination of the Regulatory Asset Base (RAB) was the most controversial issue in the implementation of the periodic tariff review process. This issue generated a number of conflicts and administrative and judicial claims by the distribution utilities. In 2002, after an intense debate in the electricity sector, ANEEL's Technical Note number 148/02 enacted by Resolution number 493/02 established DORC (Depreciated Optimised Replacement Cost) as the methodology to evaluate the Regulatory Asset Base. This methodology revaluates assets at depreciated replacement cost, with minor adjustments associated to land occupancy factors and the level of transformer use. For the second review period (2007–2010), the Regulatory Asset Base at the end of the first tariff review was shielded and rolled forward by two tariff periods. ANEEL's initial plan was to create a price reference database to value the new investments at market price. However, this idea was not developed due to operational problems faced by ANEEL. As a result, the same methodology used in the first review process has been adopted in the second review process (for further details see ANEEL Technical Note number 456/2008 SFF/ANEEL).

The cost of capital adopted by ANEEL is the same for all distribution companies in Brazil and it refers to the opportunity cost of an investment of similar risk. It corresponds theoretically to the adequate rate of return to reward the capital invested. The methodology to estimate the cost of capital is the weighted average cost of capital (WACC). According to Burns and Estache (1998), WACC methodology is the standard approach adopted by regulatory agencies and governments to set the cost of capital. In the Brazilian context, this approach considers the remuneration of equity and debt, including the tax benefits, weighted by the average leverage structure for the electricity sector (debt/equity ratio). The cost of capital in the first review process was set at 11.26 per cent per year, while in the second period it was set at 9.95 per cent (Baião, 2007).

The portion that remunerates equity is established through the Capital

Asset Pricing Model (CAPM) which is widely applied around the world (Jamasb and Pollitt, 2007). This includes the country risk, the foreign exchange risk and regulatory risk. The portion that remunerates debt arises from estimating the distribution companies' credit risk plus the foreign exchange risk and part of the country risk.

Finally, the depreciation is calculated by applying a linear rate that reflects the average accounting life of the fixed assets in service, excluding land. Therefore, depreciation is based on the straight-line methodology where a constant percentage of the undepreciated asset value is deducted from the opening asset value in each period (normally a year). The annual regulatory depreciation rates are established by a set of ANEEL resolutions, such as Resolutions numbers 02/1997, 044/1999, and 240/2006. Therefore, in the regulatory context, depreciation is a charge designed to recognise the loss of service that an asset has suffered throughout the years.

The second stage of the periodic review process is to determine the X factor, which represents the mechanism for passing distributors' productivity and efficiency to consumers through a reduction of the tariff adjustments index. The X factor is a reducer of the general market price index (IGP-M), which adjusts Part B of the utility firm's revenue; as a result, the X factor passes productivity gains to consumers in the next period. Therefore, by multiplying the IGP-M by the X factor, the maximum permitted tariff is established (Rocha et al., 2007).

ELECTRICITY SECTOR REFORMS AND THE TARIFF REVIEW PROCESS

As in many other countries, the Brazilian Electricity sector was originally based on a set of vertically integrated companies, for the most part under public ownership. Difficulties in keeping up with growing demand worsened in the 1990s. This triggered major market-oriented reforms in 1996, inspired by reforms in the United Kingdom and Latin America. The new system was designed to encourage competition in generation and retailing, while transmission and distribution remained regulated activities with provisions for open access. Other reform ingredients included the establishment of an independent system operator, as well as the privatisation of most distribution utilities and of transmission expansion (Rudnick et al., 2005).

Brazil's electricity sector went through two major reforms. The first reform took place between 1995 and 2003. The second Brazilian electricity reform started in 2004 with the introduction of a long term market which replaced the short term market introduced in the first reform. We discuss and analyse these two reforms periods in the Brazilian electricity sector by articulating those reforms with the tariff review process as a governance regime.

The First Phase of Reform: 1995–2003

The first phase of reform can be divided into two main sub-phases (Araujo et al., 2008): the first sub-phase when privatisation and reform followed nearly independent paths between 1995 and 2000; and the second sub-phase from 2000 to 2003, which was marked by correction and adjustments to the reform mechanisms, and coping with the 2001 crisis and rationing.

The Brazilian electricity sector reform started in 1995 with three distinct sets of actions (Araujo et al., 2008): First, the basic legislation was modified with the aim of altering the concession regime, forcing utilities to give up concessions and mandating open access for large consumers and independent power producers. The objective of these measures was to stimulate investments in new power plants, as well as the expansion of the network system. Second, a study to restructure the power sector was launched (RE-SEB project) which aimed to introduce competition and to divest all of distribution, transmission and part of generation. Finally, the Brazilian government stopped investing in new power plants even before any restructuring and regulatory framework had been put in place (Oliveira, 2007).

At the end of 1996, the regulatory agency for the electricity sector (ANEEL) was created (law number 9,427). Its main functions included: (1) preparing technical parameters to guarantee high quality services to consumers; (2) inviting tenders for generation, transmission and distribution; (3) establishing criteria for transmission costs; and (4) implementation and fixation of tariff reviews in the retail market (BNDES, 2002). Law number 9,648/98 created a national system operator (ONS) and a wholesale market (MAE). The latter did not settle short-term transactions until the end of 2002, because of a legal dispute among some utilities (Bajay, 2006). The national system operator (ONS) aims to improve the operation of the national interconnected power system and guarantee that all the agents have access to the transmission network.

As a consequence of this first reform, a large number of state companies were privatised. A wholesale power market was established under which large consumers (over 10 Mw and above 3 Mw after 2000) were allowed to contract electricity with generating companies, including Independent Power Producers (IPPs), in a wholesale power market. A regime of regulated third party access to the grid was established for the transport of contracted power. A new institutional framework to oversee the new system was created, with the establishment of the regulator ANEEL (Agência Nacional de Energia Elétrica – National Electricity Agency); a system operator, ONS (Operador Nacional do Sistema Elétrico – National Electric System Operator) separate from transmission assets; a market manager, MAE (Mercado Atacadista de Energia Elétrica – Wholesale Electricity Market) and a co-ordinating policy body, CNPE (Conselho Nacional de Política Energética – National Energy Policy Council) (OECD, 2008).

The first reform was mainly based on the British experience (Newbery, 2006; Littlechild, 2006): a regulator, an independent system operator, a bulk market operator, open access, a spot market, bilateral contracting, regulation of the network business, unbundling of generation, transmission, distribution and trading (Araujo et al., 2008). The reforms were ambitious but incomplete and flawed in important aspects (Araujo and Oliveira, 2005). This model was not able to attract the planned private investment thus setting the scene for the 2001 supply crisis. Installed generation capacity expanded only 28 per cent between 1990 and 1999, compared with demand growth of 45 per cent (OECD, 2008). Most of this was hydro-power, and very little was additional thermal capacity needed to secure the stability of a largely hydro-based system. One of the reasons for this under investment in the Brazilian electricity system was that the spot price signals were inadequate (Pinto Jr et al., 2007). It is expected that short-term spot price should provide the correct economic signal for the entrance of new players in the generation activity. However, in the Brazilian case, spot prices did not provide that economic signal, mostly because they were highly volatile due to the fact the Brazilian electricity sector is predominantly based on large hydro-power plants. Therefore, spot prices may be very low for several years and then increase sharply for a few months before going back to the previous levels.

This regulatory model received severe criticism because the process of reform in the electricity sector did not follow an ideal order, that is, first to create and implement a regulatory system and then to conduct privatisations and open the electricity market for foreign investors. In addition, delays in the construction and commissioning of power stations and transmission lines combined with few new investments both in hydro and thermal power plants caused a power shortage in 2001. The reason for this was a high perception of risks among private investors. According to Bajay (2006), the main problems with the Brazilian electric power section deregulation were: (1) the government priority was state debt reduction; as a result, the regulatory model did not consider a plan for generation expansion, a serious mistake that caused the electricity shortage in 2001; (2) the perception of risk was high among private investors and free consumers; (3) tariff levels were increasing; and (4) there was a lack of concerted action between the Ministry of Mining and Energy (MME) and sector's regulatory agency (ANEEL).

The second sub-phase corresponds to the 2000–2003 period and was characterised by correction and adjustments to the reform mechanisms, and coping with the 2001 crisis and rationing (Araujo et al., 2008). Therefore, from late 2000 to 2003, the Brazilian government tried to correct the flaws in the market design by introducing ad hoc measures and making policy adjustments.

As mentioned previously, the rationing in 2001 was a crisis brought on by inadequate investment in generation and insufficient diversification away from hydro-power, against the background of reforms that had failed to stimulate appropriate and timely investment, and a shortage of gas. The wholesale market was undermined by financial and contractual disputes, mostly between generators and distributors, which the institutional framework was unable to deal with (OECD, 2008). Disputes and difficulties bounced around the organisations set up to manage and control the new model, with no institution appearing to be able to take a clear lead or co-ordinate. The strategic planning and policy function that had been embedded in MME (Ministry of Mining and Energy) was dismantled, and resources for critical functions were scattered (Losekann, 2008).

A year or so before the 2001 crisis, prices in the wholesale market reached an unprecedented high that finally triggered investment in new hydro-power plants. But it was also clear that these investments would not be completed in time to prevent an electricity shortage. The government decided to intervene, and launched the emergency PPT (Priority Thermoelectricity Plan) programme in 2000, aimed at encouraging investment in gas-fired plants. But the programme was a relative failure and was never completed. Only 15 of the planned 49 plants were built. Investors stayed away partly because of the high cost of gas, but also because of continuing worries about the regulatory regime and the stability of the government's policy objectives. It was too little and too late to avoid a power crisis, the immediate trigger for which was an unusually dry summer that reduced reservoirs to a critical level at a time of growing demand spurred by economic recovery (OECD, 2008).

In May 2000, the Brazilian government set up a programme (the Emergency Electric Power Consumption Programme) and an institution (the Electric Power Crisis Management Chamber) to implement emergency measures, which lasted from June 2001 until February 2002. Power consumption was reduced by 20 per cent. Energy saving and efficiency measures taken by consumers, such as tariff bonuses for those reaching set goals, sanctions against laggards and an information campaign on television were among other measures took by this chamber (Almeida and Pinto, 2005). These measures had a sustained effect and demand did not recover to pre-crisis levels until 2004.

Therefore, the 2001 crisis required measures ranging from rationing to special contracts for merchant plants and a number of exceptions to regulation in order to encourage investment in new generation plants. A number of ad hoc contracts were signed, leading to conflicts after the rationing ended (OECD, 2008). In addition, the unexpected reduction of electricity demand had significant financial impacts on the electricity sector, in particular, the distribution companies which were negatively affected by reductions in demand and revenues (Almeida and Pinto, 2005). The reduction in demand also had an important impact on the PPT programme since the economic and regulatory uncertainties produced a very difficult environment to encourage new projects.

The Tariff Review Process During the First Phase of Reform: 1995–2003

The main feature of the Brazilian electricity sector liberalisation was that the market reforms involved independent actions characterised by the lack of planning before privatisation and ad hoc decisions made by the Brazilian government. This approach to reform the electricity sector is described by Araujo (2006) as a reform by trial and error. This approach had a significant impact on the regulatory framework adopted in Brazil. As a consequence, this also impacted on the tariff review procedures since they had to cope with this macro environment and practical issues of dissemination and implementation.

It is important to identify the major events in the Brazilian electricity sector to be able to understand the impact of this trial and error approach on the tariff review process. The first distribution company was privatised in 1995 and the first large distribution firm was privatised in 1996; in both cases this privatisation was based on ad hoc decisions, because at this time there was no regulatory framework. The regulator (ANEEL) was created in December 1996. However, the first board of directors was nominated in December 1997, when ten companies had already been privatised. Moreover, the government had problems in implementing the proposed model and the wholesale market started to operate in September 2000. In May 2001, electricity rationing started and this lasted for 10 months. As can be observed, these events put too much pressure on the recently created regulator as the demand to introduce a regulatory framework had a sense of urgency. In addition, the 2001 crisis demanded emergency measures to guarantee that the electricity system would not collapse. As a consequence, tariff review process issues were neglected. It was much more important to deal with the immediate threats than planning and discussing issues related to the tariff review as an instrument of governance.

Investors were hesitant to invest in the Brazilian electricity sector during the first reform period because there of the absence of a clear picture of the structural and regulatory framework during the first electricity reform. As a consequence, to ensure the viability of the investment, the concession contracts usually specify initial tariffs and the formula and condition for reviews and inflationary adjustments. Contracts use the same basic formula in which non-controllable costs are adjusted annually to an inflationary index and controllable costs are adjusted to the same index minus a productivity factor (X factor) (Mota, 2003). The Brazilian government decided to add ad hoc clauses in the concessions contract, such as an X factor set to zero for eight years (from 1995 to 2003), a readjustment index (IGPM, a bulk price index) correlated with commodity prices and exchange rates and lowered requirements for energy quality (Araujo, 2006). Therefore the X factor was set to zero for the first period for all distribution companies. As a consequence, the first periodic tariff review process where the X factor was not zero was conducted between 2003 and 2006 and the second periodic tariff was performed from 2007 to 2010.

It is argued that the design of the privatisation process should have ideally addressed the future information requirements of effective regulation of the new private monopoly (Estache et al., 2003). In Brazil, the regulatory process should have been designed with the future information flows between regulators and utility firms specified as part of the contractual arrangements (Estache et al., 2003). However, this was not done and the core issues in tariff review process only started to be dealt with in 2002, as the first review process was scheduled to be taking place between 2003 and 2006. This situation led to a range of problems and controversies that, to some extent, damaged the regulator's credibility and jeopardised the electricity sector development.

The most controversial issue during this period was the determination of the regulatory asset base (RAB). The proposed asset valuation (DORC) was presented in July 2002 and enacted in September 2002. However, distribution companies were reluctant to enact this and they went to court to try to change ANEEL's decision. As result, the first review process was very complicated since, for the regulator, its use of DORC methodology was a new experience. On the other hand, distribution firms were not willing to facilitate the process.

In 2003, 17 tariff review processes were carried out and none of these companies had ANEEL's approval on the regulatory asset base value.

It was argued that the distribution companies' expectations of changing the decision in court played a significant role in this result. But it seems that operational issues also played an important role, as there was not enough time for companies to incorporate this methodology in their control systems in order to adjust its controls to this new environment. As a consequence, ANEEL made ad hoc decisions in order to carry on the tariff review process on schedule. ANEEL had to find an alternative to DORC because a tariff cannot be calculated without asset value. Thus, the historical cost appeared to be a possible solution, since financial accounting uses this approach. ANEEL set temporary asset values for most of the distribution companies based on not exactly the historical cost value, but a percentage of its value. Therefore, for the majority of the firms, ANEEL established the temporary asset base value as 80 per cent of the historical cost. As the asset base was provisory, the tariff set by ANEEL was also temporary. In 2004, ANEEL made a commitment to adjust the final tariff in order to consider the definitive asset base value. In 2004, this problem happened again as 24 tariff review processes were carried out and only four companies had ANEEL's approval on the regulatory asset base value (Teixeira, 2005).

As long as the asset base value is provisional, the regulated tariff is temporary as well. Therefore, consumers can pay more when the asset base value is overestimated or can pay less if the provisory value is lower than the definitive asset base value. In the Brazilian context, for the majority of cases the asset base value was overestimated. As a consequence, consumers paid more than necessary; of course this difference was adjusted in the next period, but the damage to ANEEL's reputation was done as newspapers published the fact that ANEEL had allowed privatised distribution companies to wrongly overcharge consumers. This was a very difficult situation for ANEEL because the consumers had already faced increasing tariffs in the rationing period to compensate the distribution companies' financial losses.

Another source of controversy in the first tariff review process was the methodology to establish the operational expenditures (OPEX) value. As discussed before, ANEEL adopted the reference utility approach. In the Brazilian case, the reference utility is not based on data supplied by the regulated company or by an audit of the company. The model utility is based on external definition of efficiency standards in setting prices of regulated services. These efficiency standards are based on engineering principles. However, due to the constraint of time to develop such parameters, ANEEL decided in some cases to adopt simplistic solutions. One of them related to the fact that Brazil is a very large country where the economic situation varies greatly from region to region. ANEEL did not give this due consideration in the first review process as a number of operational cost items were attributed at the same value across the different regions of the country. In addition, no debate was held with the distribution companies on the better practices and their associated costs. Therefore, in the first review process, ANEEL did not encourage the distribution firms to participate in the process of establishing the operational expenditures methodology and criteria. This was another fault in the development of the Brazilian regulatory system as Estache, et al. (2003, p. 9) state that 'what history also teaches regulators is that they cannot afford not to educate all parties on the mechanics of regulation. It is crucial for everyone involved to understand what drives tariffs, and most important, all parts should understand and accept the tariff review process methodology.'

The Second Phase of Reform: 2004–Present

The new regulatory framework in the Brazilian electricity sector was proposed by the Ministry of Mining and Energy (MME) in 2003 and it was enacted by the Brazilian congress in 2004 (Laws number 10,847 and 10,848 from 2004 and decree number 5,163). As a result of this reform, electricity policy changed considerably in order to attract investment for sustained development of the sector. This new policy had five explicit purposes: (1) to build a stable regulatory environment; (2) to ensure enough electricity supply by reducing the perceptions of high risks in this industry, while providing a fair return to investors; (3) to promote reasonable tariff at lowest possible costs; (4) to respect contracts; and (5) to reintroduce planning in order to cope with growth of demand (Araujo et al., 2008; Bajay, 2006).

To achieve these objectives, mechanisms were introduced to enhance security of supply including: (1) a requirement that distribution companies contract for 100 per cent of their forecast demand over a five-year time period; (2) building realistic forecasts for guaranteed energy plants; (3) contracting hydropower and thermal plants in a mix that balances reliable supply and cost; and (4) permanent control over the security of supply, in order to detect imbalances between supply and demand and to take actions to restore security of supply at least cost to consumers (Araujo et al., 2008). Therefore, the second reform reinforced the role of the government in the electricity sector, as the federal government reclaimed the functions of planning and policymaking. Two features are apparent in the new arrangements: first, decisionmaking is more centralised and second, government policy is given a greater weighting than in the first reform.

Reflecting these varied objectives, the new model is a hybrid one. Two environments were created in the wholesale market: Regulated Contracting Environment (ACR) and Free Contracting Environment

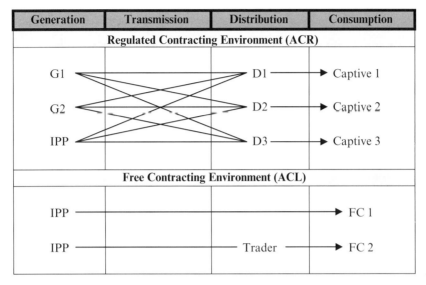

Note: G: Public Generator; IPP: Independent Power Producer; D: Distribution Company; FC: Free Consumers.

Figure 10.2   Brazilian electricity model

(ACL). The regulated market is organised around a wholesale power pool, based on long-term contracts (15 and 30 years) between generators and distribution companies serving captive consumers. The contracts underpinning the regulated environment (PPA, Power Purchase Agreement) are based on long term concessions allocated to generators and distributors for the supply of electricity to captive consumers though competitive auctions. The free contracting environment (ACL) comprises large consumers (over 3 Mw) that are free to contract directly with generating or trading companies (see Figure 10.2 above). Therefore, at the ACL, the energy is negotiated through bilateral contracts with generators and traders. The contracts are of different lengths and short-term contracts are predominant (Losekann, 2008).

The Tariff Review Process During the Second Phase of Reform

In 2004, the Brazilian government enacted the law that created a new regulatory framework. This was a response to the failure of the previous model that led to the 2001 crisis. Two main features changed in terms of the tariff review process: the legal separation of the distribution activity from generation, transmission and trading (free environment) and the end of self-dealing transactions, that is, bilateral contracting within a single economic group. These measures were aimed at facilitating controlling companies' activities and eliminating cross-subsidies between firms that are part of the same economic group.

The Brazilian government decided to adopt the separation of companies approach which requires that regulated activities and unregulated activities must be developed by different legal entities. Law number 10,848 from 2004 establishes that the distribution companies cannot perform generation, transmission and trading (free consumers) activities. In order to cope with this law, 24 Brazilian distribution companies had to separate the distribution activity from the above activities (ANEEL, 2005). As a result, different legal entities were created. The Brazilian approach is a less strict form of separation, because this requires that the generation, transmission, and trading (ACL, Free Contracting Environment) activities are performed by a separate legal entity, but it does not prohibit common ownership. Thus the utility firm's shareholders can own a subsidiary company performing unregulated activities. In fact, in the Brazilian electricity sector, a considerable number of distribution companies are part of group of companies that undertakes generation, transmission and trading activities. Therefore, each company has its own accounting system which operates independently from the parent company. In addition, Brazilian distribution utilities operate only regulated activities, that is, distribution and trading in the Regulated Contracting Environment (ACR).

During the first reform period, self-dealing (the purchase of power by distributors from their own subsidiaries) contracts were allowed within a single economic group. This generated severe criticism, as some distribution companies were allowed to adjust their tariffs to reflect the purchase of more expensive energy from a company of the same group. Araujo (2008) points out that many of the self-dealing contracts were based on the cost of thermal plants, which is much higher than the marginal system cost. As a result, the energy price that consumers had to pay with this scheme was significantly higher than the average system cost.

In order to avoid such a problem, and taking into account the challenge to regulators outlined by Bromwich and Hong (Bromwich and Hong, 2000), the second electricity sector reform forbade self-dealing or bilateral contracting within a single economic group (articles 20 and 30, law number 10,848/2004). This policy forced all purchase of energy traded by distribution companies to be done through public auctions, that is, distribution firms could only contract energy through regulated public auctions based on minimal price.

The side effect of these changes in regulation in the second reform period, and the lack of planning and discussion about the tariff review procedures during the first reform period, was an increase in the regulatory risk, that is, the risk of changing regulations and its impacts on the security of the sector and market. Robinson and Taylor (1998: 332) state that regulatory risk 'has normally referred to the risks to the utilities of being prone to regulatory intervention'. In the Brazilian case, the changes in regulations made by the government increased operational costs of the distribution companies and to some extent had a negative impact on the level of investment of these firms. However, the regulatory risk has been mitigated after the second tariff review process, as the regulator used a similar approach with minor modifications; and since the 2004 reform, the Brazilian regulatory framework has been consolidated. By using a similar approach, the Brazilian regulator has established a more stable environment and reduced the inconsistencies in its actions, which decreased the regulatory risk which materialised through the cost of capital required by investors. Finally, the trend of regulation in Brazil for the future is the consolidation of the current model with some adjustments and improvements in order to mitigate the regulatory risk. One of these improvements in tariff review methodology will be the utilisation of a reference regionalised database to determine the regulatory asset base; this will occur in the third tariff review which starts in 2011. This constitutes an improvement because the regulator will not need to use information provided by each company and this can reduce the asymmetry of information between utility companies and the regulator.

CONCLUDING REMARKS

The privatisation process in the electricity sector was severely criticised, as the reforms during the Cardoso administration (1995–2002) followed nearly independent schedules, instead of the 'text-book' sequence of restructuring-regulation-privatisation (Araujo, 2006). The problem in the Brazilian reform process was that the government's main priority at the beginning was to generate revenue for the treasury. As a consequence, the government paid little attention to market development and overall efficiency gains in the industry. In addition, the privatisation started before a regulatory structure had been organised and established by law. This sense of failure was exacerbated in 2001 when Brazil experienced its worst electricity supply crisis in 50 years. This crisis was caused by under-investment in generation and transmission, aggravated by severe drought conditions. As a result, a rationing of electricity consumption by 20 per cent was imposed from June 2001 to March 2002. In order to deal with these problems, the new administration established a new model in 2004.

This model views electricity as a key public service that needs to be upheld by a strong state role, as well as delivering a pragmatic assessment of the weaknesses of the first reforms, and the need to establish a regulatory system that delivers investment for reliable power and thus avoid another electricity shortage.

This chapter examined the tariff review process in an attempt to understand its development and its importance during the electricity sector reforms in Brazil by highlighting how the tariff review process as a governance regime affected the outcomes of the Brazilian electricity sector under the two reform phases. The evidence we have provided shows that tariff review process issues developed in the same way that the Brazilian regulatory system developed, that is, based on ad hoc decisions with limited time to discuss and plan its development,because it was much more important to solve the immediate problems caused by the flaws in the first model than planning and discussing issues relating to tariff reviewing. However, it is important to highlight that after the second reform in 2004, the tariff review issues have been consolidated and the trend for the future is that these issues will only be refined in order to mitigate the regulatory risk.

Cubbin and Stern (2006) point out that for the electricity sector in developing economies, regulation should focus on providing sufficient supplies, which typically means increasing investment and capacity. As a result, an effective regulatory framework could be expected to reduce the constraint on the operation of the market, increasing supply and moving the outcome closer to the market equilibrium (Cubbin and Stern, 2006: Ugur, 2009; Kirkpatrick and Parker, 2004; Zhang and Thomas, 2009). The better the regulatory framework, the greater the expected increases in capacity and technical efficiency and productivity of the system, which are the two main measures to evaluate regulation according to Cubbin and Stern (2006). In the context of Brazil, in particular regarding the tariff review process, it was observed that price cap regulation became more complex and provided distorted signals to the market. The lack of planning and discussion about the tariff review process during the first review period was one of the main contributors to the lack of investment and under-expansion of the electricity capacity which led to the 2001 crisis. This argues against one of the main reasons for promoting independent regulatory agencies in electricity and similar utility service industries, which is: 'sizable increases in investment flows (domestic and foreign) to developing economy electricity industries' (Cubbin and Stern, 2006: 117).

After the second reform in 2004, the tariff review issues have been consolidated and the trend for the future is that these issues will only be refined in order to maintain the stability and consolidate the present regulatory framework. This new regulatory framework was able to attract investment flows to support the expansion of the Brazilian electricity systems, in terms of generation, transmission and distribution. In addition, the quality of the electricity system – measured by two main quality indicators DEC (equivalent length of electricity interruption per consumer) and FEC (equivalent frequency of electricity interruption per consumer) – has improved after the second reform (ABRADEE, 2009). However, the present tariff review process has been criticised because it led to a considerable increase on the electricity tariff and distribution companies' profit. The electricity tariff started to grow much faster than the consumer price index, leading to discontentment, pressures on the budget of poorer households and an increase in defaulting and other commercial losses (Araujo et al., 2008). As a result of the increase in the consumers' tariff, the profit of the electricity companies in Brazil increased considerably, leading to greater remuneration for the private owners. According to Santos et al. (2008), the electricity tariff increased five times after privatisation and the dividends of the electricity companies rose by the same proportion after privatisation. Therefore, the regulator's challenge is to refine and consolidate the regulatory framework and the tariff review issues in order to reduce the Brazilian electricity tariff which is among of the highest in the world.

REFERENCES

ABRADEE (2009), Associação Brasileira de Distribuidores de Energia Elétrica, available at http://www.abradee.org.br (accessed 10 June 2009).

Almeida, E.L.F.D. and H.Q. Pinto (2005), 'Reform in Brazilian electricity industry. The search for a new model', *International Journal of Global Energy Issues*, **23**, 169–187.

Alvarez, L.F. (2007), 'Brazilian discos price cap regulation', paper presented at *IEEE Power and Energy Society General Meeting*, doi 10.1109/PES.2007.385944.

Amann, E. and W. Baer (2005), 'From the developmental to the regulatory state. The transformation of the government's impact on the Brazilian economy', *The Quarterly Review of Economics and Finance*, **45**, 421–431.

ANEEL (2005), 'Aprovada reestruturação societária das distribuidoras', *Boletim Energia*, **189**.

ANEEL (2009), Agência Nacional de Energia Elétirca, available at http://www.aneel.gov.br (accessed 8 June 2009).

Araujo, J.L.R.H.D. (2006), 'The case of Brazil: reform by trial and error?', in F.P. Sioshansi and W. Pfaffenberger (eds), *Electricity Market Reform. An International Perspective*, Amsterdam and London: Elsevier.

Araujo, J.L.R.H.D. and A.D. Oliveira (2005), *Diálodos da Energia: Reflexões Sobre a Ultima Década, 1994–2004*, Rio de Janeiro: 7letras.

Araujo, J.L.R.H.D., A.M.D.A.D. Costa, T. Correia and E. Melo (2008), 'Reform of the reforms in Brazil: problems and solutions', in F.P. Sioshansi (ed.), *Competitive Electricity Markets: Design, Implementation, Performance*, Amsterdam and London: Elsevier.

Bajay, S.V. (2006), 'Integrating competition and planning. A mixed institutional model of the Brazilian electric power sector', *Energy*, **31**, 865–876.

BNDES (2002), *A Privatização no Brasil: O Caso dos Serviços de Utilidade Pública*, Rio de Janeiro, Brazil: BNDES (Banco Nacional de Desenvolvimento Economico e Social).

Boubakri, N. and J.C. Cosset (1998), 'The financial and operating performance of newly privatized firms. Evidence from developing countries', *Journal of Finance*, **53**, 1081–1110.

Branston, J.R. (2000), 'A counterfactual price analysis of British electricity privatisation', *Utilities Policy*, **9**, 31–46.

Bromwich, M. and C. Hong (2000), 'Costs and regulation in the UK telecommunications industry', *Management Accounting Research*, **11**, 137–165.

Burns, P. and A. Estache (1998), 'Information, accounting and the regulation of concessioned infrastructure monopolies', *The World Bank Policy Research Working Paper*, **2034**.

Cole, B. and C. Cooper (2006), 'Deskilling in the twenty first century: the case of rail privatisation', *Critical Perspectives on Accounting*, **17**, 601–625.

Cubbin, J. and J. Stern (2006), 'The impact of regulatory governance and privatization on electricity industry generation capacity in developing economies', *The World Bank Economic Review*, **20**, 115–141.

Estache, A., M.R. Pardina, J.M. Rodriguez and G. Sember (2003), 'An introduction to financial and economic modeling for utility regulators', *Policy Research Working Paper Series*, **3001**.

InstitutoAscendeBrazil (2007), 'Política tarfária e regulação por incentivos', *Caderno de Política Tarifária*, **1**.

Jacobs, K. (2009), 'Beyond commercial in confidence: accounting for power privatisation in Victoria', *Accounting, Auditing & Accountability Journal*, **22**, 1258–1283.

Jamasb, T. and M. Pollitt (2007), 'Incentive regulation of electricity distribution networks: lessons of experiences from Britain', *Energy Policy*, **35**, 6163–6187.

Jaruga, A. and S.S.M. Ho (2002), 'Management accounting in transitional economies', *Management Accounting Research*, **13**, 375–378.

Johnson, G., S. Smith and B. Codling (2000), 'Microprocesses of institutional change in the context of privatization', *The Academy of Management Review*, **25**, 572–580.

Kang, J., D.L. Weisman and M. Zhang (2000), 'Do consumers benefit from tighter price cap regulation?', *Economics Letters*, **67**, 113–119.

Kirkpatrick, C. and D. Parker (2004), 'Regulatory impact assessment and regulatory governance in developing countries', *Public Administration and Development*, **24**, 333–344.

Lima, J.W.M. (2002), 'Distribution pricing based on yardstick regulation', *IEEE Transactions on Power Systems*, **17**, 198–204.

Littlechild, S. (2006), 'Foreword: the market versus regulation', in F.P. Sioshansi and W. Pfaffenberger (eds), *Electricity Market Reform. An International Perspective*, Amsterdam and London: Elsevier.

Losekann, L. (2008), 'The second reform of the Brazilian electric sector', *International Journal of Global Energy Issues*, **29**, 75–87.

Mota, R.L. (2003), 'The restructuring and privatisation of electricity distribution and supply business in Brazil: a social cost-benefit analysis', *Cambridge Working Papers in Economics*, **CWPE 042**.

Newbery, D. (2006), 'Electricity liberalization in Britain and the evolution of market design', in F.P. Sioshansi and W. Pfaffenberger (eds), *Electricity Market Reform. An International Perspective*, Amsterdam and London: Elsevier.

OECD (2008), *Brazil: Strengthening Governance for Growth*, Paris: OECD.

Ogden, S.G. (1995), 'Transforming frameworks of accountability: the case of water privatization', *Accounting, Organizations and Society*, **20**, 193–218.

Ogden, S.G. (1997), 'Accounting for organizational performance. The construction of the customer in the privatized water industry', *Accounting, Organizations and Society*, **22**, 529–556.

Oliveira, A.D. (2007), 'Political economy of the Brazilian power industry reform', in D.G. Victor and T.C. Heller (eds), *The Political Economy of Power Sector Reform: The Experiences of Five Major Developing Countries*, Cambridge and New York: Cambridge University Press.

Pinto Jr, H.Q., E.L.F.D. Almeida, J.V. Bomtempo, M. Iootty and R.G. Bicalho (2007), *Economia da energia: fundamentos econômicos, evolução histórica e organização industrial*, Rio de Janeiro: Elsevier.

Robinson, T.A. and M.P. Taylor (1998), 'The effects of regulation and regulatory risk in the UK electricity distribution industry', *Annals of Public and Cooperative Economics*, **69**, 331–346.

Rocha, K., F. Camacho and G. Braganca (2007), 'Return on capital of Brazilian electricity distributors: a comparative analysis', *Energy Policy*, **35**, 2526–2537.

Rudnick, H., L.A. Barroso, C. Skerk and A. Blanco (2005), 'South American reform lessons: twenty years of restructuring and reform in Argentina, Brazil and Chile', *IEEE Power and Energy Magazine*, July/August, 49–59.

Santos, G.A.G.D., E.K. Barbosa, J.F.S.D. Silva and R.D.S.D. Abreu (2008), 'Por que as tarifas foram para os céus? Propostas para o setor elétrico brasileiro', *Revista do BNDES*, **14**, 435–474.

Teixeira, D. (2005), 'Regulators' challenge in the price ceiling – the valuation of regulatory assets in the Brazil's electricity ratemaking', Working Paper, The George Washington University, **April**, 1–37.

Thomas, S. (2006), 'The grin of the Cheshire cat', *Energy Policy*, **34**, 1974–1983.

Tozzini, S. (2008), 'Benchmark regulation in Brazil: potential strategic implications for electricity distribution utilities', *International Journal of Energy Sector Management*, **2**, 52–74.

Tsamenyi, M., J. Onumah and E. Tetteh-kumah (2010), 'Post-privatization performance and organizational changes: case studies from Ghana', *Critical Perspectives on Accounting*, **21**, 428–442.

Ugur, M. (2009), 'Regulatory quality and performance in EU network industries: evidence on telecommunications, gas and electricity', *Journal of Public Policy*, **29**, 347–370.

Varela, R. and E. Redolfi (2007), 'Compared regulations: the tariff review process in Brazil, Panama and Peru', paper presented at *IEEE Power and Energy Society General Meeting*, doi 10.1109/PES.2007.385944.

Zhang, Y.F. and M. Thomas (2009), 'Regulatory reform and governance: a survey of selected developing and transition economies', *Public Administration and Development*, **29**, 330–339.

Index